BENIN

BENIN

LORDS OF THE RIVER

PHILIP KOSLOW

CHELSEA HOUSE PUBLISHERS • New York • Philadelphia

Frontispiece: A 17th-century bronze plaque depicting a group of officials serving in the royal palace of Benin.

On the Cover: An artist's interpretation of a bronze head from Benin; in the background, a royal procession moves through the streets of 17th-century Benin City.

CHELSEA HOUSE PUBLIHERS

Editorial Director Richard Rennert
Executive Managing Editor Karyn Gullen Browne
Copy Chief Robin James
Picture Editor Adrian G. Allen
Creative Editor Robert Mitchell
Art Director Joan Ferrigno
Production Manager Sallye Scott

THE KINGDOMS OF AFRICA
Senior Editor Martin Schwabacher

Staff for Benin
Assistant Editor Catherine Iannone
Editorial Assistant Erin McKenna
Senior Designer Cambraia Magalhães
Picture Researcher Ellen Dudley
Cover Illustrator Bradford Brown

First Printing
1 3 5 7 9 8 6 4 2

Library of Congress Cataloging-in-Publication Data

Koslow, Philip.
  Benin : lords of the river   Philip Koslow.
    p. cm.—(The Kingdoms of Africa)
Includes bibliographical references and index.
  ISBN   0-7910-3133-0.
           0-7910-3134-9 (pbk.)
    1. Benin (Nigeria)—Civilization—Juvenile literature. 2. Benin (Nigeria)—History—Juvenile literature. [1. Benin (Nigeria)—History. 2. Bini (African people)] I. Title. II. Series.   95-12343
DT515.9.B37K67 1995   CIP
966.9'32—dc20   AC

CONTENTS

Titles In
THE KINGDOMS OF AFRICA

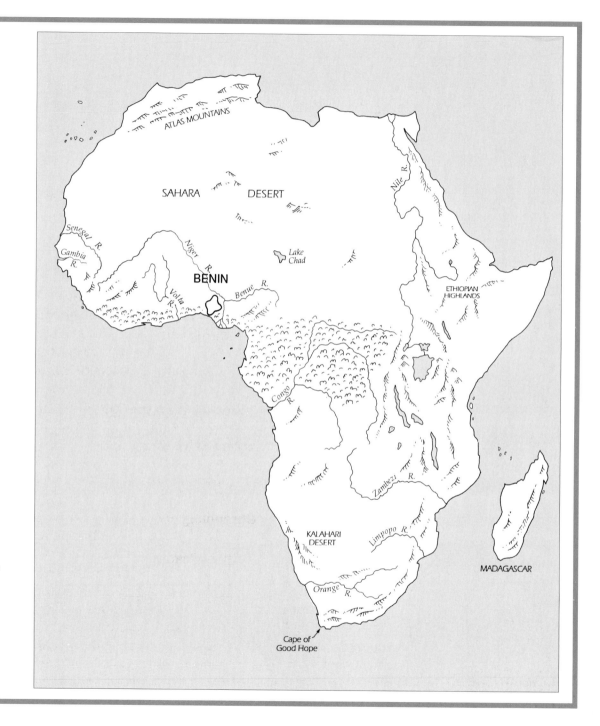

"CIVILIZATION AND MAGNIFICENCE"

On a sunny morning in July 1796, Mungo Park, a Scottish doctor turned explorer, achieved a major goal of his long and difficult trek through West Africa when he reached the banks of the mighty Niger River. Along the river was a cluster of four large towns, which together made up the city of Segu, the principal settlement of the Bambara people. The sight of Segu dazzled Park as much as the spectacle of the broad, shining waterway. "The view of this extensive city," he wrote, "the numerous canoes upon the river; the crowded population; and the cultivated state of the surrounding country, formed altogether a prospect of civilization and magnificence, which I little expected to find in the bosom of Africa."

7

Park's account of his journey, *Travels in the Interior Districts of Africa*, became a best-seller in England. But his positive reflections on Africa were soon brushed aside by the English and other Europeans, who were engaged in a profitable trade in slaves along the West African coast and were eventually to carve up the entire continent into colonies. Later explorers such as Richard Burton, who spoke of the "childishness" and "backwardness" of Africans, achieved more lasting fame than did Park, who drowned during a second expedition to Africa in 1806. Thus it is not surprising that 100 years after Park's arrival at Segu, a professor at England's Oxford University could write with bland self-assurance that African history before the arrival of Europeans had been nothing more than "blank, uninteresting, brutal barbarism." The professor's opinion was published when the British Empire was at its height, and it represented a point of view that was necessary to justify the exploitation of Africans. If, as the professor claimed, Africans had lived in a state of chaos throughout their history, then their European conquerors

A relief map of Africa, indicating the territory once controlled by the kingdom of Benin.

This head of an oba (king) from 18th-century Benin is one of the countless great artworks produced by the peoples of Africa before European powers began to dominate the continent during the late 19th century.

could believe that they were doing a noble deed by imposing their will and their way of life upon Africa's people.

The colonialist view of African history held sway into the 20th century. But as Africans gained their independence from the European powers, more enlightened scholars began to take a fresh look at Africa's past. As archaeologists (scientists who study the physical remains of past societies) explored the sites of former African cities, they found that Africans had enjoyed a high level of civilization hundreds of years before the arrival of Europeans. In many respects, the kingdoms and cities of Africa had been equal to or more advanced than European societies during the same period.

Modern scientists also reject the idea—fostered by Europeans during the time of the slave trade and colonialism—that there is any connection between a people's skin color and their capacity for achievement and self-government. Differences in pigmentation, scientists now recognize, are based solely upon climate and have nothing to do with intellectual ability. When the human species began to develop in the torrid regions of Africa some 7.5 million years ago, humans were all dark skinned because dark pigmentation protected them from the harmful ultraviolet rays of the sun. However, when some Africans began migrating to colder regions where there was far less sunlight, heavy pigmentation became a drawback—it prevented the skin from absorbing the amount of sunlight needed to produce vitamin D, which is essential for the growth of bones and teeth. Hence lighter skin began to predominate in Europe, with the peoples of Asia, the Middle East, and North Africa occupying a middle ground between Europeans and dark-skinned Africans. Rather than indicating superiority, therefore, lighter skin can be viewed as a deviance from the original skin color of all human beings.

As early as the 5th century B.C., when ancient Greece was enjoying its Golden Age, West African peoples had developed a highly civilized way of life and were producing magnificent works of art. By A.D. 750, ancient Ghana, known as the Land of Gold, emerged as West Africa's first centralized kingdom. When Ghana began to decline in the 12th century, power shifted to the empire of Mali, and Mali was in turn supplanted by Songhay, Kanem-Borno, and the fortress kingdoms of Hausaland. All these great nations were located in the central region of West Africa—the wide, sun-baked savanna that borders the vast Sahara Desert. To a large extent, they owed their wealth and grandeur to trade with North Africa and the Middle East. Because of this ever-widening economic and cultural contact, the fame of the Bilad al-Sudan ("land of the black peoples" in Arabic) spread throughout the world.

However, the rich saga of the savanna states does not represent the entire history of West African achievement. Indeed, much of the region's wealth derived from the gold and ivory supplied by the peoples of the lush forest belt that extends along the southern coast of West Africa. The forestland communities had emerged at least as early as those of the savanna, but their distant location and rugged terrain ensured that they would be known to few outsiders before the arrival of European mariners in the 15th century. Their history forms a unique chapter in the development of African civilization, and some of the most remarkable contributions to that civilization were made by the kingdom of Benin, which ruled the Niger Delta for more than 1,000 years.

Chapter 1 | "RULERS OF THE SKY"

A view of the Benin River in the present-day nation of Nigeria. This thickly forested region has for thousands of years been the home of the Edo people, farmers and warriors who founded the kingdom of Benin in A.D. 900.

The Niger River begins its majestic 2,600-mile course through West Africa in the mountains of Fouta Djallon on the Atlantic coast. From Fouta Djallon the Niger flows northeast into the rain-starved savanna. Reaching its northern limit at Timbuktu, the legendary center of African trade and learning, the river makes a wide bend to the south, forming a vast inland delta—when the rains finally fall in the summer months the river overflows its banks, turning the parched and tawny landscape into a green and fertile expanse where farmers can plant their crops and wandering herders can graze their cattle. The river then runs southeast, cutting across the lands of the Hausa and Yoruba and plunging from savanna country into dense tropical rain-forest. At last, the Niger empties its wa-

ters into the Gulf of Guinea, forming another massive delta where numerous smaller rivers and streams meander through groves of squat, thick-rooted mangrove trees.

North of the coast, the landscape is dominated by massive 100-foot-tall trees, hanging vines, and thick undergrowth covering the forest floor. But this region of Africa is far from hostile to human life. The waters of the delta abound with fish, and the forest provides game for skillful hunters. The giant African snail also furnishes a ready source of protein. Palm trees yielding a nutritious oil grow wild here, as does the kola tree, whose nuts contain a highly prized stimulant. Natural clearings in the forest—often made by herds of elephants—provide farmers with fertile ground for the planting of

This striking mask, representing a water spirit, was carved by an artist who was a member of the Ijo people. Inhabiting the dense mangrove swamps of the Niger Delta, the Ijo were skilled at fishing; they traded part of their catch to the Edo of Benin in return for agricultural products such as yams.

crops such as yams. Thus it is not surprising that for at least 4,000 years the Niger Delta region has been home to several ethnic groups. Among these are the Edo—one of the most significant peoples in the history of the continent.

The Edo (also called the Bini) are closely related to the Yoruba, their northern neighbors. At some point in the past, the two peoples may have even inhabited the same territory. According to their own traditions, the Edo lived for a time at Ile Ife, the sacred center of Yorubaland. This is entirely plausible because the Edo and the Yoruba worship many of the same gods. Like the Yoruba, the Edo trace their origin to Olodumare, the creator god, who sent his son Oduduwa to Ile Ife, commanding him to create land upon the waters and populate the world with humans. A party of Edo hunters later ventured south from Ile Ife in search of land of their own. They established a new homeland on the western banks of the Niger, just above the delta.

For many centuries, the Edo lived in scattered villages without any form of central government. Each village was organized around clans, or descent lines. People who traced their family lineage to a common ancestor lived together in large compounds, adding new buildings as various family members married and had children. Each compound was headed by the oldest member of the clan. The head of the largest clan normally served as the chief of the village, with the elders of smaller clans serving as a council of advisers.

Throughout their early history, the Edo traded with other Africans—not merely their immediate neighbors but also those living in distant lands. In the challenging climate of Africa, people in a given region often found it difficult to supply all their needs, so they looked to other areas in order to supplement their diet. For example, many coastal fishing communities wished to obtain grains and cereals from the savanna, while savanna dwellers needed fish, meat, oil, and kola nuts. From earliest times, trade routes sprung up, linking the forestlands with the interior. Enterprising peoples, such as the Dyula of the western savanna and the Hausa of the central savanna, prospered by carrying goods back and forth along these routes. At the same time, the need to provide safety for travelers led to more complicated forms of political organization; scattered collections of villages gave way to larger states whose rulers saw to it that trade routes were free of bandits.

The Edo kingdom, which became known as Benin, dates back to A.D. 900, when a chief named Igodo took the title *ogiso*. (*Ogiso* means "ruler of the sky," an indication that the first kings sought to establish a link with Olodumare, thus giving their rule the sanction of the gods.) Little is known of Igodo's character or reign, but his son and successor, Ere, had a powerful impact on the development of Benin. The Edo chief Jacob Egharevba, in his *Short History of Benin* (first published in 1934), has described the achievements of Ere's rule:

> He was a lover of peace and concord. For instance, if there was fighting or quarrelling among his people a crier would be sent out by him to announce to the fighters the term *"A wua ne Ere"* meaning "quarrelling is forbidden by Ere" and at once peace would be restored. . . . He founded many villages . . . and the groups of craftsmen known as Onwina [carpenters] and Igbesamwan [carvers in wood and ivory]. . . . It was Ere who introduced the royal throne (*ekete*), the chief's rectangular stool (*agba*), the round leather fan (*ezuzu*), the round box (*ekpokin*) made of bark and leather, the swords of authority (*ada* and *eben*), beaded anklets (*eguen*) and collars (*odigba*), and a simple, undecorated form of crown. He also

13

A 19th-century engraving of a village on the banks of the Benin River. The Edo lived in isolated villages for many centuries before creating a centralized kingdom headed by rulers known by the title of ogiso.

14

introduced such domestic articles as wooden plates and bowls; mortars and pestles, which were carved by the Onwina; and the wooden heads, carved by the Igbesamwan, which are placed on ancestral shrines. Ere died peacefully after a successful reign.

The traditions of Benin account for 15 ogisos. The last ogiso, Owodo, was banished from the realm during the late 13th century because of various im-

proper acts, including the execution of a pregnant woman. The elders of Benin could not agree on a new ogiso; instead, they appointed a man named Evian to run the government in a role similar to a modern president or prime minister. Evian governed successfully for a time, but when he attempted to act like a king and designate his son Ogiamwen to follow him, Benin entered a period of turmoil in which a number of factions vied for power. Some of the Edo supported Evian; others insisted on a republican form of government in which there would be no king.

The solution to this conflict came from without. According to tradition, the Edo sent word to Ile Ife and invited Prince Oranmiyan, the son of Oduduwa, to rule Benin. Oranmiyan married an Edo woman, Erinmwinde, who soon gave birth to a son. "After some years of residence here," Chief Egharevba writes, "[Oranmiyan] called a meeting of the people and renounced his office, remarking that the country was a land of vexation . . . and that only a child born, trained and educated in the arts and mysteries of the land could reign over the people." Oranmiyan then returned to Ile Ife, but he left his son to rule in his place, and this son became known as Eweka I.

Though not all historians agree that Oranmiyan was the actual founder of a new dynasty in Benin, the Edo tradition accurately describes what became a defining event in the history of the kingdom: during the period of instability brought on by Evian's attempt to start his own dynasty, a powerful group from Yorubaland took advantage of Benin's weakness and imposed their will on the Edo. As the historian Basil Davidson has written, such political events were not unusual: "There is scarcely an African people without a more or less vivid tradition that speaks of movement from another place. Younger sons of paramount chiefs would hive off with their followers, and become paramount themselves in a new land. Stronger peoples would conquer those who were weaker, marry their women, merge with them, weave yet another strand in the fabric of African life." The developing saga of Benin, given new life by the arrivals from the north, proved to be one of the most dramatic in African history.

15

Chapter 2 | "LAND OF THE POWERFUL OBA"

This 17th-century engraving shows the oba of Benin (center, on horseback) accompanied by warriors, musicians, dwarfs, and leopards as he leaves the royal palace to attend a communal celebration. Benin's yearly religious festivals were the only occasions on which the oba was seen by his subjects.

Eweka I took the title *oba* when he began to rule Benin, and the obas were to reign in an unbroken line for nearly 700 years. According to Chief Egharevba, "Eweka had a long and glorious reign but he had many children who were always quarrelling among themselves. He sent some of them away to be chiefs (*enigie*) of famous villages. . . . Eweka I was the creator of Councillors of State or Kingmakers, afterwards known as *Uzama Nihinron*. . . . He made their titles to be hereditary and ordered that every Oba of Benin should be crowned by [them] . . . because it was they who sent to Ife to fetch Prince Oranmiyan." The uzama remained powerful throughout Benin's history, providing stability for its complex political system.

Other important traditions date from the reign of Oba Ewedo, Eweka's grandson. Ewedo created posts for a number of royal officials, including the keeper of the oba's wardrobe, the recorder of deaths, and the keeper of the harem. He also took pains to enhance the personal prestige of his office, decreeing that only the oba could have a sword of state carried before him in the street and that all the Edo chiefs were to stand in his presence, so that only he remained seated in assemblies. Ewedo began a number of building projects, including the royal palace and prison, which survived into the late 19th century.

Perhaps the greatest of all the obas was Ewuare, who came to the throne around the year 1440. In the Edo language, *ewuare* means "it is cool" or "the trouble has ceased," suggesting that the new oba was a man of peaceable nature. When his ambitions were aroused, how-

In this 19th-century sculpture of an oba, the ruler wears the traditional crown, collar, and beads associated with his office. In his left hand he carries a royal staff; in his right hand, he holds a ceremonial sword.

18

ever, he was far from docile. Ewuare's original name had been Ogun, and he was the son of Oba Orobiru, a capable ruler well loved by his people. As Chief Egharevba recounts, Orobiru's death touched off a violent sequence of events:

> The throne was vacant for several months because Ogun, the rightful heir, had been banished from the City with his younger brother, Uwaifiokun. It is said that Ogun sent Uwaifiokun to the City to find out whether the elders would like him to return home or not. Uwaifiokun, however, told the elders that he had not seen Ogun since their departure from the City, and he induced them to make him Oba, thus usurping the throne. Ogun therefore armed himself, and after lying in wait at the Oba's market at a ceremonial performance, murdered Uwaifiokun at night.

In spite of this bloody beginning, Ewuare proved to be an energetic and farsighted ruler. Like most successful African monarchs of the time, he was first and foremost a powerful military commander. His troops ranged far and wide into Yorubaland to the north and Igboland to the east, conquering more than 200 towns and forcing the local rulers to pay tribute to him. The Ekiti people of Yorubaland began to say of Ewuare, "The oba of Benin wages war on the earth below and [the god] Ogbomudu wages war in heaven." The neighboring Igbo now spoke of Benin as *Idu ala Eze ike*, "the land of the powerful oba."

With the wealth he gained from tribute, Ewuare expanded his capital, Benin City, building new roads and thoroughfares. As Egharevba relates, "It was he who had the innermost and greatest of the walls and ditches made round the City and he made powerful charms and had them buried at each of the nine gateways to the City, to nullify any evil charms which might be brought by people of other countries to injure his subjects." Much of the city was laid out in a grid pattern, with the streets running at right angles to one another. Some of the streets were as much as 120 feet wide, suitable for royal processions and other public spectacles.

Whereas Edo villages were organized mainly around descent lines, Benin City was divided into wards based on crafts and occupations. Thus blacksmiths would live in one ward, weavers in another, leatherworkers in a third. Within the wards, living space was divided into family compounds that were similar to those in the villages, with each compound being surrounded by a wall to define its boundaries. All the inhabitants of Benin City were considered retainers of the oba: that is, they lived under his protection, and their primary function was to provide for his needs and add to his glory.

The most formidable wall in Benin City loomed above the broad avenue that separated the oba's palace from the remainder of the city. This arrangement shielded the oba from public view and bolstered the belief that he was a sacred being gifted with powers of magic. (As in many West African kingdoms, the monarch's subjects were never allowed to see him performing ordinary human activities, such as sleeping and eating.) A number of ceremonies were designed to reinforce the aura surrounding the oba, and these were the only occasions on which he allowed himself to be seen by the people, who would come to the capital by the thousands from the surrounding countryside. Among the greatest occasions were the Igue festival, designed to reinforce the oba's spiritual powers, and the New Yam festival, celebrating the harvest. One of the most striking rites, according to Egharevba, commemorated an event from the time of Ewuare's exile:

> During the night, while [Ewuare] was resting under a tree, he felt something

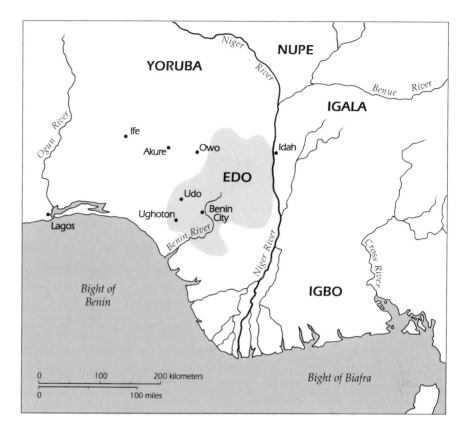

dripping on his head like water. In the morning he was greatly surprised to see it was blood, and on looking up he saw a leopard on the tree with blood dripping from its mouth. He got up hurriedly and then saw that he had been lying during the night on a snake. He killed both the leopard and the snake, and planted an *ikhimwin* tree on the spot, vowing that if ever he should become Oba of Benin he

A map showing the boundaries of Benin and the major ethnic groups of the lower Niger region.

19

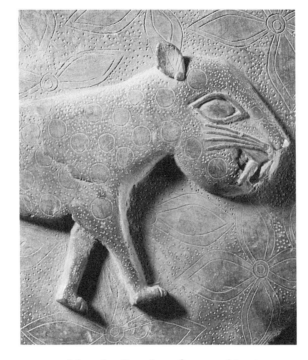

The head of a leopard from one of Benin's magnificent bronze plaques. Beginning with the reign of Ewuare the Great in the 15th century, the obas of Benin sacrificed a leopard each year to commemorate a miraculous event in Ewuare's early life.

20

would make it a place for worshipping the gods of his destiny. This vow he fulfilled by placing people there to watch the spot, and every year of his reign he sacrificed a leopard, and this example was followed by his successors.

Ewuare was aware that his personal aura alone could not sustain an expanding kingdom such as Benin. For this reason, he created the State Council to assist him in the process of governing. The State Council consisted of three distinct groups: the chiefs of the major towns; the palace chiefs, whose titles were created by the oba; and the powerful uzama, the six hereditary chiefs whose duty it was to install each new oba. Ewuare also took measures to establish an orderly succession to the throne. He created the title *edaiken* (crown prince) for his eldest son and appointed the edaiken to the State Council as an equal of the uzama.

Ewuare is credited with encouraging the art of carving wood and ivory, but in this area he was only continuing the great artistic tradition that had begun during the reign of Ere in the 10th century. Indeed, Benin had inherited a rich legacy that began with the vanished civilization now known as the Nok culture. As early as the 5th century B.C., the artists of the Nok culture—which flourished to the north of Yorubaland—were producing terracotta figures that rivaled the sculpture of ancient Greece. When the Nok culture died out around A.D. 200, the expertise of the Nok artists passed to the Yoruba, who produced astonishing lifelike heads for the sacred shrines of Ife.

Considering the close ties between Ife and Benin, it was only natural that the artists of Ife should export their skills to Benin City. The main work of Benin's artists was to sculpt the heads of deceased obas. The heads were displayed in funeral ceremonies and then placed in shrines, where current rulers could honor those who had previously held the throne. For three or four centuries the sculptors worked in wood or terra-cotta. Sometime during the 14th century, the art of working in bronze (a mixture of copper and tin) came to Benin by way of Ife.

In order to create their bronze sculptures, African artists employed a sophisticated technique known as the lost-wax method.

The artist would first make a clay model of the sculpture. When the clay dried, he would apply a thin layer of beeswax and carefully etch all the details of the sculpture into the wax. Then he would cover the wax with several more layers of clay, forming a thick mold. When the entire form was heated over a fire, the middle layer of wax would melt and drain off through the bottom of the form. At this point, the sculptor poured molten bronze into the top of the mold through a series of tubes. The bronze filled the space where the "lost" wax had been, conforming to all the fine details now baked into the surrounding clay. When the bronze cooled and set, the outer layers of clay were carefully broken, and the finished sculpture emerged.

21

The dramatic and expressive works produced by the Edo artists attest to the refinement of Benin's culture at a time when the kingdom had only limited contact with the peoples who lived beyond the forest belt and none at all with the world beyond Africa. By the time of Ewuare's reign, however, Europeans had already visited the western coast of Africa. When they reached the forestlands, they would help stimulate the artists of Benin to achieve their greatest period of creativity. But they would also bring ideas and practices that would ultimately cause the downfall of many African societies.

An early engraving shows Africans engaged in the art of metalworking. When the sophisticated technique of bronze casting reached Benin during the 14th century, the kingdom's artists began to produce magnificent sculptures in bronze.

Chapter 3 | WORLDS IN COLLISION

The top of this 17th-century bronze box is modeled after the roof of Benin's royal palace. The birds in the design represent the oba's magical powers, while the warriors bearing firearms indicate the growing importance of European weapons in the affairs of Benin.

Throughout the Middle Ages, which extended roughly from A.D. 500 to 1500, there was little outward difference between the kingdoms of Africa and the kingdoms of Europe—apart from the skin color of the people. On both continents, states were ruled by kings and queens whose power, in the eyes of their subjects, came directly from the Supreme Being. At the same time, a complex system of checks and balances operated in these states; monarchs ruled through the cooperation of local leaders—chiefs in Africa, barons in Europe—and many decisions were made by state councils rather than by the whim of an individual. Despite these similarities, Africans had no conception of Europe; the only light-skinned peoples they knew of were the Berbers of North Africa, who crossed the Sahara in great caravans to trade with the peoples of the savanna. Europeans, on the other hand, held a vague and generally alluring image of Africa as a mysterious and far-off land containing great riches, especially in gold, and fabulously wealthy kings such as Mali's Mansa Musa. Indeed, there were periods during the Middle Ages when Africa appeared to enjoy a level of prosperity far ahead of Europe's. During the 14th century, for example, when Europe was ravaged by the Black Death and the Hundred Years War, African empires such as Mali and Songhay were enjoying peace and prosperity.

Nevertheless, by the end of the Middle Ages, Europeans were sailing to the coast of Africa, whereas West Africans had yet to venture beyond the confines of their own continent. In later centuries, many Europeans would take this as proof of their racial superiority. However, to unbiased students of history, the varying fortunes of Europe and Africa indicate a far more complex set of causes.

Though political organization in both Africa and Europe appeared to have developed in a similar fashion, Europe's physical environment had always provided many advantages for its inhabitants. Early humans first discovered these advantages about 40,000 years ago when they developed the ability to make clothing and build shelters; this enabled hunting groups to migrate from Africa and other hot-weather regions, following game animals into colder climates. As William H. McNeill has written in his book *Plagues and Peoples,* "In leaving tropical environments behind, our ancestors also escaped many of the parasites and disease organisms to which their predecessors and tropical contemporaries were accustomed. Health and vigor improved accordingly, and multiplication of human numbers assumed a hitherto unparalleled scale."

Initially, moving to colder climates had drawbacks. Wild animals were less abundant, and humans found far fewer wild food plants than they had been used to in tropical climates. However, as McNeill points out, the absence of disabling diseases such as malaria and sleeping sickness allowed humans greater opportunity to find ways of altering their environment, "giving a much wider scope to cultural invention than had been attainable within the tighter web of life from which naked humanity had originally emerged." In other words, the challenge for Africans was adapting to their environment, which they had done brilliantly, evolving ways of life and thought that emphasized tradition, continuity, and balance. Europeans, on the other hand, had the opportunity to develop a restless, competitive outlook that would impel them to change their world.

By the Middle Ages, Europeans had learned to exploit their land to the fullest. They had adapted hand-held farming tools into the plow. Pulled first by oxen and then more efficiently by horses, the plow could cultivate far more land in a short time than could the muscle power of the African farmer, who was still using the iron-bladed hoe of his ancestors. Africans practiced hoe agriculture not

(Continued on page 29)

24

IMAGES OF ROYALTY

The art of sculpture in Benin dates back to A.D. 950, when Ere, one of the kingdom's first rulers, encouraged the creation of specialized guilds for craftspeople. Heirs to a great artistic tradition that began with the Nok culture in the 5th century B.C., Benin's artists displayed their mastery in a variety of materials, including wood, ivory, terra-cotta, and bronze.

A terra-cotta head from Benin. Working in terra-cotta required great skill because the sculpture had to be heated at exactly the right temperature; if the air inside the hollow mold became too hot, the resulting pressure would cause the figure to disintegrate.

This striking head dates from the early period of bronze casting in Benin (14th to 15th century). Sculptors created such heads to honor deceased obas; after being publicly displayed during funeral ceremonies, the sculptures would then be placed in a royal shrine.

A small ivory mask from 16th-century Benin, designed to be worn as a royal ornament. The mask itself portrays an oba, but the row of tiny heads adorning the oba's crown have Portuguese features.

This bronze head depicts a
queen mother (iyoba). The
queen mother, who had her
own court and her own
officers, played an important
role in the affairs of Benin.
Normally, the oba could
depend on his mother for
support, although Ose, a 19th-
century iyoba, joined forces
with the enemies of her son,
Oba Obanosa.

SCENES FROM THE PALACE

During the 16th century, when European traders brought large amounts of copper and iron into Benin, Benin's sculptors were able to work on a grand scale. Using the same techniques they had employed to produce individual heads, the artists now created hundreds of decorative plaques that adorned the interior rooms and passageways of the royal palace in Benin City.

This 17th-century plaque depicts one of the drummers who made up Benin's corps of royal musicians. The floral designs in the background were inspired by patterns woven into Portuguese textiles.

XVII,4

An oba supported by two attendants. By casting the oba's legs in the form of mudfish, the artist expresses the Edo belief that the oba is the human counterpart of Olokun, the sea god.

Three hunters attack a leopard. Because the fierce jungle cat was so closely associated with the early life of Ewuare, the greatest of all the obas, it is featured in a number of Benin artworks. In addition, leopard-skin cloaks and necklaces made of leopards' teeth were highly prized items of apparel.

XVIII, 6.
98
1-15
51

This 17th-century plaque
depicts an Edo chief whose
high rank is indicated by the
massive beaded collar he wears.
The chief is accompanied by
two heavily armed soldiers and
a pair of musicians, one
blowing a horn and the other
playing a pair of wooden
clappers.

(Continued from page 32)

munication between monarchs of equal stature:

> We have heard Dom Jorge, your ambassador, in all that he has said to us on your behalf. We were much pleased with his coming to us, so that from him we might learn of the goodwill which you profess touching our service. . . . Be assured that, because of our constant desire to further your interests, you may command and make use of all that is ours as though it were your own.

Esigie, who is remembered as one of the greatest obas, accommodated the Portuguese in their desire to trade for pepper, gold (mined by the Akan peoples of the forest belt), textiles, ivory, and slaves (many of them prisoners of war captured in the campaigns of Oba Ozolua). He also permitted some Christian clergymen to operate in Benin, teaching Portuguese and converting Africans to Christianity. (The influence of the Christian fathers, however, was not widespread—most of them died of malaria, to which many Africans had developed a natural resistance over the centuries.) In allowing missionaries access to his people, Esigie was no different from the rulers of many savanna states, who adopted and fostered the religion of Islam as a means of creating bonds with their North

37

This 16th-century ivory casket from Benin, created for European customers, dramatically portrays a pair of Portuguese soldiers. With their beards, pale skin, and prominent noses, the visiting Portuguese clearly appeared strange and rather sinister to Africans.

A pair of bowmen brandish their weapons in this dramatic bronze plaque. Benin's powerful army, the scourge of the lower Niger region, ensured that visiting Europeans would be on their best behavior while conducting business in the realm of the obas.

38

African trading partners. This contact between cultures was often beneficial to the savanna kingdoms, and the Portuguese presence was certainly a stimulus to the people of Benin. The most lasting evidence of that influence are the magnificent works of art produced by Benin artists, beginning with the reign of Esigie and lasting for the next 100 years.

Among the Benin masterpieces from this period are carvings in ivory, many of them depicting Portuguese visitors. Even more impressive are the ceremonial bronze plaques created by the lost-wax method and displayed in the numerous reception chambers and inner rooms of the oba's palace. Most of the plaques depict obas, palace guards, warriors, court musicians, and other members of the royal entourage. Previously, the output of Benin's artists had been limited by the scarcity of copper, which had to make its way to Benin from North Africa through overland trade routes. Once they could obtain large amounts of copper directly from the Portuguese ships, the Edo were able to work on a larger scale than ever before and produce plaques by the hundreds. Some of the designs and techniques used in the plaques show that the sculptors adopted patterns common in Portuguese textiles and also studied the illustrations in European books.

When other Europeans learned of Portugal's profitable trade with West Africa, they were eager to follow suit. By the middle of the 16th century, the British and Dutch had made their way to the coast of Africa; being richer nations with more powerful navies, they were able to displace the Portuguese in many areas and take the lion's share of the African trade. Initially, the advent of new trading partners promised benefits for the Edo and other Africans. But before long, the interplay between Europe and Africa assumed a sinister and destructive nature.

Chapter 4 | THE SLAVE COAST

Throughout the 17th century, the people of Benin traded with British and Dutch merchants as equal partners. The trade developed to such an extent that the Edo devised sophisticated procedures to govern the trading process. In *Benin and the Europeans*, Alan Ryder describes these procedures:

> At the arrival of a ship at Ughoton [Benin's main port], the chief of that town dispatched a messenger to inform the Oba, as had been the practice in the sixteenth century. But instead of the Europeans being taken to Benin City, two or three *Iwebo* officials [palace chiefs] and twenty or thirty traders arrived to deal with them at Ughoton. . . . For their first visit to the Dutch merchants, the officials wore a dignified dress with strings of beads . . . around their necks. Kneeling they delivered salutations from the Oba, his mother and the three chief counsellors . . . presented some gifts of food in their name, and paid many compliments. Next they enquired after the state of the visitors' country, the progress of its wars and like subjects. Finally, after accepting a drink of spirits, they took ceremonious leave, without once mentioning questions of trade. . . . On subsequent days the officials returned in order to fix prices for any goods which had never been traded before; other items remained at the prices previously agreed upon. Keen bargaining ensued, sometimes lasting several weeks.

Those rare merchants who did have a chance to visit Benin City were impressed with the size of the capital, the arrangement of the streets, and the qual-

In this engraving, slaves are transported to a European ship anchored off the West African coast. By the mid–18th century, the transatlantic slave trade had taken a drastic toll on the societies of West Africa.

ity of the houses. One trader passed on the following account to Olfert Dapper, who included it in his *Accurate Description of the Regions of Africa*:

At the gate where I went in on horseback, I saw a very big wall, very thick and made of earth, with a very deep and broad ditch outside of it. . . . Inside the gate, and along the great street just mentioned, you see many other great streets on either side, and these are also straight and do not bend. . . . The houses in this town stand in good order, each one close and evenly placed with its neighbor, just as the houses in Holland stand. . . . The king's court is very great. It is built around many square-shaped yards. These yards have surrounding galleries where sentries are always placed. I myself went into the court far enough to pass through four great yards like this, and yet wherever I looked I could still see gate after gate which opened into other yards.

Dapper's book appeared in 1668, but not more than a century later, the entire picture had changed. Europeans had begun to think of Africans as a lower order

This bronze plaque depicts an Edo trader of the 17th century. In his right hand, the trader holds a staff indicating his authority to conduct business on behalf of the oba; in his left hand he holds a manilla, a C-shaped metal bracelet used as currency in Benin's trading operations.

of humanity, and many West African societies had declined from their former grandeur. The driving force behind these dramatic changes was the transatlantic slave trade.

Slavery has existed in human society since ancient times, encompassing all parts of the world and all races, including the city-states of ancient Greece, the great kingdoms of Egypt, and the Roman Empire. Black Africans had enslaved one another long before they even knew that Europeans existed. Many of these slaves were prisoners captured in warfare; others had been convicted of serious crimes. Most often, the captives were incorporated into the armies or households of rulers or other powerful men—in a few cases, such as those of Kanem-Borno, the Akan states of the forest belt, and the larger city-states of Hausaland, slaves were also organized into communities of laborers. The trade between the savanna states and the Muslims of North Africa had always included a certain number of black slaves, desired by the Muslims as soldiers and household servants.

It was entirely natural, then, for Africans to offer captives to their European trading partners. But for the first 200 years of their dealings with Africa, Europeans' interest in buying slaves was outstripped by their desire for items such as pepper and ivory. The transatlantic slave trade would never have developed if not for the growth of European involvement in a distant part of the world—the Americas.

Beginning with the first voyage of Christopher Columbus in 1492, the nations of western Europe began to seize islands in the Caribbean Sea as well as great tracts of land in North and South America. Whereas in earlier years Europeans had voyaged to Asia and Africa to obtain spices and precious metals, they now found that these valuable commodities were theirs for the taking, once they had subdued the Indians of the New World. In order to establish gold and silver mines and plantations for crops such as sugar, however, the Europeans needed laborers, and the conquered Indian populations could not fill this need. Unused to such labor and prey to the diseases carried by Europeans, the Indians died in such numbers that in many parts of the New World their once-thriving populations all but disappeared.

Europeans soon realized that Africans could fill their needs for labor. Africans were strong and hardy, often skilled in

43

mining and tropical farming, and highly resistant to many diseases. Thus, as the economy of the New World expanded, European traders demanded more and more slaves from their African trading partners; captives began to play such a large part in the bargaining that Europeans soon referred to the lands bordering the Bight of Benin as the Slave Coast. By 1600, the total slave exports of West Africa had amounted to about 10,000 a year; by 1750 the annual total had risen to 100,000. All in all, during the entire duration of the transatlantic slave trade (1500–1900), about 12 million Africans were shipped from their homeland to the Americas. As Patrick Manning has pointed out in his 1990 book *Slavery and African Life,* the slave trade represented "the largest migration in human history to that time."

The slave trade had a powerful impact on the population of West Africa. Because many of the slaves were men in the prime of life, women began to outnumber marriageable men in many regions of Africa, and birth rates declined. Manning explains that although Africa's population may not have actually declined during the slave-trade era, it certainly did not grow. He calculates that in the normal course of events, the population of sub-Saharan Africa should have been 100 million by 1850, yet in fact it was only 50 million. During the same period, the populations of Europe and North America enjoyed substantial growth, and the wealth of both continents grew enormously, in large part because of African labor.

If population were the only way of judging the effects of the slave trade, Benin itself would not have suffered disastrously, at least compared with other areas of West Africa, such as Igboland and Senegambia. In 1789, for example, when British ships loaded 20,000 captives from Igboland in the eastern Niger Delta, they took only 1,000 from the ports of Benin. Most of that 1,000 would have been non-Edo who had been captured by Benin's army, and thus Benin itself would not have suffered severe population losses. However, as Benin's neighbors to the east and west grew wealthy from the slave trade and acquired firearms from the Europeans, the balance of power along the lower Niger shifted. Towns that had previously paid tribute to the obas ceased doing so, and their new firearms gave them the ability to raid Benin's territory and take on the more numerous Edo armies. Benin, along with many other African states,

A group of captives being transported overland by African slave traders. When the captives reached the coast, they were purchased by European merchants and loaded onto ships for transport to the Americas.

was forced to acquire firearms to maintain its military strength, and the Europeans, realizing their advantage, would only give firearms in exchange for slaves. The growing instability in the delta inevitably decreased the power of the obas and the prosperity of their kingdom.

In broader terms, the slave trade corrupted the society of Benin, just as it corrupted the society of every other African nation involved in it—no matter whether that nation was primarily selling slaves or losing its people to the slavers. Unlike other avenues of trade, the slave trade provided no wealth for African soci-

46

This copper sculpture from Benin depicts an Edo musketeer. By the 18th century, Benin and other African kingdoms were dependent on European firearms for defense against their enemies; they could obtain these weapons only by providing a steady supply of slaves in exchange.

ety. The money and goods exchanged for slaves remained in the hands of a narrow class of rulers and slave merchants. No benefits accrued to hardworking families as they did when textiles or other goods were exchanged; indeed, many families lost some of their most productive members without getting anything in return.

The Benin praised by Dutch visitors as late as the 1650s began to show a different face after only half a century of intense slaving. In 1700, for example, the Dutch merchant William Bosman wrote of Benin City, "Formerly this village was very thick and close-built, but now the houses stand like poor men's corn, widely distant from each other." As the historian Basil Davidson has pointed out, the art of Benin also began to decline in quality and sensitivity, and he links this change to the kingdom's political fortunes: "Moreover, this process of coarsening can be shown to have continued: the heads became clumsier and more gross in shape and feeling as the slaving years passed by and the old skills were overborne and set aside."

In light of all these factors, it is not surprising that European attitudes toward Africa began to change. In part, the change took place because those who profited from slavery felt the need to jus-

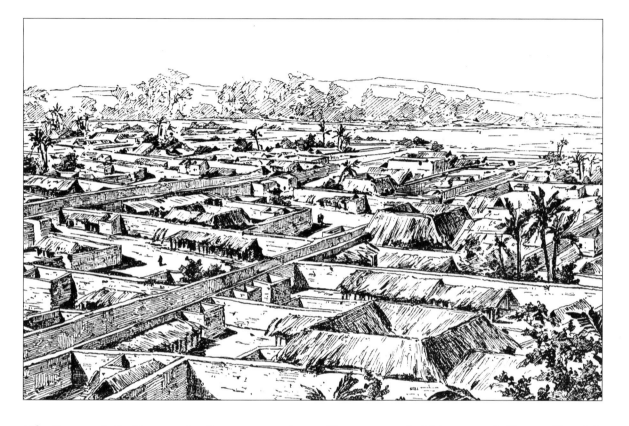

This engraving of Benin City was made by a British artist in 1897, when the once-grand capital of the obas had suffered greatly from the effects of war and political upheaval.

47

tify the exploitation and often unspeakably brutal treatment of so many human beings. If they could convince themselves (and others) that Africans were "backward" and "naturally servile," white slave traders and slave owners could even claim that they were providing these poor "savages" with a better life in the New World. And as the slave traffic progressed, the growing disparity in wealth between Europe and Africa—and the noticeable coarsening in African society—gave credence to European and North American feelings of racial superiority. Having once been an equal trading partner, Africa was now looked upon only as a ripe source of plunder. This drastic change would finally contribute to the overthrow of societies that had flourished for centuries.

Chapter 5 | "FAREWELL, FAREWELL!"

An Edo chief and two young hunters, photographed in the early 20th century. Though Benin was at this time part of the British empire, the Edo staunchly maintained their traditions and their pride.

By the beginning of the 19th century, the transatlantic slave trade became less profitable, due in part to the growing availability of cheap industrial labor in Europe and the Americas. The traffic in human beings in the Bight of Benin entered its final phase in 1809, when the British Parliament declared it illegal. The gradual decline of transatlantic slaving, however, was only the prelude to new forms of European exploitation.

In Benin and its surrounding territories, the British turned their attention to other goods, principally palm oil. Obtained from the nuts of the many palm trees growing wild in West Africa, palm oil was desired in Europe to lubricate machinery and for the manufacture of soap, candles, and margarine. The palm oil trade required the work of many individuals, who were needed to harvest the nuts, extract the oil, pour it into barrels, and transport the barrels to the ports for shipping. This commerce achieved such a scale that the British began to refer to the waterways of the Niger Delta as the Oil Rivers.

However, the Africans employed in the palm oil trade were not, in many cases, free laborers whose wages could usher in a new era of African prosperity. Europeans may have called a halt to slavery, but they had accustomed powerful men in Africa to profiting from their weaker neighbors, and this practice continued long after 1809. In many areas,

50

Workers harvest palm nuts to be used in the production of palm oil. After the abolition of the transatlantic slave trade in the early 19th century, palm oil became the major export from the coast of West Africa.

African rulers and slave merchants continued to take large numbers of captives. Instead of being sold to Europeans, the captives were now put to work along the Oil Rivers. In addition, black slaves were still in demand in North Africa, and the trans-Saharan slave trade continued unabated.

Now antislavery activists in Europe demanded the elimination of slavery within Africa. The British government in particular felt obliged—or believed it could be profitable—to act on these demands. In order to root out slavery completely, the British clearly needed to delve farther into the African interior. Before the 19th century, this had been largely impossible, because Europeans had virtually no resistance to malaria. (For many decades, Europeans referred to the African coast as "the white man's grave.") European slavers had mostly remained in their ships and relied upon African merchants to bring the slaves to the wharves. However, the development of the drug quinine in 1830 provided an effective treatment for malaria. The British could now push inland from the Niger Delta, both to search out illegal slavers and to further their commercial interests.

In 1849, the British established a consulship for the coastline of the Gulf of

Guinea, and in the ensuing years they steadily increased their influence in the region, forcing their will on Africans who resisted them. In 1885, the major European powers met in Berlin, Germany, and agreed on a plan to divide up Africa. According to this plan, the entire Niger Delta region was to become part of the British Empire, which by now included India and much of the Middle East.

In 1892, the British government persuaded the new oba of Benin, Ovonramwen, to sign a treaty by which he accepted the "gracious favor and protection" of Queen Victoria. In return the oba pledged, among other things, to have no dealings with other European powers, to grant wide authority to British consuls, to permit free trade between the British and other peoples in the delta, and to welcome Christian missionaries. Despite the one-sided nature of the treaty, the British government apparently intended to gain control over Benin in a gradual and peaceful manner. However, this was not the attitude of their main official in the area, Sir Ralph Moor.

An ambitious man, Moor wanted to advance his career by getting quick results in Benin. When the oba called a halt to trade in the delta because he was unhappy with the terms being offered, Moor saw an opportunity to create a confrontation. He dispatched his newly appointed deputy, James Phillips, on a mission to Benin City, with instructions to persuade the oba to lift his trade embargo. Phillips organized a party of eight Englishmen and numerous Itsekiri porters and set out for Benin in January 1897. Inexperienced in Africa, Phillips had little idea of the provocation he was creating.

While the Phillips party was en route, emissaries from Benin City informed them that the oba was taking part in the monthlong Igue festival and that he could not receive any visitors. Nevertheless, Phillips decided to follow his orders from Moor and press on. When Ovonramwen learned that the Englishmen were coming ahead, he ordered that they be given a peaceful reception. However, the war chiefs believed that Benin was being invaded by hostile forces, and they directed their troops to set up an ambush along the main road to the city. When the Phillips party approached, the Edo greeted them with a fusillade of rifle fire. Two men managed to escape into the forest and eventually made their way back to the coast. Phillips and the other six Englishmen died, either on the road or later in Benin City.

51

52

British troops firing on Edo troops during the final assault on Benin City in February 1897. Though the Edo defended their capital valiantly, their antiquated muskets were no match for the machine guns and artillery of the invaders.

When reports of the so-called Benin Massacre reached England, the public was outraged, and the government could no longer forestall the use of force. A squadron of British navy vessels, carrying detachments of soldiers and marines, was dispatched to the Benin River with instructions to take Benin City by force. The Edo did everything within their power to halt the advance of the British troops through the forest, and when this failed, they defended their capital with volleys of rifle fire and shells from the ancient cannon they had obtained many years earlier from the Portuguese. In the end, however, the outmoded weapons of the Edo were no match for the rapid-fire machine guns and powerful artillery pieces employed by the British. On February 18, 1897, the attackers mounted a final assault and captured Benin City.

Among the first acts of the conquerors was the looting of thousands of artworks from the royal palace and from nearby shrines. This action deprived the Edo of much of their artistic heritage and made it impossible for scholars in later generations to fully understand the development of Benin's world-class art. Reflecting on his countrymen's behavior in his 1982 book *City of Blood Revisited*, the historian Robert Home wrote: "For all their assumptions of racial superiority, the British at Benin did their best to destroy a remarkable artistic achievement, like the Mongols when they pillaged medieval Baghdad." Desecration was followed by destruction: a fire broke out on February 21, and by the time it had burned itself out, the royal palace and much of Benin City lay in ruins. As Home remarks, "The British always maintained that the fire at Benin was accidental, though the Edo never believed them."

Ovonramwen had fled the city before the final assault, and he remained a fugitive until August, when he surrendered to the British forces and was put on trial. The six war chiefs responsible for the ambush on the Phillips party were condemned to death. Two of them escaped execution by committing suicide, and a third was pardoned because of his youth. Ovonramwen himself was cleared of any involvement in the massacre and was offered the opportunity to continue as oba under British supervision, provided that he spend some time at the British colonial headquarters at nearby Calabar, where he would be instructed in the

Oba Ovonramwen wears a rueful expression as he sits on the deck of a British yacht in 1897, sailing into exile. He was obliged to remain in Calabar, a British outpost east of Benin, until his death in 1914.

53

ways of the British colonial system.

Believing that the British meant to keep him in Calabar, Ovonramwen fled again, going into hiding in the compound of an influential chief. However, after the British threatened the leading chiefs with death, they agreed to surrender their oba. This time the British

A map of present-day Africa. The shaded area indicates the former territory of the kingdom of Benin, now Bendel State in the nation of Nigeria.

54

sentenced Ovonramwen to permanent exile in Calabar, and he left his kingdom with sad and bitter words:

> I appeal to the Almighty and the Spirits of the departed Obas of Benin, my fathers, to judge between me and the Binis who ill-advised and cunningly sold me into the hands of the British troops. . . . Oh! Benin, Merciless and Wicked! Farewell, Farewell!

By the time of Ovonramwen's death in 1914, Benin had been incorporated into the larger British colony of Nigeria. The British preferred to govern their colonies by "indirect rule" through traditional leaders, and upon the death of Ovonramwen they appointed his son Aiguobasimi to be the new oba and restored him to Benin City. Aiguobasimi took the title Eweka II, forging a link with Eweka I, the first oba of the Oranmiyan dynasty in the 14th century. Eweka II rebuilt the royal palace on a smaller scale and reigned until his death in 1933, when he was succeeded by his son, Akenzua II.

When Nigeria obtained its independence from Britain in 1960, the Edo constituted one of the new nation's most important ethnic groups. Benin City became the capital of Nigeria's Mid-Western State, now known as Bendel State. (The modern nation of Benin, located just west of Nigeria, corresponds to the former state of Dahomey and has no relation to the former Edo kingdom.) Today, Benin City is a sprawling urban center with a population of more than 160,000. In the royal palace and the National Museum (erected in 1973), the remaining artworks from Benin's great periods of creativity are on display. Despite the many changes brought about by 20th-century technology and politics, the Edo continue to celebrate the Igue festival and the New Yam festival as their ancestors did. Their neighbors may no longer refer to Edo country as the "land of the powerful oba," but the Edo can proudly contrast their 1,000 years of imperial grandeur to the swift passage of the colonial empires that once imposed their will on Africa.

CHRONOLOGY

c. 2000 B.C.	Edo people migrate from central Nigeria to the Niger Delta region
A.D. 900	Kingdom of Benin emerges under Igodo, who takes the title *ogiso*
c. 950	Ere begins reign as ogiso; Benin's artists begin to carve in wood and ivory
late 13th century	Reign of ogisos comes to an end; Edo try republican form of government under Evian; Evian's ambitions cause political crisis
c. 1300	Edo send to Yorubaland for Prince Oranmiyan and invite him to become the ruler of Benin; Oranmiyan declines the throne, but his son, Eweka I, becomes the first *oba* of Benin
c. 1325	Reign of Oba Oguola begins; bronze-casting techniques come to Benin from Yorubaland
1355–80	Reign of Oba Ewedo, who creates new posts for royal officials and undertakes numerous building projects
1440–73	Reign of Ewuare the Great, who increases the wealth and power of Benin by military conquest and expands the capital, Benin City; Portuguese mariners begin to explore the Atlantic coast of West Africa

1485	Portuguese emissary João Afonso d'Aveiro visits Benin City; Oba Ozolua sends ambassador to Portugal
1504–50	Reign of Oba Esigie, who fosters trade and cultural relations with Portuguese; art of Benin enters its golden age as sculptors produce hundreds of bronze plaques for the royal palace; British and Dutch begin to replace Portuguese as trading powers in West Africa
1650–1850	Traffic in slaves dominates relations between Europeans and West Africans; millions of Africans are shipped to the Americas; Benin and other African societies begin to decline; Europeans develop racist views of Africa
early 19th century	British Parliament outlaws slave trade; palm oil trade replaces slaving in commerce between Benin and Britain
1849	British establish consulship for Gulf of Guinea and extend their influence in Benin
1892	Oba Ovonramwen signs treaty that further expands British power in Benin
1897	British delegation is ambushed en route to Benin City; British forces retaliate by occupying Benin City and exiling Ovonramwen; kingdom of Benin ceases to exist
1960	Nigeria gains independence; Benin City becomes capital of Mid-Western (now Bendel) State

FURTHER READING

Connah, Graham. *African Civilizations.* Cambridge: Cambridge University Press, 1987.

Dark, P. J. C. *Introduction to Benin Art and Technology.* Oxford: Clarendon Press, 1973.

Davidson, Basil. *Africa in History.* Rev. ed. New York: Collier, 1991.

———. *The African Genius.* Boston: Little, Brown, 1969.

———. *The African Slave Trade.* Rev. ed. Boston: Little, Brown, 1980.

Davidson, Basil, with F. K. Buah and the advice of J. F. A. Ajayi. *A History of West Africa, 1000–1800.* New rev. ed. London: Longmans, 1977.

Egharevba, Jacob. *A Short History of Benin.* 3rd. ed. Ibadan: Ibadan University Press, 1960.

Forde, Daryll, and P. M. Kaberry, eds. *West African Kingdoms in the Nineteenth Century.* Oxford: Oxford University Press, 1967.

Freyer, Bryna. *Royal Benin Art.* Washington, D.C.: Smithsonian Institution Press, 1987.

Gimpel, Jean. *The Medieval Machine: The Industrial Revolution of the Middle Ages.* New York: Penguin, 1976.

Hodgkin, T. H. *Nigerian Perspectives: An Historical Anthology.* Oxford: Oxford University Press, 1975.

Home, Robert. *City of Blood Revisited: A New Look at the Benin Expedition of 1897.* London: Rex Collings, 1982.

Hull, Richard W. *African Cities and Towns Before the European Conquest.* New York: Norton, 1976.

McEvedy, Colin. *The Penguin Atlas of African History.* New York: Penguin, 1980.

McNeill, William H. *Plagues and Peoples.* New York: Anchor, 1976.

Manning, Patrick. *Slavery and African Life.* Cambridge: Cambridge University Press, 1990.

Oliver, Roland, and Brian M. Fagan. *Africa in the Iron Age.* Cambridge: Cambridge University Press, 1975.

Park, Mungo. *Travels in the Interior Districts of Africa.* Reprint of the 1799 edition. New York: Arno Press / New York Times, 1971.

Ryder, A. F. C. *Benin and the Europeans, 1485–1897.* New York: Humanities Press, 1969.

Shaw, Thurstan. *Nigeria: Its Archaeology and Early History.* London: Thames and Hudson, 1978.

Smith, Robert. *Warfare and Diplomacy in Pre-Colonial West Africa.* 2nd ed. Madison: University of Wisconsin Press, 1989.

UNESCO General History of Africa. 8 vols. Berkeley: University of California Press, 1980–93.

Webster, J. B., and A. A. Boahen, with M. Tidy. *The Revolutionary Years: West Africa Since 1800.* New ed. London: Longman, 1980.

GLOSSARY

bronze
a metal created by the combination of copper and tin; used by Benin artists to create numerous sculptures

caravel
a light, maneuverable sailing vessel developed by Portuguese shipbuilders during the 15th century

delta
a wide, flat plain, usually at the mouth of a river, covered by a network of waterways

edaiken
title used by the crown prince of Benin

Edo
black African people who created the kingdom of Benin; one of the major ethnic groups of Nigeria

Igue festival
monthlong rite through which the oba of Benin increases his spiritual powers

lost-wax method
technique of metal casting with which Benin artists created bronze sculptures

malaria
deadly parasitic disease transmitted by various mosquitoes; common throughout the West African forest belt

Middle Ages
period of European history extending roughly from 500 to 1500

missionary
one who attempts to spread the teachings of a particular religion among people who observe a different religion

oba	title used by the rulers of Benin since 1300
ogiso	title used by the rulers of Benin between 900 and 1300
palm oil	oil obtained from the nuts of African palm trees; important trade item during the 19th and early 20th centuries
sleeping sickness	a deadly parasitic disease transmitted to both humans and animals by the tsetse fly, which breeds throughout the West African forest belt
transatlantic slave trade	traffic in human beings that lasted roughly from 1500 to 1900 and resulted in the shipment of 12 million Africans from their homeland to the Americas
uzama	hereditary Edo chiefs who have the responsibility of crowning the oba

INDEX

63

PHILIP KOSLOW earned his B.A. and M.A. degrees from New York University and went on to teach and conduct research at Oxford University, where his interest in medieval European and African history was awakened. The editor of numerous volumes for young adults, he is also the author of *El Cid* in the Chelsea House HISPANICS OF ACHIEVEMENT series and of *Centuries of Greatness: The West African Kingdoms, 750–1900 in Chelsea House's* MILESTONES IN BLACK AMERICAN HISTORY series.

PICTURE CREDITS

CROAKED!

CROAKED!

DICK LOCHTE

FIVE STAR

An imprint of Thomson Gale, a part of The Thomson Corporation

Detroit • New York • San Francisco • New Haven, Conn. • Waterville, Maine • London

LIBRARY OF CONGRESS CATALOGING-IN-PUBLICATION DATA

Lochte, Dick.
    Croaked! / Dick Lochte. — 1st ed.
      p. cm.
    ISBN-13: 978-1-59414-525-4 (alk. paper)
    ISBN-10: 1-59414-525-3 (alk. paper)
    1. Men's magazines—Employees—Fiction. 2. United States—History—1961–1969—Fiction. 3. California, Southern—Fiction. I. Title.
PS3562.O217C76 2007
813'.54—dc22
                                                     2006038244

First Edition. First Printing: April 2007.

Published in 2007 in conjunction with Tekno Books and Ed Gorman.

Printed in the United States of America on permanent paper
10 9 8 7 6 5 4 3 2 1

For all those, here and gone, who followed the white rabbit to wonderland . . . thanks for the memories.
A special tip of the Ogle hat to Seth Greenland for suggesting the title.

PROLOGUE

Several events of varying importance occurred in the United States during the first six months of 1965.

The Reverend Martin Luther King, Jr. led a march of 25,000 to the Alabama State Capitol to hand a petition to Governor George Wallace, demanding voting rights for African Americans. The 1961 conviction of entrepreneur Billie Sol Estes, a close, personal friend of President Lyndon Johnson, was overturned by the Supreme Court on the grounds that the television broadcast of the trial may have affected the jurors, the witnesses and the judge.

The initial U.S. mass bombing raid of the Vietnam War took place with Guam-based B-52s attacking a Vietcong stronghold just north of Saigon. And, as American involvement in the war proliferated, so did the number of student protests on campuses throughout the country.

The discovery of cosmic background radiation confirmed the "Big Bang" theory.

The Record of the Year Grammy was awarded to Stan Getz and Astrid Gilberto for their "The Girl from Ipanema." The film based on Boris Pasternack's novel of the Russian Revolution, *Dr. Zhivago*, was considered an artistic and commercial blockbuster.

Astronaut Edward White II became the first American to take a walk in space, possibly to make sure Soviet cosmonaut Aleksei Leonov left things as they were during his breakthrough spacewalk three months before.

And, at 8 p.m. on a typically mild and smoggy June night in Hollywood, California, on the first floor of a five-story office building slightly past its prime, the stockholders of OPI, a privately owned corporation responsible for the publication of *Ogle*, a monthly magazine devoted to "the masculine pleasure-principle," were gathered around a conference table discussing a proposed change in editorial policy.

"So, do we or do we not go pubic?" Milton Zephyr Armstead asked, his hawk-like profile softened by an air of insouciance as he slouched in his contour chair. "Ida?"

Ida Connor considered the question. A former UCLA campus beauty queen, she was, at forty-something, a handsome, fair-haired woman bearing a strong facial resemblance to the actress Patricia Neal. But while her physical attributes were appreciated, it had been her agile mind and her ability to seek and find logical solutions to the most illogical of problems that had won her a seat at the *Ogle* executive table in the dual role of CFO and Personnel Director.

"Do we know Mr. Hefner's thoughts on the subject?" she asked, referencing the founder and creative force behind the country's leading men's magazine.

"My Chicago spies tell me he's giving his airbrushes a rest," Armstead said. "That's why we can't afford to beat around the bush, so to speak."

"I assume, Milton, your people in Promotion can handle the attending flak from women's rights groups and the usual right-wing guardians of morality," Ida said.

Armstead shifted his emaciated, Pierre Cardin–wrapped frame on the chair and said, "Who cares what those trogs think?"

"The big money advertisers care," John Bingham said from across the table. A sturdy, florid man with a barrel chest that tested the buttons of his Hickey-Freeman suit coat, he was the picture of a college jock softened by too much good life. "I busted my ass getting GM to at least consider using the magazine. We'll kiss them and every other major advertiser good-bye if we do this thing."

"So we lose some ads," Armstead said. "We've got enough cigarette and booze pages to keep us in clover. Our readers are into foreign sports cars, anyway."

"Our readers like to look at sports cars," Ida said. "They don't buy them. They buy Fords and Chevys."

"Exactly," Bingham said.

"You can count on losing some key contributors, too," the magazine's editor, Kevin Dobbs, said. He'd been living in Southern California for the past seven years but had steadfastly maintained his Manhattan pallor. He ran an anxious hand through his greying blond crew cut for, by Ida's count, the twentieth time since the meeting began. "You can't expect me to ask a National Book Award–winner to—"

"We feed your literary lions damn well," Armstead said. "They're not gonna slink away from the money trough just because of a little patch of fuzz."

"*The New Yorker* feeds them better," Dobbs said.

"Jesus, Kevin, don't start with your *New Yorker* bullshit," Armstead said. "The magazine of choice for college girls and fags! If you're so fond of the bloody *New Yorker* why don't you go work there?"

"I did, for nearly nine years," Dobbs said. "Happy days."

Ida sighed and turned to the remaining v.p., the man responsible for *Ogle*'s circulation. Nick Hobart was a six-foot-four mass of bone and muscle wearing a tweed jacket so rumpled it looked as if he'd been in an alley fight. That was an actual possibility, she knew, considering that he'd started out in the magazine business as a strong-arm, traveling around the country tipping over racks and terrorizing store managers into placing his former employer's publications in prime point-of-sale position.

Hobart was staring at an object at the center of the table—a foot-tall bronze statue of an anthropomorphic frog standing upright on a lily pad. It was a particularly dapper amphibian, wearing a snap-brim hat at a jaunty angle, lifting a cocktail in one webbed hand while the other held a sport coat draped over its scrawny shoulder, Sinatra-style. The magazine's logo in 3-D.

"What about you, Nick?" Ida asked, causing Hobart to shift his gaze lazily from the statue. "Any thoughts on the pubic issue?"

"Sure," Hobart said. "Bottom line: we go hairy and *Ogle* gets tossed out of drugstores and supermarkets."

"So frigging what?" Armstead said.

"Eighty percent of our circulation is single copy," Hobart said. "We lose the racks, we could drop from 2 million copies a month to 400,000, just like that." He didn't bother to snap his fingers.

"That's a . . . a city magazine number," Armstead said, visibly shaken. "It's a worst case scenario, right?"

"Wake up and smell the mood of the country, pal," Bingham, the ad man, said. "People out there are pissed off. They can't do anything about Vietnam. They can't do anything about their beatnik kids. They can't do anything about rock and roll or crime in the streets or marijuana. So what do they do? They find stuff they can change and zero in on it. They picket. They complain. They write letters of protest. We do anything to flag their attention, they'll be on us like rabid dogs."

"One racker drops us, they all drop us," Hobart said. "I've warned our leader about this before." He gestured toward an empty chair that ordinarily would be supporting the tall, trim body of Trower J. Buckley, *Ogle*'s publisher. "Where is the big guy, anyway?"

Armstead used fist and middle finger gesture to pantomime copulation. Ignoring him, Ida said, "He had a conflicting appointment. I'll be phoning him with our recommendation . . . which seems to be heading toward a thumbs-down, correct?"

They all nodded.

"Buck may not listen," Armstead said. "Unlike us mere mortals, he's not in this for the loot. In his current savior-of-the-oppressed mode, he might see it as a freedom of expression issue."

"Which brings us to the real reason for this meeting," Kevin Dobbs said, freckled hand going through his crewcut once again.

"Real reason?" Hobart asked, turning to Ida. "I don't think I got that memo. What real reason?"

"I'm sorry, Nick," Ida said. "I was remiss—"

"It's about our shares of OPI stock, Nick," Bingham said with some impatience. "You are aware of the company's ownership structure?"

Ida had purposely kept Hobart out of the loop on the new plan, waiting for some inspiration as to how to sell him on it. Of one thing she was certain: Bingham, a supposed expert salesman, was making a lousy pitch.

"I don't suppose I need a college degree to figure it out," Hobart said. "The company was split up among the founders. Buck, Milton, Ida and . . . I can't remember the other guy, the one had the heart attack."

"Remy Lagerloff," Ida said.

"Yeah, Lagerloff," Hobart said. "The three of them put up five hundred bucks apiece. I don't know if I ever heard what you contributed, Ida."

She smiled at his sarcasm. He was getting back at her for not giving him the full story on the meeting. He knew most of the things she'd done to earn her piece of *Ogle*. How she'd found a lawyer to handle the legal work off the books and cajoled both

11

paper stock supplier and printer to produce the debut issue on the cuff. All part of the company lore.

He'd heard the stories about her keeping her three partners in food and drink while they worked nineteen- and twenty-hour days and nights creating the debut issue. And, finally, that she'd sought out a promising novice photographer and, wearing a flowing brunette wig, a see-through peignoir, fake horn-rimmed glasses and an appropriately placed copy of Kinsey's *Sexual Behavior in the Human Female*, had been the magazine's first nude centerfold.

"My contribution was hard-earned," she said.

"Probably harder earned than your other partners here might suspect," Hobart said. "Anyway, Buck cut you in for a piece of the pie along with Milton and the dead guy, Lagerloff. As I understand it, Lagerloff's stock was automatically acquired from his estate by OPI. That's what got split up between me and Dobbs and Bingham when we came aboard."

"The salient point," Armstead said, "is that Buck has always maintained a controlling interest."

"It's his baby," Hobart said.

"Not completely," Bingham said. "Forty-eight percent belongs to the five of us."

"So? I'm sure as hell satisfied with my share," Hobart said.

"What about the future?" Armstead said.

"What about it? Circulation's up," Hobart said. "Naked broads are not gonna go out of style."

"There are other things in the magazine besides the naked . . . nudes," Kevin Dobbs said. "And that's where Buck has lost his touch."

"Lost his mind, you mean," Bingham said. "Publishing articles about politics, the war, race relations. Now he's starting to spout mumbo-jumbo about business ethics and morality. Our readers want fantasy, not reality."

"You're worryin' over nuthin,' John," Nick Hobart said. "The numbers are up. The magazine's in better shape than Raquel Welch."

"We have to start thinking beyond the magazine," Armstead said. "Hefner's got his clubs. We want to open things up, make a public offering of OPI shares and use the loot to expand the *Ogle* empire to television, books, movies. Go worldwide. Put out international editions. Give that new Brit skin mag Penthouse some competition."

"Buck's not the kind of guy wants to worry about what some stockholder from Iowa has to say about the magazine," Hobart said. "He'll never go public with *Ogle*."

"That's the problem precisely," Bingham said. "That's why we feel it's time to take the ball away."

"He's got a pretty tight hold on it."

"No, he doesn't," Bingham said. "He doesn't have a tight hold on anything, including his sanity."

"It's for his own good," Dobbs said. "We'll be stopping him before he hurts himself."

"I get it," Hobart said. "You're not thinking about making a killing, you're just thinking of Buck's mental health. You in on this, Ida?"

"I'm finding it difficult to poke holes in their argument," she said.

"The guy's gone weird," Dobbs said.

"Weird how?"

"He's . . . forgetful," Bingham said. "Confuses the present with the past. Quotes the Scriptures."

"He . . . fondles himself in public," Dobbs said. "While quoting the Scriptures."

Hobart stood up. "This is bullshit," he said heatedly. "Nothing's wrong with Buck. If he is acting whacky, I wouldn't put it past you greedy bastards to have slipped some happy dust into his martini."

"It's important we stand together on this," Armstead said.

"Yeah? Well, brother, count me out of the togetherness," Hobart said and stormed off.

"That worked well," Ida said.

"He'll go straight to Buck," Dobbs said.

Armstead shrugged. "So fucking what? We deny, deny, deny. Who's Buck going to believe? His oldest and closest or some thug whose father once carried a gun for Mo Annenberg?"

In a fury, Hobart charged up the stairwell to his office on the third floor where he paused, breathing hard, trying to calm himself. There was nothing that infuriated him more than disloyalty. True, it had been Ida Connor who'd brought him into the company. And God knows he owed her a hell of a lot. But it was Buck who'd welcomed him warmly and who always made him feel part of the *Ogle* team.

Armstead and Dobbs and that sonofabitch Bingham walked around with their goddamned noses in the air most of the time, but Trower Buckley, born to one of Southern California's oldest and wealthiest families, was the kind of aristocrat who didn't think he had to shove it in your face. Nothing high-hat about the man.

The publisher knew most of Hobart's history, mainly that he'd dropped out of school at fourteen to work in the circulation department of the *Philadelphia Inquirer;* the job reputedly had been part of a debt the newspaper's owner, Moses Annenberg, owed Hobart, Sr. for using his gun during the infamous Chicago circulation wars.

Hobart himself had carried a gun early in his career, though he was no killer. He'd done a lot of things he wasn't proud of, but there was one rule handed down by his old man that he never broke: you honor the guy who signs your paycheck. That was a tie stronger even than love.

He tossed his coat on a nearby chair and headed for the shelf where he kept the Bell's Eight-Year-Old. He poured an inch, shot it down and then headed for his desk.

On the way, he paused beside his white couch and patted one of its cushions. He'd been using that cushion as a sort of safety deposit box, a repository of interesting facts. He was following another of his father's bits of advice: "Always know who the fuck you're dealing with, kid."

Hobart sat down at his desk and wondered how he was going to tell Buck that the people he trusted most were conspiring to take away his magazine.

He reached for the phone, but stopped himself. This wasn't something you handled by phone.

He scribbled a note to Buck, requesting a meeting the next morning. He folded it, slipped it into an interoffice envelope and was about to drop it into the OUT box, when he noticed a stack of pages the number-crunchers in research had left in the IN box, the most recent newsstand sales figures from across the country. He drew the pages toward him, a man infatuated by circulation figures.

The final numbers were encouraging enough to lift his spirits, at least momentarily.

He picked up a pencil and began to go through the report line by line.

But his thoughts continued to drift back to this new development. It wasn't enough that Buck's top guys were turning against him, there was this other, really rough thing he deserved to know about. Hobart should've told him the minute he found out.

He grabbed the phone and dialed Buckley's apartment in the building's penthouse.

Five rings and Buckley's recorded voice was saying, "If the

phone's been ringing, then I'm off swinging. Try me later."

With a sigh, Hobart replaced the receiver.

He glanced down at the circulation figures and smiled. At least he could offer Buck a little good news to go with the bad.

Two hours later, he tried Buckley's number again, got the swinging message and decided to call it a night.

By then the building was pretty much deserted.

He passed the empty reception desk where T.J. the night watchman usually sat in that dumb outfit they made him wear—a forest green version of a cop uniform with an empty holster and an *Ogle* frog logo patch on his sleeve. Probably on his rounds. His current choice of literature was spread open on the desktop, a paperback titled *The Galton Case* with a cover drawing of a gun-toting guy in a trench coat. Hobart knew a lot of gunmen but none of them wore trench coats unless it was raining buckets. It was hard enough drawing your weapon past your jacket.

As he descended the short flight of stairs to the front door, his right knee began making clicking noises again. He'd popped it years before, kicking out the glass front door of a drugstore that had refused to put his magazine, *Global News*, near the cash register next to rivals *Time* and *Newsweek*. What goes around, he thought.

He unlocked the front door and stepped into the night.

Under the building's marquee, he waited to make sure the door popped back into a locked position.

That's when he heard a scraping noise overhead.

Scowling, he took a few steps backward along the sidewalk and stared up at the marquee that had been designed to resemble a huge lily pad. Atop it was a twenty-foot-high stone statue of the *Ogle* frog.

By light of day, the figure seemed amusing. But at night, in the bloodred neon light from the bar across the street, the frog, with its bulging eyes and smirking lips, looked demonic and obscene.

Hobart was stunned to see it suddenly hop forward. It leaned over the edge of its lily pad and leered down at him.

By the time the circulation manager realized what was happening, it was too late for him to do anything about it. Even as he raised his arm to guard his head, he knew that skin and bone would be no protection against the plummeting stone figure.

It easily snapped his wrist and drove him to the ground, crushing his upper body and shattering his cranium, sending shards of bone into his no-longer-functioning brain.

1.

Harry Trauble's day began with a phone call from his mother in Hot Springs. "Did I wake you, son?" Micki Trauble asked.

"Not exactly," he said, groping for and finding his watch on the bedside table. He blinked to clear the sleep fuzz from his eyes and tried to make out the time in the drapery-darkened apartment. It looked like 6:45 a.m.

"I wanted to catch you before you left for work. You know I don't like to phone that . . . place."

"Well, you caught me, mom," he said. "What's up? You and dad okay?"

"We're fine," she replied chirpily. "But your brother Vaughan was shot by a sniper."

Harry sat straight up, wide awake. "How bad?" he asked.

"His shoulder. Evidently they removed the bullet and it went well. This all happened three days ago, but he or the Army didn't think it necessary to notify us until this morning when he called."

"How'd he sound?"

"In good spirits, I think. You know Vaughan, how closed-in he can be. And he seemed rather woozy."

"They probably gave him something for the pain."

"Oh, Harry, you know very well your brother stopped doing drugs after the accident." The "accident" was his mother's way of referencing the evening a few years before when Vaughan Trauble, high on elephant tranquilizer, had driven the family

18

Chrysler into a tree, breaking his collar bone and demolishing the car.

"Are they sending him home?" Harry asked.

"I would have thought so, but Vaughan says the wound isn't one of those thousand-dollar things."

"Million dollar, mom. A million-dollar wound."

"Have it your way," she said. "In any case, your brother says we shouldn't worry. This was the bullet with his name on it and he's survived."

Harry heard yelling in the background. "Is that dad?" he asked.

"Yes. He wants to know if you've satisfied your pagan lust at that porno magazine and decided to get a real job."

"Still full of pagan lust."

He heard her repeating the comment to his father.

"It's nearly seven here," Harry said. "I'd better get going."

"President Johnson was on the TV last night, saying he's increasing the draft. Doubling it. I hope you don't wind up over there with Vaughan, getting shot at. There could still be a bullet with *your* name on it."

"I'll hold that thought, mom."

"Just a minute. Your father is telling me something."

Harry crawled out of the bed, wondering why he was still wearing his suit pants from the night before.

"Your father wants me to remind you that the Lord says it's better to spill your seed on the ground than to put it into the belly of a whore."

"Tell dad not to worry," Harry said. "Keeping my seed on the ground."

"I pray for you, son. I pray for both my boys."

"Thanks, mom. And thanks for letting me know about Vaughan."

"I know how close you and your brother are."

19

It was only after he'd hung up the phone that he began to wonder what made his mother think he and Vaughan were close. He couldn't remember a time when that was true. It wasn't just that they were separated by four years—the difference between childhood and puberty, high school and college, adolescence and adulthood. Theirs was an even more distancing separation—lifestyles. His brother was one of the chosen few who exuded cool, settling on a steady wardrobe of tight jeans, tomato-red windbreaker and aviator sunglasses while barely in his teens. Never at a loss for words. Never at a loss for pals or female companionship. Harry, an awkward loner, had spent much of his home life envying and resenting his popular younger brother.

But that didn't mean he wanted Vaughan to wind up in an Army hospital in Vietnam with a bullet hole in his shoulder.

His brother occupied his thoughts through shave, shower, coffee and three-day-old Danish and remained on his mind until being chased away by the sight of a pretty girl leaning against his convertible in the apartment building's underground parking area.

He'd noticed her before. In her early twenties. Short red hair, feather-cut. Her face had a vaguely kewpie doll look—round, with a cute upturned nose and dimpled cheeks. Her emerald green eyes were enhanced by long lashes that curled upward at their tips and an artfully applied smoky purple liner. Her body, wrapped in a clinging black skirt and white silk blouse, added to what was an undeniably sexy presence.

Still, the automobile was a two-month-old racing green Mustang ragtop, the first new car he'd ever owned, well he and the Bank of America. His immediate thought was that she was smudging the wax job.

"You got any gum?" she asked, her tongue sliding across the area between her teeth and her puffy, port wine–colored lips.

She wrinkled that cute little nose and said, "My mouth tastes like the Vietcong just marched through it."

"No gum. Sorry."

"Tic Tac?"

He shook his head.

"The engine of my bug's turned to shit," she said. "I was hoping you could give me a lift to the office?"

"The office?" he asked dully.

"You're the new guy in Promotion, right?"

"I've been there three months," he said. "You work for *Ogle*, too?"

His lack of recognition seemed to deflate her. "I'm a receptionist," she said. "On three."

"Oh, sure. I recognize you now," he lied. "I don't know why they're hiding you up on three. You ought to be at the lobby desk."

"Well, aren't you sweet," she said, her smile returning. "I'm Terry O'Mara." She extended a pale hand with fingernails that matched her purple lipstick. It was dry and warm and squeezed his when he told her his name.

"Terry Trauble," she said. "Sounds good. I always check out the name thing when I meet somebody promising."

He was surprised and a little thrown by this bit of flirtation. "Uh . . . I guess we oughta get moving," he said.

He opened the door for her, a gesture she repaid by running her hand down the length of his arm as she got into the car. "I'm a pushover for chivalry," she said.

Harry had discovered that the Santa Monica Freeway offered the fastest route from Bay City to the *Ogle* Building just off La Cienega in Hollywood. While he weaved in and out of the morning traffic, Terry spent the first few minutes fiddling with the radio before clicking it off with a sigh. "They just don't give a darn about news in this city," she said.

From the corner of his eye, he saw her pull up her dress and begin to adjust her dark pantyhose. He couldn't remember the last time he'd had a hard-on before nine o'clock in the morning.

"What's it like working for Milton Armstead?" she asked, smoothing the dress down again. "Difficult, would be my guess."

"I don't have much contact with him," Harry said. "I get my assignments from Maurice Grumbacher or Larry Beagle."

"You're lucky," Terry said. "Milton is not what you'd call a nobleman. Not at all like Nick. Nick was a real gent."

"Nick?"

"Nick Hobart," she said. "He was the boss on my floor."

"Oh, yeah. He died the week I started."

"He was a big old bear. Grumbled a lot, but was really very sweet."

The late Circulation Department V.P. hadn't given Harry that impression. With his obviously broken nose and scarred knuckles, Hobart had reminded him of the union leg breakers who beat Marlon Brando to a pulp in *On the Waterfront*.

"I suppose you've heard the rumors," she said.

"What kind of rumors?"

"That Nick's death might not have been an accident."

Harry frowned as he sent the Mustang down the La Cienega off-ramp. "The statue fell on him," he said. "How could that not be an accident?"

"What made the statue fall, just when Nick was leaving the building?"

"You mean somebody might have been up there on the marquee? That seems like a stretch."

"Nick told me a little about his past," she said, lowering her voice. "He had family ties to mobsters in Chicago."

"Mobsters would more likely use guns, not a frog statue,"

Harry said. "The police probably checked that out, anyway, before they called it an accident."

"Maybe," she said. "But, you know, the sculptor who put the statue on the marquee says there's no way it could have come loose by itself."

"He would say that, right?" Harry said. "With the magazine suing him and all."

"I suppose. Well, if somebody did kill Nick, I know who I'd pick."

"Who?"

"Milton."

"He and Hobart didn't get along?"

"Oh, I wouldn't know about that," she said. "It's just that Milton is the only person I can think of who might be capable of murder."

"What makes you think so?"

"Any guy who'd throw you out of his beach house at four in the morning, naked as a jay bird, is capable of anything."

"Armstead did that to you?" Harry asked.

She nodded. "But he has this guy, Manfred, like a butler, who took pity on me and got my clothes and drove me home.

"There's a parking spot."

It was a block from the *Ogle* Building, but Harry took it.

As they walked down La Cienega, he said, "You . . . slept with Milton Armstead?"

She rolled her eyes. "Like who hasn't?" she said.

Turning the corner, they saw that something was going on at the *Ogle* Building. Two men were on the marquee, sharing the lily pad with the new frog statue.

Arriving workers warily rushed to the lobby giving them and the marquee as wide a berth as possible.

"Looks like they're taking pictures of the new frog," Harry said.

"It's Joe and Orlando," Terry said. "Joe Tobella is the sculptor of the original frog. Orlando Royale is his assistant slash boy-friend."

Across the street from *Ogle,* the usual crowd of early-morning inebriates loitered in front of Herkie's Wonder Bar and Grill verbally harassing the magazine's more voluptuous employees. Harry expected them to do a number on Terry as they approached. Instead, they opened up a path to the bar's front door.

One of them, a particularly grizzled stewbum, took her hand, kissed it and said, "Welcome, Terry gal. Yer breakfast awaits within."

She turned to Harry and asked, "Toddy for the body?"

"A little early for me," he said.

She winked at him, then turned and strolled into the bar. He heard her ask, "Anybody got a stick of gum?"

Crossing the street, Harry saw that one of his supervisors, Maurice Grumbacher, *Ogle*'s Assistant Promotion Manager, had joined the tableau at the entrance.

"Enough with the camera," he was shouting to the young man in denim on the marquee taking photos.

"Ignore the jackass, Orlando," the other lily pad occupant said. "You jus' keep snappin' the pictchas." He was tall, of medium weight, with long hair and the fresh start of a beard. He was wearing bright pink pants and a white shirt, unbuttoned to display a purple, yellow and red tie-dyed T-shirt underneath.

"You two greaseballs got no permission to be on these premises," Grumbacher said. "Come down from there."

"Fauk you, fat boy. You guys sue Tobella. Tobella gets photos to prove his statue don't fall by itself. This building been through so many quakes, it shake like a leaf. I say all this to you when I start my work, warn about earthquakes. Even little ones.

You such a smart-ass, you say not to worry."

"I said no such thing," Grumbacher yelled. "Come down here, dammit."

Tobella turned to his associate. "Pitchas of everything, Orlando. The joints. The struts. This piece of plaster shit, too."

His reference was to the new statue, which had been crafted by the magazine's art department. It weighed much less than the original and, supposedly, was better anchored to its lily pad. Still, Harry assumed it would be capable of considerable damage in a free fall.

"Hit the sidewalk now, you bastards, or I send for the fuzz," Grumbacher said. He seemed so frazzled Harry decided to hang back from his line of sight.

"Fauk you and fauk ya fuzz."

Grumbacher's round face turned crimson. "Down here, now," he shouted, "or I'm coming up."

"Whoooo. Fat boy, you make me so scared."

"We done here, Joe," Orlando said.

"Good. I wouldn't wanna get caught up here in a quake."

The two men descended the ladder.

"Hand over the film," Grumbacher said.

"Fauk you, asino," Tobella said. He was brushing away the soot and cobwebs from his pink pants.

Grumbacher took a step toward him and Tobella straightened belligerently and said, "You touch me, I bust yo' face for you."

That stopped the Promotion man.

Tobella and his assistant folded the ladder and carried it and the camera down the street.

Grumbacher watched them go, his anger melding into a mood Harry couldn't quite identify. Concern, maybe. Or fear.

"Morning, Maurice," he said, moving close enough now to get the full musky blast of Grumbacher's Canoe cologne. "You okay?"

Grumbacher looked up at the leering frog. "We . . . have to protect ourselves."

"From what?"

The Assistant Promotion Manager glared at Harry. "We can't let any yahoo with a dime-store shutterbox shinny up on our marquee. We're liable if anything happens to the assholes. Our insurance is in jeopardy, as is. Buck should never have put another damn statue up there. You'd think one death would be . . . ahhh, the hell with it."

Grumbacher charged through the front door, pushing lesser employees aside.

Harry took another look at the frog. He thought he understood why Trower Buckley, *Ogle*'s creator, had put up a new one after Nick Hobart's death. Buckley was so personally involved in every aspect of the magazine, it was as if he and *Ogle* were one. The frog was his symbol, too. Taking it down or moving it somewhere else would suggest that its original placement had been a mistake. His mistake.

Still, the new plaster-based version wasn't nearly as impressive as Tobella's. Or as substantial. Like its predecessor, it would tumble down sooner or later. It didn't seem right to make *Ogle*'s employees walk beneath it each day with the same attitude of preordained destiny as the soldiers in Vietnam, waiting for the bullet with their name on it.

Which brought his brother to mind again.

He was thinking about sending Vaughan some copies of the magazine to ease his stay in the hospital when someone touched his shoulder.

It was a man of ordinary appearance, except for his black suit, black tie and white shirt. He looked like a clergyman in search of a church. If so, he was definitely at the wrong address. "I beg your pardon," he said. "Is this the *Ogle* Magazine Building?"

"None other," Harry said. He made an upward gesture with his thumb. "But the frog's not safe. You don't want to stand out here too long."

The man looked at him in obvious confusion.

"Follow me," Harry said and double-timed it under the marquee, the man in black at his heels.

Inside the neon-and-chrome lobby, Harry gave the man a nervous smile and, satisfied that his obligation toward the perplexed stranger was at an end, left him in the lobby to fend for himself.

2.

The man in black watched Harry take the simulated marble stairs to the first-floor landing where he hurried past a voluptuous brunette receptionist who appeared to be in a state of suspended animation. He saw Harry wish the woman "Good Morning, Iris" and, receiving no reply, continue on through an open doorway.

The man in black's attention shifted to a stunning blonde who hip-switched across the floor to him and said, "Morning, Father."

Her face was meticulously made up to highlight her peaches-and-cream complexion, but she didn't seem to be quite as careful with her manner of dress. She was, in fact, wearing some sort of bathrobe, sashed at the waist, which did little to hide the fact that she was naked underneath except for a lacy black garter belt, its tendrils flapping against bare thighs.

She saw him gaping at her and held up a thin dime. "Got to feed the meter," she said, high heel pumps clattering on the simulated marble as she bounced to and through the front door.

Only after she had exited did the newcomer check himself, deciding that, man of the cloth or not, he had no business staring at such an apparition.

At the reception desk, Iris, the elaborately quaffed receptionist, asked, "What can I do for you, Father?" Her face was immobile except for the slight motion of her lips, reminding him of those movie short subjects featuring talking animals.

"Not 'Father,' miss," he replied, swaying slightly. "I'm of the Anglican persuasion, an archbishop. That is, I was an archbishop. I'm here to see a Mr. Maurice Grumbacher."

With jerky motion, the girl lifted her telephone handset and balanced it in her palm. She continued to stare at the man in black, taking in his flat brown hair, his bland face, his puzzled manner. "Who shall I say is calling?"

Ignoring her faulty grammar with difficulty, he said, "Archbishop Alphonse L. Hewitt."

"Is Mr. Grumbacher expecting you?"

"I don't have a specific appointment," he said. "But I—"

"Mr. Grumbacher never sees anyone without an appointment."

"But he has to see me. I've come all the way from Buzz."

"Buzz?"

"In West Virginia. South of Wheeling. Its original name was Buzzard, but . . ."

He stopped talking because Iris was obviously not listening to him. She was dialing a phone with dark red fingernails longer than the ones on Fu Manchu's daughter. She waited a beat and said into the receiver, "There's an Archbishop Buzz here to see Mr. Grumbacher. Sans appointment."

"No, no," the man in black said. "Hewitt is the name. From Buzz, West Virginia."

Iris frowned. "Now he claims his name is Hewitt," she said.

There was a brief, silent moment before the receptionist announced, "Mr. Grumbacher's secretary says he never heard of you."

"But he must have." The man in black searched his pockets frantically, finally withdrawing a rumpled piece of stationery bearing the *Ogle* frog letterhead that he thrust into the receptionist's blank face. "He sent me this only last week."

"He's got a note from Mr. Grumbacher," she relayed into the

telephone. "It says something about a reprint of a letter he sent in . . . Yeah . . . that's it."

She turned to the archbishop. "Take a seat, Mr. Buzz," she said, pointing the phone toward a visitor alcove. "Mr. Grumbacher will see you in a minute."

Archbishop Alphonse Hewitt did as he was told. He found a comfortable Naugahyde and chrome chair next to an ersatz mulberry bush and there he sat for forty-five minutes, watching an assortment of sales people get turned away by the seemingly affectless receptionist.

By the time Grumbacher's secretary, a perky blonde identifying herself as Mavis, came to summon him, Archbishop Hewitt had chewed away most of the inside of his mouth. He was a worried man.

Mavis led him through a maze of wood and glass cubicles and offices past *Ogle* employees engaged in various activities. The females, ranging from attractive to beautiful, read the morning papers; one young male lay on the floor of a darkened office, another was busy applying nose drops. A tough old bird in a chauffeur's uniform was daubing clear polish on his fingernails.

The few non-self-absorbed enough to notice the archbishop eyed him with curiosity and suspicion.

Grumbacher greeted him at the door to his executive office with a broad cheery smile, an outstretched hand and a nearly overpowering musky cologne scent. "Archbishop Hewitt. Great to see you, pal. How was the flight?"

"A trifle unnerving, actually."

"Swell," Grumbacher said. "Love the big bird, myself. Zip, zap and you're there. Bring the little woman along?"

The archbishop found himself staring at a scattering of dry yellow spots all over Grumbacher's shirt and tie. They looked like egg stains. "My wife left me," he said. "After nearly twenty-five years of marriage . . ."

"Could be a blessing in disguise," Grumbacher said. "My wife's a lush. Ever sit across the breakfast table from a dame in hair curlers, sipping Schnapps while you're digging into your Rice Crispies?" Grumbacher shuddered.

"Everything's happened so fast, Mr. Grumbacher," Hewitt said.

"Take a load off," Grumbacher said, pointing to a Naugachrome chair that looked no more comfortable than the one at reception. It wasn't. But it did distance him somewhat from the effects of Grumbacher's ghastly cologne.

"Buzz, West Virginia," Grumbacher said. "Drink a lot of coffee there?"

"No. The town was originally named Buzzard. Karl Buzzard was one of the founders, but—"

"Okay, here's how it plays," Grumbacher said, not even aware he'd interrupted the archbishop. "You sent us a fan letter. You said you were fractured by our fiction, awed by our art, ecstatic over our Eyefuls. Not in those words, of course. We gave your prose a little zing."

"Eyefuls?"

"Center-spread cut-ups. The babes in the buff. Don't play coy, Arch boy. You said yourself, in your letter, that there was nothing immoral about nudity, that our magazine was as close to God as the Bible. You're not gonna tell me that wasn't your John Hancock at the bottom of the page."

"I did sign the letter," the archbishop said with a sigh.

"Well, it hit here at just the right moment. We're this close to cracking the Fortune 5'er."

"I don't see—"

"Don't see the problema? In a nutshell: there are squareheads who think we're putting out porno. Not right thinkers like you and me."

"Well, actually—"

"Anyway, our sales reps needed a door opener and your letter appeared, like manna for us poor starved Persians. Naturally we made promo hay. Your letter, Arch, wound up on the desk of every captain of industry in the country."

"Including the bishop," the man in black said. "And it wasn't even my letter."

"Come again?"

"I didn't write it. James Peregrine, my assistant, placed it in with a batch of correspondence and I signed it without even noticing its contents."

"Too much trust is no good. Tell me about this cat, Peregrine."

"A man several years younger than myself, in his early thirties, a recent addition to our church in Buzz. Very ambitious, as you may imagine."

Grumbacher's eyes narrowed. "I don't suppose you could give him a little of his own medicine, slip a similar letter past him?"

"I'm afraid not," the man in black said. "I'm no longer allowed on church grounds. There has been no official declassification, but I now feel like an imposter wearing this black suit."

"Then dump it. Trade it in on some classwear."

"I . . . it's quite difficult to remove the vestiges of a religion to which I've devoted my whole life."

"The toothpaste has left the tube, daddy-o. Time to look forward. Our Fashion Department will fix you up with some threads." Grumbacher paused to light a thin cigar.

"I . . . I was hoping that your magazine would print some sort of retraction."

"No chance," Grumbacher said, adding a blast of sweet cigar smoke to the toxicity of his cologne. "Look, the key thing is you're at liberty now. I've worked out a plan to make things right for you."

How could this insensitive fool make things right for him, the archbishop wondered? Grumbacher neither knew nor cared what he had been through. Martha, locking him out of the house. The bishop delivering a two-hour sermon condemning him before a congregation that included his mother and two younger sisters. Years of work, dedication, study gone irrevocably down the drain. How could this foul-smelling fool make it right for him?

"We have a paper for you to sign that'll put a new roof on the henhouse, as it were," Grumbacher said, exhaling more smoke as he extended a multipage document.

The archbishop glanced at it with watery eyes. "This looks like an employment contract," he said.

"Ordinarily, they'd handle this up in personnel, but you're kinda like our special project here in Promotion. You're gonna love it at *Ogle*. Good pay. Good benefits. Good times. So do that thing you do: sign the paper."

"I'm not sure . . . What kind of work would I do?"

"The same thing you were doing in Buzz," Grumbacher said, "workin' for the man upstairs."

"God? Here?"

"Mr. Buckley. Fifth floor. He wants the magazine to cover all the bases where men are concerned. We been a little light in a few areas. Sign the paper, daddy-o. What else you got going?"

Alphonse Hewitt picked up a pen. He was about to use it when someone entered the office, the young man who'd guided him into the building.

Grumbacher glared at the newcomer. "I'm busy, Harry. Later, 'gator."

Harry was carrying a two-foot by three-foot drawing of the frog that had been perched over the building's entrance. "This is important," he said. "You signed off on this, Maurice. But the frog is facing the wrong way."

Grumbacher examined the drawing. "What's Larry say?"

"That he couldn't be bothered and to show it to you," the young man said.

"I can't get my goodies in an uproar about it, Harry. Why don't you take it back to your office and run it through the old think-tank uno mas?"

The young man turned to Archbishop Hewitt. "Sorry to have disturbed you," he said.

"No bother," the archbishop said.

"Harry prepared the brochure that went out with your letter, archbishop," Grumbacher said. "He's one of our best copywriters."

The young man picked up the art board. "There's only one other copywriter," he said.

3.

That was the problem with the job, Harry Trauble thought. Everybody was so busy watching their butts nothing ever got done. He carried the art board back to the tiny office he shared with a wiry, balding copywriter named Roger Weeks.

The room was in darkness. Weeks was on the floor, lying on his back. Next to him was a slide-film projector that was throwing a full-color picture of a naked girl on the ceiling.

"What's up?" Harry asked.

"What's it look like?"

"Alright. Why on the floor?"

"The tile is cool and it's very restful," Weeks told him. "And I think I get a better projection on the ceiling. The walls are too dark."

Harry hopped over body and machine and sat down at his desk. He leaned back as far as his chair would allow and watched the color slides for a while. Then he said, "There's an archbishop in Maurice's office."

"Doing what?"

"He had an employment contract in his hand. He's the one that got booted out of his church because of that letter."

"What's he going to be doing here?"

"Probably something in Special Projects," Harry said.

With the room in darkness, Harry couldn't ponder the flopped frog. He leaned back and watched a few more slides, but his mind was elsewhere.

"Roger?"

"Huh?"

"You think Nick Hobart's death was an accident?"

"Whoa. Where's that coming from?"

Harry didn't want to mention Terry, the third-floor reception-ist, because Weeks would then batter him with questions about the girl. Instead, he said, "The sculptor, Tobella, was up on the marquee this morning, taking pictures. Looking for something. Maurice got all shook up about it."

"So you think Maurice killed Hobart?"

"No. I just . . . hell, I don't know anything about it."

"Apparently."

Harry watched a few more slides and asked, "Did I get any calls?"

"The phone rang a couple times," Weeks said, "but it might have been for me."

"You didn't answer?"

"And get up off the floor? If it's important, they'll call back."

Harry shrugged and rose from his chair. "I'm going to the Art Department. Anybody calls, they can reach me there."

"I'll be sure to tell them," Weeks lied.

4.

It had not been one of Maurice Grumbacher's better days. Seated at breakfast, much earlier, he had stared at the neatly cut, buttered toast on the table in front of him and the two-minute egg that was on his grey sharkskin lap, its bright yoke seeking lower levels. He could not think of one thing to say.

"Oh, Moe," his wife got out between chuckles, "I'm so sorry."

"I'd believe that if you'd stop your goddamn laughing," he told her. He stared gloomily at his lap. "I don't have time for another, I guess? For my plate this time."

"There aren't any more," Henny Grumbacher told her husband. "No more eggs, no more milk, no more sherry. We're going to hell in a hand-me-down handcar, Moe."

"We're doing what?"

"Isn't that the way you'd put it, dear?" she said, staggering toward the Frigidaire. "My master of the tired cliché."

Grumbacher got up from the table and went to their bedroom to change his trousers before taking the long, crowded drive from Studio City in the Valley to the office. He decided not to worry about the shirt and tie.

At *Ogle,* where he usually found some sort of surcease from personal problems, he was confronted by the sculptor jumping up and down on the marquee, probably trying to cause the whole damn thing to come tumbling down.

Even worse, he no sooner had arrived at his desk than Larry Beagle, Manager of the Promotion Department, had dumped an assignment on him.

"We need a lucid and concise essay outlining the *Ogle* Magazine credo," Beagle had said.

"Credo?" Grumbacher had asked, painfully aware of Beagle's dull eyes behind rimless glasses taking in the dried egg splatter on his shirt and tie.

"Buckley's finally decided it would be a good idea, since the world is undergoing such incredible social change, to define our purpose as something more than a stroke book."

"Social change?"

Beagle was a stocky man of medium height with a ruddy complexion and wispy grey-black hair. "You do watch the news occasionally, Maurice?" he asked.

"If I get home early enough."

"Well, perhaps you've heard of Vietnam, student rebellion, strained race relations? Women demanding equal rights?"

"What's that got to do with us?" Grumbacher had asked.

Beagle's round face registered an expression of painful tolerance that raised Grumbacher's hackles. "We're in publishing," Beagle told him slowly. "It behooves us to stay on top of current affairs."

"We're at the goddamned cutting edge," Grumbacher said. "Movies, fashion, the good life. All part of our package."

"That may be," Beagle said, "but our boss feels it's time to explain to our critics that *Ogle* is, well, relevant."

"Good word," Grumbacher said, scribbling it onto a desk pad.

"This is going over Buck's signature," Beagle said, "so give it a special effort."

"Larry, I really don't think—"

"Don't think what?"

"Well . . . I've never actually met Buck, Larry. I don't think I'm qualified to say why he feels the magazine is relevant."

"You've been here four years and never met Buckley?"

"I've passed him in the hall a couple times. Larry, you know him. Maybe you should—"

"I don't really feel the magazine is relevant, Moe," Beagle said. "Fact is, I doubt that Buckley, in his heart of hearts, thinks it is. But a fellow like yourself, you believe in this bullshit, which makes you the man for the job."

He paused at the door to add, "We need the piece like yesterday."

Maurice Grumbacher stayed with his problem for the better part of ten minutes after Beagle had gone, at which time Archbishop Hewitt arrived, further complicating his day.

Now he watched the archbishop sign the contract. He snatched it from under the man's pen and slipped it into a desk drawer.

"Perhaps this makes sense," the archbishop said. "I just don't know anymore."

"It's one baby-doll of a company to work for. Believe you me, Arch boy, it beats pickin' with the chickens." He stood up, prompting the archbishop to do the same. "There's no room for you down here, so we've set up an office for you on four. Same floor as all the other editors. I'll get Mavis to show you the way, get you set up."

He pushed the buzzer on his desk. His door opened and a young woman with jeweled cat's-eye glasses, a towering mouse-brown beehive and breasts the size of casaba melons burst into the room. "Florence," Grumbacher said with a grimace, "Mavis not out there?"

"On her break, Maurice. Something I can do for you?"

"Archbishop Hewitt has just joined the *Ogle* fold. Archbishop, Florence Proneswagger, from our Photography Department. Florence, archbishop."

"Pleased," she said, absently pumping the ex-clergyman's hand.

"Give him the dollar-fifty tour, honey, and lead him to his office. It's on four."

"On four? Really," she said, impressed.

"Behind the stairs."

"Oh. Well, after I've shown the archbishop around, I'll hurry back here, in case you need me for something else, Maurice."

"Carlos will probably need you more," Grumbacher said. "I'll be tied up with a writing assignment the rest of the day."

"All work and no play?" she said, making a moue.

"Afraid so," he said.

5.

Miss Proneswagger began her tour on the first floor, explaining to Hewitt that "these are the offices for the Promotion and Publicity Departments of the magazine."

She pointed to a row of two closed doors stretching out past Grumbacher's. "We call this Executive Row."

She nodded in the direction of the desks stationed to the right of each door. They were all empty. "These are where the executive secretaries sit. The girls are all on a break right now, as you can see."

"Yes," the archbishop said. "I can see that."

"Mr. Grumbacher, as you know, is the Assistant Promotion Manager. He's such a wonderful man, and the cross he bears with that wife of his. . . ." she pantomimed the raising of a bottle to her lips. "Mr. Grumbacher's other titles include Director of Special Projects, Thought Coordinator, Copy Chief and Image Controller. Mr. Grumbacher wears many hats."

"What sort of hat is Image Controller?" the archbishop asked.

"Well, we have this image you know. Of sophistication. Mr. Grumbacher is responsible for this."

"I'm not sure I understand."

"That's alright," she said. "You'll catch on. Next to Mr. Grumbacher is Mr. Beagle. He's the Promotion Manager. Mr. Beagle was a decorated soldier during World War II and, if his door were open, you would see many souvenirs of that great war on his desk and about his office. We can take a peek in later when he's at lunch. He's a very private person, but a real gentle-man.

"Next to Mr. Beagle is Mr. Armstead. He's our Vice-President in charge of . . . ," she giggled. "He likes to say in charge of vice." She giggled again. "Actually, he's really in charge of all promotion and public relations activity."

She suggested they take the stairs to the second floor. "The elevator has this lurch that, frankly, scares the wee-wee out of me."

"The stairs by all means, then," the archbishop said.

On level two, they entered what appeared to be a tasteful oasis from the chrome and tile reception and promotion areas. Indirect lighting. Classical music played, Couperin's "Nightin-gale in Love," if the archbishop was any judge.

The floor was covered wall-to-wall by a thick beige carpet on which several exquisite Oriental rugs had been placed by a designer's hand. The few pieces of furniture were antiques, French provincial the archbishop thought: six chairs, in a row against one wall, a stunning, elaborately carved desk with a velvet top that matched the color of the rug on which it rested.

The only human in the large room was seated behind the desk, a handsome bespectacled woman in silk blouse, her brown hair drawn back in a bun. Her fingers danced across the keys of an electric typewriter.

The walls were a restful dark brown and absent the framed nudes prevalent throughout the rest of the building. Instead, someone had selected paintings by famous contemporary artists who had accepted small fortunes to allow their works to ac-company the magazine's fiction pieces.

The only thing disturbing the elegance of the area was the rear view of the giant frog statue on its lily pad just outside the window bank.

"What goes on here?" the archbishop asked.

"This is Ida Connor's domain," Miss Proneswagger said. "She's the company's Chief Financial Officer as well as the Vice President in charge of Personnel. A role model for all us gals.

"Shall we head up—?"

"Could we linger just a moment?" he asked. "It's such a tranquil—"

The mood was suddenly shattered by the appearance of a tall man with thick blond hair who raced into the room from the reception area, shouting, "Some sick son of a bitch sabotaged my sofa."

The woman at the desk looked up from her typing, her eyes wide as the intruder rushed past her and disappeared into a corner office. The seat of the man's blue trousers was covered with white powder and the archbishop noticed that his feet were bare.

"That was Mr. Bethune," Miss Proneswagger continued calmly. "Manager of our Circulation Department. He took over after the frog killed poor Mr. Hobart."

"I see," said the archbishop, who didn't see at all.

6.

Howard Bethune flew into Ida Connor's office trailing powder clouds behind him.

Ida was at her desk studying an employment application. She looked up at him, maddeningly unflappable. "Hello, Howard. I hope this isn't about Nick Hobart's stock shares. As I've told you, there's been no decision—"

"This isn't about stock," the blond man said. "Ida, they've gone too far this time."

"Perhaps you should sit down, Howard. Not on the blue velvet, please. There's powder all over your ass."

"Exactly. There's powder all over my ass. And how did it get there?"

"How did it get there, Howard?"

"I don't know, Ida." He seemed close to tears. "Nothing like this ever happened in all my three-plus years at the Digest or eight-plus with Arthur Murray. First it was those strange rock and roll records that kept turning up on my hi-fi. Then it was the corn flakes under my desk. Ida, you know how I like to kick my slip-ons off during the day."

"Of course, Howard," Ida said soothingly. "Take your shoes off whenever you want. I told you that when we hired you."

"Can you begin to imagine how it feels, stepping on corn flakes? With dancer's feet as sensitive as mine? And now, I settle back on my nice white couch and get powder all over my ass."

Ida clucked understandingly. "What can I do to help, Howard?"

Bethune leaned closer, his eyes wide. "I think there are dark forces at work here."

A tiny frown furrow appeared on Ida's usually unlined face. "What . . . sort of dark forces?"

"Murderers."

Ida's frown came to full blossom. "Quite an accusation, Howard. Please specify."

"You know I've been going through the bound copies of circulation figures, year by year, trying to get up to speed?"

"Yes."

"Tucked in the most recent pack, I found an interoffice envelope that I'm guessing Nick Hobart stuck there. His name was on it. Inside was a scribbled warning."

Ida Connor's face tightened, but she maintained her smile. "What did it say, Howard?"

"I've memorized it, word for word. 'Must talk. Treacherous bastards out to get you. And something personal you deserve to know.'"

"What do you think it means?" Ida asked.

"I know what 'treacherous' means," Bethune said. "And considering what happened to Hobart and this stuff that's happening to me, I'm getting the idea something is very wrong in the Circulation Department."

"What happened to Nick was . . . terribly unfortunate, but it was a cruel quirk of fate. Nothing more sinister than that. The police made a full investigation and that was their official finding."

"Yeah, well they might change their mind when they hear somebody tried to warn Hobart that treacherous bastards were out to get him."

"That's a rather hasty interpretation of the note's intent, Howard."

"How else would you interpret it?"

"I can assure you that Nick did not behave like a man afraid. The note could be years old, referencing something from his rather checkered past."

"It was in an *Ogle* interoffice envelope," Bethune said, "stuck in between circ figures."

"I suppose we should try to identify the writer."

"According to the envelope, it was sent by Maurice Grumbacher," Dobbs said.

As remarkable as Ida's self-control was, it began to show signs of fraying. "They . . . the envelopes are constantly reused. They collect many names."

"I know," Bethune said. "That's why I decided to make sure Grumbacher was the man."

"You spoke to Maurice?"

"No, ma'am," Bethune said. "I gave the envelope and the note to Kevin Dobbs."

Ida blinked. "Kevin? Why?"

"You remember that article in the magazine, '*How to Tell the Heat of Her Pants*'?"

"I recall the title," she said warily.

"Well, as you know, it was written by this handwriting expert. I figured if he knew how to tell if a woman wanted sex by the way she dotted her 'i's, he sure as hell could say definitely if Grumbacher wrote the note. So I went to Kevin to find out how to get in touch with this guy and he said he'd take care of it."

"Ah, so Kevin is on the case," she said. "I suppose we'll just have to wait and see. Meanwhile, I promise to look into the matter of the corn flakes and powder. But these do seem like harmless pranks, don't they, Howard?"

"Why should I be subjected to pranks? This is an office, not a schoolyard."

"It's a little of both," she said. "It's why we pay our executives such exorbitant salaries."

"And some get shares of stock," he said.

"When I hired you, I made no promises. Nick had been a vice president of the company."

He considered that and nodded. "Thanks for hearing me out," he said. At the door, he turned. "Do you suppose a maintenance man might vacuum the couch?"

"Of course," Ida said. "I'll tell him to have his machine give your trousers a little kiss, too."

7.

As soon as Howard Bethune had departed, Ida Connor was on the phone to Kevin Dobbs, asking why he had said nothing to her about the so-called warning note.

"It's all handled," *Ogle*'s editor said. "The note no longer exists. I burned the damned thing."

"Some might construe that as destroying evidence."

"What evidence?" Dobbs asked. "You were at the meeting that night. It had to have been Nick himself who wrote that note. It was his warning to Buck. He probably was going to hand-deliver it the next morning."

"It's still evidence," she said.

"Of what?"

"Of Nick's intent to expose our little cabal to Trower. A suspicious person might call that motive for murder."

"Except that Nick wasn't murdered," the editor said. "It was an accident."

"I'm beginning to wonder," she said. "There's so much money involved. Perhaps one of us felt threatened enough to climb out on that marquee and wait for Nick and . . ."

"Christ, Ida, you're supposed to be the level-headed one. Save the goddamn fiction for the magazine."

"I'd hate to think Howard was in any mortal danger," she said.

"Why would he be . . . whoa, you're warning me not to harm Howard? What do you take me for?"

"Someone who has destroyed evidence in what may have been a murder."

"For the record, Ida," Dobbs said angrily, "I don't kill people. It's not in me. In fact, I was a pretty moral type fella until I succumbed to the lure of *Ogle* lucre. You may remember I wasn't all that keen on taking part in our little mutiny."

"My recollection is that you rolled over faster than last month's centerfold," Ida said. "But that's neither here nor there, Kevin. What you'll have to do now is come up with some way to keep Howard from gumming up the works. Killing him is not an option. He's hoping to snag all or part of Nick Hobart's *Ogle* stock. That might keep him happy, if we can convince Buck to give it to him."

"When your hired-gun shrink gets here," Dobbs said, "why not put him to work on Bethune as well as our loony leader?"

"That's a very interesting suggestion, Kevin," she said. "I might say murderously clever."

"What a lucky lady you are, that I'm not inclined toward homicide."

Ida allowed Dobbs the last word, self-amused at having shaken his cage. She took a moment to think about their conversation, then summoned her secretary.

"Take a memo, Darlene," she said to the smartly dressed young woman seated across from her. "To Trower J. Buckley. Trower, comma, it looks as though matters discussed in our meeting of last week have finally come to a head, period. I suggest we get to work immediately on the new cap Executive cap Tests, period. I will arrange for cap Doctor cap Magnus to be here tomorrow morning at ten, period. Would you care to see him then, question mark?

"That's it, dear. I'll sign it by hand."

Darlene folded her steno pad. "Is something wrong with Mr. Bethune?"

"Just in need of a little fine-tuning," Ida said. "Nothing he can't waltz through quite gracefully."

8.

Harry Trauble stood at a long white counter in the Art Department observing the flopped frog with Scotty Lemming, the magazine's Art Director. Somewhere behind them the members of Lemming's ragtag crew gathered to eavesdrop on the discussion, not because it interested them especially, but because it gave them an opportunity to stop working.

"There is a reason for everything we do here, Trauble," Scotty said. "We've been trained in the graphic arts for as many years as you were trained at a regular college. Not that we don't make mistakes, but just because you don't understand an artistic con—"

"The frog is flopped," Harry said impatiently.

Scotty smiled patiently. "Do you know about Art Nouveau, Trauble?"

"Do you know left from right?"

"You're on my home court now, so be polite. You say the frog is facing the wrong way. I say that, for artistic purposes, the frog is facing the only way it can."

"Then you agree it's flopped?"

"Of course, of course," Scotty said. "That's how I ordered it."

"Then you'll take full responsibility for it?"

"I always take full responsibility for everything that comes out of this department," Scotty said.

"You didn't the last time Buckley blew a gasket over a flopped frog. The guy whose job I have, Leroy Grimes, got canned because of it."

Scotty turned to see the artists who were hanging on every word. "Back to the boards, guys," he said. "I don't want Mr. Buckley coming in here and seeing you loaf around like the promo people."

He said to Harry, "In my office."

When Lemming had shut the door behind them he said, "Dammit, you ought to be thanking me for getting rid of Grimes."

"I just don't want to follow him out the door."

"He was an oaf. You're smart, Trouble."

"You gonna fix the frog?"

"Give me one good reason and I'll do it."

Harry didn't even have to think. The words seemed to be in his mouth all the time. "You don't want to screw around with the *Ogle* image."

Scotty reacted as if he'd been kicked in the groin. He began to perspire and his eyes searched the corners of the room. Then his face changed and a smile broke through the confusion. He reached up and put his arm around Harry's shoulders.

"Consider it done, Harry. After all, we're here to make you guys look good. But let's wait a day. Give the kids out there a chance to forget we had this talk. They feel insecure if I give in too quickly. No hard feelings?"

"None," Harry said.

He left the Art Department with a strange sense of having evoked a deity through the use of that word. Image. It carried a lot of power within those walls.

The advertising salesmen never used it, for it seemed that same "image" was what kept many influential clients out of the magazine's pages. On the other hand, everyone else spoke of it in hushed tones, as if "image" were *Ogle*'s primary life force.

He had first experienced this on the day he had been hired. Armed with the best samples turned out by a newly defunct advertising agency, he had appeared at Ida Connor's desk well-groomed and ready.

Ida had been watching a small television set nestled atop a window-ledge bookshelf near her desk. She clicked it off and faced him, dabbing at moist eyes.

"Soap opera?" Harry asked.

"Jimmie Lee Jackson's funeral," Ida had replied. "So sad. So tragic."

Harry had seen the newscasts describing the fatal shooting of the civil rights activist by Selma, Alabama, policemen. Jackson had traveled to the racially troubled town to take part in a demonstration demanding voter registration for blacks. Harry had experienced the shock and dismay many men and women felt when hearing of the reprehensible act. But at the moment, his only thoughts about the martyred man's funeral were centered on how they might negatively affect his job interview.

He needn't have worried. When he offered his samples, the Personnel V.P. dismissed them with a wave of her hand. She made one final dab at the corner of her right eye, tucked the kerchief up her sleeve and turned her lovely patrician face toward him. "May I call you Harry?"

"Sure."

"Well, Harry, tell me why you left your previous employment."

"The ad agency was bought out by a larger one in New York City. Some of the people were asked to go along. I wasn't."

Ida shook her head. "Harry, please. Honesty is a lovely policy, but this is a job interview. What you meant to say, I'm sure, was that you did not desire to leave this beautiful city of eternal sunshine for the cold, concrete towers and unpleasant lower life forms on that distant and uninhabitable island called Manhattan."

Harry nodded dumbly.

"Now, what made you think of *Ogle*?"

"I . . . there was an ad in the paper. For a copywriter."

"I imagine you were also impressed by the youth of our Executive Staff and by the chance for growth in such a dynamic, upwardly mobile company."

"Yes, ma'am," he answered.

"What about the military?"

"Beg pardon?"

"How do you stand with the draft board? We don't want you running off to Vietnam or some other God-awful spot a month after we hire you."

"I went through the Coast Guard OCS program at New London, Connecticut," he said. "I'm a lieutenant, junior grade, in the Reserve."

"That's a white uniform, like the Navy? With brass buttons?"

"The dress uniform, yes."

"So you won't be drafted and you wear a white officer's uniform. Very, very good. Ordinarily, I would give you a series of little tests. It's quite the thing to do. But in your case, I think we can dispense with such boring formalities. When can you start?"

"Next Monday?" he asked hesitatingly.

"Fine. We're shorthanded right now. Your predecessor left rather abruptly."

"What happened?"

"He . . . just didn't fit in," she said. She gave him a warm smile. Harry rarely found older women sexually attractive, movie stars excepted of course, but Ida Connor's smile was definitely having a profound effect on his libido.

"Anyone can tell you have frog prince potential," she said.

"Huh?"

"You're a frog prince. It's my little nickname for a promising junior executive, a handsome young man like yourself who fits the image perfectly."

What image would that be? he wondered, but was wise enough not to ask.

"There is one thing," Ida Connor said. "You have to understand that our work here is our own business. Our competition is growing faster than Fidel Castro's beard. We're giving the Great White Rabbit in Chicago a run for his money and to continue we absolutely must maintain our major circulation advantage over *Dude, Nugget, Swank* and the rest of the pack.

"You are not to associate with anyone working for those magazines, particularly not any women with whom you might have sexual congress and engage in pillow talk. We are quite sensitive to the possibility, make that probability, of company espionage and demand one hundred and fifty percent loyalty from our employees. I trust you will not object to signing a loyalty oath to keep mum on anything you might see or hear in the course of your employment?"

"No objection at all," Harry had replied.

On the day of that interview, the day Jimmie Lee Jackson was put to final rest, he had had no idea that within weeks he would begin to write an exposé of the company that would, he hoped, be his ticket out and up. On that interview day, in a state of elation and confusion, he had agreed to everything asked of him.

During his initial week at *Ogle,* inspired by Ida Connor's talk about his frog prince potential, he had worked diligently and creatively, skipping lunches and staying late. That ended when Maurice Grumbacher burst into the small office he occupied with Roger Weeks and ordered him to confine his activity to normal working hours.

"This isn't a hotel, Trauble," Grumbacher said, his cologne, as potent as it was, no longer masking his flop sweat.

"What's the problem?" Harry asked. "I'm not charging overtime or anything. I just want to get the jobs done."

"If you can't swing that in eight hours," Grumbacher said, "we'll have to find somebody who can. An employee like Weeks, here, who's out enjoying his second happy hour martini by five."

"If we had a secretary," Weeks said, "I bet Harry would be joining me for those martinis."

"Yeah? I'll see if we can work something out," Grumbacher said.

When the Assistant Promotion Manager departed, Weeks began waving his hands trying to clear the air. "Get that man some industrial strength Five-Day pads," he said.

"They could use that musk and BO combination to fight the Vietcong," Harry agreed.

"You know why he wants you out of here at five?"

"Not a clue," Harry said.

"The conference room is right next door."

"So?"

"Sometimes they use it to hold executive councils and crap. Usually after office hours. Grumbacher's worried some V.P., maybe even Buckley himself, will notice you in here, actually earning the money you're being paid. The big G. is convinced everybody is after his job. That includes you. He wants us all lower-than-low profile."

"Got it," Harry said.

Weeks continued to stare at him. "I guess I haven't been the friendliest guy in the world."

Harry nodded. Weeks hadn't said more than a word to him since he'd moved in.

"I liked having the office to myself," Weeks said.

"The copywriter who left wasn't in here?"

"He didn't just leave," Weeks said. "He got caught in a piss-ing match between that asshole Scotty Lemming and Armstead over a frog drawing. When he wound up the fall guy, he actually punched Armstead in the schnoz. So Milton got two guys from the mailroom to take him into the alley and stomp the shit out of him.

"But I digress. No, he didn't work in here. They're using his office for a storeroom. A lot of my crap is in there, lamps, a little TV, a leather chair—stuff I sort of appropriated from other offices. They moved it to make room for your desk."

"I don't blame you for being pissed," Harry said.

"It's not your fault," Weeks said. "And now that Grumbach-er's on your ass, I see I was wrong about something else."

"What's that?"

"I thought they might have put you in here to spy on me."

"Spy on you? Get serious."

"Hey, why should I be the only one at *Ogle* not paranoid?" Weeks said. "Anyway, we all have our little secrets."

Harry shrugged and turned to his typewriter, not at all interested in Weeks' secrets and eager to convey that fact.

"*Ogle* may seem like a swingin' place to work," Weeks said, "but it's got elements that are more conservative than Barry Goldwater's barber."

Harry nodded, "I had to sign a loyalty oath."

"Working here is like eating a peanut," Weeks said. "You've gotta figure out a way of cracking the shell to get to the good parts. Dig?"

"Not really."

Weeks looked at his watch. "It's past four," he said, standing. "Time to punch out and keep the big G. happy. Let's go grab a couple of brews and I'll tell you about my latest nutcracker of a plan."

Dick Lochte

It was the beginning of the two copywriters' frequent sojourns to a dark little bar called Los Tres Marinos. The establishment was only a few blocks away from the office, but there they felt free to discuss Weeks' "nutcrackers" without worrying about being overheard by anyone else from the magazine since the joint was déclassé and mildly odiferous and managed by a couple of burly Mexican brothers who belched and farted a lot and hardly fit the *Ogle* image.

9.

When Milton Zephyr Armstead walked into the office that afternoon, he found a desk covered with little blue papers informing him of people who expected a return call. He removed his coat, screwed a black cigarette into a gold holder and swept the little papers into the wastebasket. Then he called for his secretary.

She was away from her desk.

Fiddling with a miniature plaster head of Adlai Stevenson given him for meritorious contribution to the great campaign of 1956, he unhooked the phone and dialed Kevin Dobbs.

After several rings, *Ogle*'s editor answered.

"You acting as your own secretary?" Armstead asked nastily.

"She must be away somewhere. What do you want, Milton?"

"Ida's got you pegged as a hit man, chum."

"Oh, Christ," Dobbs moaned. "She called you?"

"At home, she was so upset," Armstead said. "You should never have told her you destroyed the damn note. We definitely don't want her sticking her lovely nose into what you were up to that night."

"You mean what *we* were up to," Dobbs said.

"My advice is: scribble out another note and take it to her. Tell her you were bullshitting when you said you burned it and let her do whatever the hell she wants with it."

"That might work," Dobbs said begrudgingly. "And what do we do about Bethune?"

"The waltzing asshole? What we don't do is give him a piece of *Ogle*. I told Ida what a lousy idea that was. Let me handle him," Armstead said. "Oh, by the way, congratulations."

"About what?"

"I was having dinner with Jennings Lang; he tells me Universal is interested in that novel of yours, the one about the black quadruple amputee in France."

"*A Vet in Vichy?* Jennings Lang? Universal? My God! You must be kidding."

"Actually, I am," Armstead said and killed the connection.

Chuckling, he dialed Beagle. "Get your ass in here right away," he ordered.

He sat back, screwed another black cigarette into place and turned on the tape recorder he kept in his bottom drawer. By the time the Promotion Manager, Larry Beagle, had puffed into the office, Armstead had hidden the mike in the OUT basket under a sheaf of papers.

"Something, Milton?" Beagle asked nervously.

"What kind of an office you running here, Beagle?"

"I'm afraid I don't understand."

"Where are the secretaries who are supposed to be sitting out front?"

"On a break, I suppose."

"You suppose. You suppose. God supposes and man disposes. Or something to that effect. What about the powder all over Howard Bethune's couch? I don't suppose you know who put it there?"

"This is the first I've heard about it, Milton. That's not even our department."

Armstead took a long drag on his cigarette. "We're Promotion and Publicity. We're supposed to be on top of everything. I put the powder on Bethune's couch. Teach that faggot a lesson. Did you know he used to be a dance instructor? That's the kind of executive manpower we're getting around here. We ask for chess players and get checker players. You play chess, Beagle?"

"No, sir. A little bridge. . . ."

"Bridge?" Armstead threw up his hands. "Well, so be it. Which of your cretins is working on the *Ogle* Credo."

"Maurice," Beagle answered.

"Perfect. A do-nothing nitwit assigned to one of the most important tasks we've ever been asked to handle."

"The task is daunting," Beagle said. "That's why I gave it to my top-ranking officer."

"Ranking officer. Jesus Christ, man, this isn't the frigging Army. It's a magazine."

"Noted," Beagle said, feeling his stomach begin to churn.

"Buck is a bear when it comes to material going out over his signature," Armstead said. "The Credo is a tar baby. I wanted Dobbs and his effete intellectuals to get stuck in it. Not us."

"We didn't ask for it," Beagle said. "Buck tossed it in our laps."

Armstead waved a dismissive hand, "Enough about our master's little letter. What's happening in Des Moines?"

Beagle quivered. He closed his eyes to think. Finally, he said, "I don't know of anything that's happening in Des Moines."

"The sales meeting, Beagle. Dammit, are you on pot? The sales meeting in Des Moines."

"The sales meeting is in Chicago, Milton. It's all taken care of."

"Oh, Chicago then. Taken care of, eh? Good. Now that that's settled, what about Des Moines?"

Beagle's body stiffened. He began to tremble. "I . . . I don't understand."

"Am I speaking in some unfamiliar patois?"

"No."

"Then what is it you don't understand? Des Moines? It's a

city. In the Midwest, I think."

"Could I be excused, Milton? My stomach . . ."

"What about your stomach?" Armstead bellowed.

"Pains. I need a pill."

"Of course. Go take your pill. Take ten pills. But don't let me see your sickly face around here until you can give me a full report on Des Moines."

Beagle scuttled from the office clutching his heaving belly. He rushed first to his desk for his Maalox and popped several of them into his mouth. Then he leaned against the wall chomping them into peppermint-flavored powder that he swallowed with a sigh.

He staggered to the water cooler where, because of his shaking hands, he had difficulty getting the fluid to his lips.

For three years in the Marines, from boot camp at Paris Island to the big guns in the Pacific, never once did he break under fire. Cool, collected L.B., they called him.

He looked at his hands. Once they carried an M1 across war-torn earth, tore barbed wire apart, snapped many a Nip spine. Now having trouble lifting a Dixie cup.

He walked slowly to his office. As he passed Armstead's door his cautious glance caught the Vice President pressing his ear to a radio-like machine, doubled up with laughter. Beagle thought he heard a familiar voice coming from the machine. It sounded like his father. But his father had died years ago. He decided that he'd better get a grip on himself.

At his desk he took a few deep breaths, then dug into his correspondence file hoping to unearth some letter or memo that would offer some clue at to what was happening in Des Moines.

He had the papers neatly assorted on his desk when Weeks came in.

"What can I do for you, Roger?" he asked wearily.

"You remember our little discussion last month, Larry, about those cards that get sent out to get people to subscribe to *Ogle*?"

"The subscription cards," Beagle said.

"Right," Weeks said. "You told me all about how we make it easy for the rubes to subscribe by sending them an order form with their name already typed out on one side and our name and address printed on the other?"

Beagle nodded, not wanting to hear what was to come.

"Well, in my haste, I'm afraid I forgot to have our return address printed on the form. There's nothing on the piece that would let a subscriber know where to send his money."

"Throw them away, Roger. Start fresh and make sure the new bunch is done properly. If Milton were to—"

"They've all been mailed," Weeks cut in.

"If he were to discover we had made such a mistake . . . what did you just say?"

"The pieces have all mailed."

"The whole two million?"

"Two million, two hundred thousand. And forty-six."

Beagle lowered his head until his chin touched his chest. "Milton will get his sample copy," he said.

Weeks nodded. "I was too close to it, Larry, too intent on getting everything correct, like the girlie pictures and the prices and codes and everything."

"Armstead will roast my ass."

"Maybe you could tell him it was a test," Weeks said.

"A test?"

"Yeah. We were trying to see how strong the *Ogle* selling power really is. What other magazine would think of pulling such a subscription stunt? I mean, it's like saying we don't give a damn if the guy subscribes or not."

"You sincerely think Armstead will buy that?"

"Not really. He'll probably chew your head off. You could tell him it was my fault . . ."

Beagle frowned. "You know me better than that," he said, and Weeks nodded that he did. "I don't suppose, Roger, that, in your skulking around you've heard anything about the Des Moines matter?"

"What Des Moines matter?"

"Never mind. When you get back to your office, ask Harry to come see me."

10.

Weeks was almost past Executive Row when he heard Armstead shout, "YOU!"

"Me, sir?"

"Yes, you. Come in here."

Weeks walked cautiously into the office.

"What's your name, son?"

"Roger Weeks, sir."

"You in the Art Department?" Armstead asked, his long finger scratching the side of his carrion nose.

Weeks' eyes unwittingly focused on the finger. "No, sir. I can't draw a straight line with a French curve."

"Then you have no business looking like an artist. Get a god-damned haircut."

"Yes, sir," Weeks said, backing out of the door. "Only it's getting a little thin in front and I'm trying to compensate for it by—"

"What the hell is it you do, Weeks?"

"I'm a copywriter, sir. In charge of subscription materials," he added and immediately realized his mistake.

"Then you're responsible for this," Armstead said, waving the foolish subscription order form before Weeks' popping eyes. "Can you explain this to me, copywriter Weeks?"

Weeks took the order form. "Of course I can explain it," he lied. "But let me ask you something first?"

"Out with it."

"It's about the archbishop who's been walking around the building all day."

"What archbishop?" Armstead leaned across his desk.

"The one that's been walking around the building all day looking for a job."

"Looking for a job? What the hell does he think this place is, the Salvation Army? Or maybe he wants to save our souls. Picture this, Weeks. We've got this broad in Photography, she's not wearing a stitch, dig? Big, luscious naynays in full view of the camera.

"The photographer focuses, starts to snap her picture and this bead rattler darts in. He sticks a hymnal right between those big, luscious lungwarts and . . ."

The phone rang, cutting off Armstead's parable. He grabbed the receiver. "Yeah?"

Weeks had no idea who the caller was. He only knew that this was his chance. Armstead was caressing the phone and speaking softly into the mouthpiece. Weeks edged forward, cupping his ear like a deaf man trying to hear a pin drop.

Armstead shot him a cold glance. He pulled the phone away from his ear. "Get the hell out of here, Weeks, and don't come back until summoned."

Weeks tiptoed out of the office, shutting the door behind him. He knew that the chances were in his favor that Armstead would forget his name or the incident or, with luck, both.

He noticed that he was still holding the ill-conceived subscription order form. He hastily tore it into tiny pieces and shoved the pieces into his pocket.

Another crisis averted.

11.

As Armstead had fantasized, the archbishop was in the Photography Studio, but, alas, sans hymnal. He was on the last leg of a building tour that had taken him through the vast *Ogle* Empire as it existed in that five-story ex-warehouse that shimmied with the passing of each semi.

He had seen it all, except for the private confines of Trower J. Buckley on the fifth floor where *Ogle*'s creator worked and lived.

The archbishop thought that he had observed much of humanity back home among the flock in Buzz, but certainly he had never come in contact with the likes of Jones, the big Jamaican who was in charge of the mailroom and who carried a leather thong whip that he smilingly referred to as his "air-mail special." Or Wilbur Terhue, the gaunt Manager of the Accounting Department, ("Snake Willy" as his underlings called him behind his back) who each day wore one of three handmade suits dyed to match U.S. mint green. Or even Angus Flood, eighty-one last month, whose sole task at *Ogle* was to keep a watchful eye on the Great Dummy, the massive white scrapbook that was filled each month with rough pages from the issue currently in production.

Miss Proneswagger had also introduced him to Kevin Dobbs, *Ogle*'s Editorial Director, who without removing his pipe or rising from his chair, nodded wordlessly. As the archbishop edged toward the door, he noticed a sign taped to the wall which read, "Nothing is won without compromise."

"I've been learning a lot about that since I've arrived here," the archbishop said.

Dobbs looked up, puzzled, and the man in black pointed to the sign.

To his surprise, Dobbs leapt from his chair in a fury and ripped the placard down. Then he took the archbishop by the elbow and impolitely escorted him from the room.

Outside the writers and junior editors ignored Archbishop Hewitt's presence. They were busy studying photos of naked girls or reading magazines other than *Ogle*. The man in black liked the no-nonsense way they went about their tasks. But he did wonder why, in an Editorial Department, there were no typewriters.

When he asked Miss Proneswagger, she replied, "These people are editors, not writers."

Miss Proneswagger was a good person, he decided, but he thought she was wasting her time pining for Mr. Grumbacher who struck him as anything but a romantic figure. In fact, he felt that in the great sea of life, Mr. Grumbacher was a man treading water.

He wasn't at all sure it had been a smart move to let Mr. Grumbacher push him into signing the employment contract. He didn't know if he could be happy living in this big, impersonal, sprawling city, working for a sexually liberated magazine.

He was still mulling over his future when he realized Miss Proneswagger had led him into a bone-white space filled with harsh lighting and what appeared to be white inverted umbrellas.

He followed her to a section of the room where a bearded and shaggy-haired, middle-aged man in dark brown suede pants and shirt caressed a camera while a very pretty blonde lady, topless, was stepping out of her step-ins.

"We usually don't allow employees up here during a shooting session," Miss Proneswagger said. "Just once, right, Carlos?"

The man in suede turned and grinned, reminding the archbishop of a pesky gopher he'd had to remove from the church lawn. "Thas right, Flor-jence," he said. "Hon'y once."

"Look at that body, Archbishop," Miss Proneswagger said. "Have you ever seen anything so perfect?"

His throat was dry. He had to cough before replying, "She's quite . . . impressive."

"The archbishop is a new staffer, Carlos," Miss Proneswagger said.

"Ah," Carlos said and re-positioned his camera.

"Glad to have you with us, honey," the blonde said to Hewitt. "Can always use another handsome guy around here."

The archbishop blushed.

"Harch-bis-jup, wou' you mine helping me hout, pliz?" Carlos asked. "Hif you coul' brush dat smudge from Angel's shoulda . . ."

"Oh, I don't think . . . I mean, she's not wearing . . ."

Suddenly, Miss Proneswagger pushed him forward. Disoriented, blinking in the glare from the suddenly brighter overhead lights, he lost his balance and fell against the naked blonde.

"Calm down, poppa," she cooed. "Angel's here."

Her arms wrapped around him and he felt himself drawn in to her comfortable warmth. Her flesh was both soft and firm and smelled of lilac powder. She took his right hand and placed it over a large, firm breast. Her tongue was in his ear and one of her legs wrapped around his.

From a far distance he heard the flutter and click of the camera and Carlos's sardonic chuckle and Miss Proneswagger's nervous giggle.

The bright lights bore into his skull. The blonde's lilac perfume filled his nostrils. "Ohhh, baby," Angel whispered in his ear, and he felt her hand working the zipper of his trousers.

Aching with passion, he offered no resistance when she drew him to the tile floor.

Visions of martyrs flickered through his mind, ending with the plain, incredibly sad face of a woman with lank brown hair who was probably not even close to giving up her life for her faith.

"Dearest God, this is wrong," he said, pulling back from the blonde's grasp. His belt was undone and his pants slid to his knees. His feet were ensnared by thick electric cords.

He was having trouble standing. Couldn't see. His ears exploded with the sound of people laughing. At him, he presumed, at the pathetic figure he made.

He felt strong arms push him back under the lights and down on the floor again. He felt the warmth of a female body once more. His body suddenly relaxed. "That's more like it, sweetie," the blonde cooed. "Oh, yeah, baby."

He clenched his hand into a fist and struck out blindly. "Martha," he screamed. "You vile bitch, Martha."

There was a cry and he felt something strike the back of his head. He lost consciousness for what seemed like only a few seconds, during which time the anger, spirit-like, deserted his body.

He lay on the tile floor, limp as a rag, his head aching.

From a great distance, he heard the blonde whining, "He bruised me, the asshole. He's crazy. Called me Martha, whoever the hell that is."

The archbishop's closed eyes filled with burning tears as he wondered in his self-pity why his God had so deserted him, wondered even more how he could ever have mistaken a vulgar, sensuous, stunningly beautiful young woman for his angry and bitter and unfaithful former wife, Martha.

★　★　★　★　★

Some time later, he struggled back to full consciousness to find the room lighted normally, vacated except for Miss Proneswagger seated on a nearby chair looking concerned.

"I'm sorry, archbishop. It got kinda out of hand."

"I don't . . . understand."

"It's Carlos's little game," she said. "He plays it with every new male employee. Usually they don't mind."

"It was . . . a cruel joke," the archbishop said, wiping his eyes on his coat sleeve.

"It wasn't a joke. You must never think that. It's Carlos's check on the guys. His photos give him the upper hand. If you wanted to get the best of him, you couldn't very well do it now, could you?"

"Why would I want to get the best of him?"

"You must resent him, possibly even hate him, for putting you through this."

"I . . . Right now, I hate everyone, myself included. I suppose I do hate Carlos."

"You probably want to see him fired."

"Would that make him unhappy?"

"The magazine is his whole life."

"Then I will do everything in my power to have him dismissed. I shall go to Mr. Buckley's office and describe the iniquities that have been forced upon me."

"That's what I've been trying to explain," Miss Proneswagger said patiently. "If you went to Mr. Buckley, Carlos would show him the pictures of you and Angel. Angel is Mr. Buckley's fiancée and he's a very jealous man. If he were to see those pictures, he might possibly kill you."

"S-s-surely that's an exaggeration," the archbishop said.

"Not really. His wrath is a terrible thing. That," she said, "is why Carlos always has the upper hand. Now, I'll show you to your office. But you may want to zip up your fly first."

12.

When Howard Bethune's world grew too complex or disturbing, as it was now with concerns about his predecessor's grim demise and a developing paranoia about his co-workers, he liked to escape into music. Returning from a two-martini lunch at The Losers, he shut his office door and drew the drapes against the harsh glare of the smoggy Hollywood afternoon.

He placed a Percy Faith album on the hi-fi. He checked the couch for powder and, finding none, eased himself onto its length.

And heard a crunching noise in the cushion beneath his head.

What now?

He sat up, poked the cushion and created another crackling sound.

Observing the pillow more carefully in the dusky light, he saw that it had been placed upside down on the couch, zipper side showing, probably by the maintenance person who had cleaned off the powder.

Curious about the source of the sound, and a bit fretful over its prank potential, he unzipped the cushion and warily withdrew two folded pieces of paper. Both had a little age on them. The larger had been yanked from the center of an old *Ogle*. He took a quick, appraising glance at that month's naked Eyeful, refolded it quickly and stuck it back into the cushion, wondering why his predecessor, the late Nick Hobart, had put it there. Maybe the second piece of paper would explain . . .

He only had to see the name "Trower Buckley" on it to jam it back into the cushion, too. He wanted no more to do with whatever weird freakiness Hobart had been party to, freakiness that possibly had cost him his life.

He turned the cushion over and exchanged it for the one at the other end of the couch. Then he leaned back again, kicked off his tasseled loafers and shut his eyes, letting the music drive the discontent from his mind.

Before long his inner eye saw the soft yellow glow growing larger and larger until . . . he was back in that wonderfully elegant dreamland ballroom among dazzling women and handsome young men dancing to a waltz orchestra that had never heard of the frigging Rolling Stones. Round and round the couples swirled in unison, their bodies never touching, never touching.

"Your skin is like the smoothest alabaster," he was saying to the exotic brunette in his arms, the woman who graced all of his dancing dreams.

"You move divinely," she answered. "Even better than, than . . . what's his name?"

"Fred Astaire?" he prompted.

"No," she said, her forehead wrinkled in thought. He had always awakened before his partner could reply. But now, for the first time, it seemed that the dream would continue. "Bobby Van. That's the dancer you remind me of."

Well, Van wasn't exactly Astaire, but he was no slouch.

Round and round Bethune and the Bobby Van–loving beauty whirled. She was light as gossamer.

But just as he seemed to be waltzing into a state of ecstasy, the music stopped and the room turned cold. His partner drew back, a grimace of horror robbing her face of its beauty.

He turned to see a figure staggering toward them. A large man, his face covered in blood from an open gash in his skull.

74

Bethune had only a vague idea what Nick Hobart looked like, but he had no doubt about the identity of the ghastly apparition.

Hobart's corpse opened its mouth. But just as it was about to speak, to convey some message of dire importance, Bethune felt himself zooming to the surface of consciousness.

He awoke to the sound of someone knocking on his closed door.

He hopped from the couch and, still in his stocking feet, walked to the window, drawing back the drapes.

"Come in," he said, staring at the door, half expecting it to open on the nightmare corpse.

But the door didn't open. Instead, a white envelope was shoved under it.

He hopped to the door and threw it open.

There was no one in the vicinity.

He picked up the envelope; saw that his name had been typed on it.

Inside was a folded note, also typewritten, that read: "Keep talking about Nick Hobart and you'll be joining him."

Bethune blinked at the warning. His fear was so overwhelming it made him light-headed. As he walked toward his desk, he paused to turn off the hi-fi. Not even Percy Faith could help him now.

13.

"It's a bit cozy," Florence Proneswagger said.

The room was about the size of the side altar of the archbishop's former church. The ceiling was at a forty-five degree angle to accommodate the building's stairwell, which meant that one could stand upright only near the exterior wall.

Archbishop Hewitt cast a despairing eye on the oddly shaped space with its industrial grey furniture and industrial grey carpet. There was one window. It looked out on dirty brick.

"If you brought in a radio, I doubt anyone would mind," Miss Proneswagger said. "You're sort of by yourself back here."

On each floor of the building, in the spaces beyond the stairwell that had been of absolutely zero interest to *Ogle*'s interior decorator, almost hidden cubicles had been slapped together in a makeshift manner. The basement was taken up by two cots that allowed the maintenance crew and the mailroom lads the luxury of catnaps during the day and at eventide. On the first floor, a noisy, usually dysfunctional copying machine held sway. Soft drink and candy dispensers occupied the second-floor nook. Floor three was storage. No one really knew what went on in the space on five, it being part of Trower Buckley's apartment.

Judging by the way Miss Proneswagger had carried on about the fourth-floor niche, the archbishop had been expecting something equaling a pasha's playroom. He could see no sign of hookah or harem, but he supposed it would serve his purpose, whatever that might be, and told her so.

"Brilliant," she said. "Now, I'll be getting back to . . . my work."

"I wonder what *my* work will be," he said, easing onto the chair behind the desk.

"Oh, nothing terribly strenuous, I imagine. Ta, now."

He watched her toddle off and, still woozy from the nightmarish episode in photography, he leaned back and shut his eyes.

It had seemed as if only minutes had passed before he opened his eyes again. But the sun had journeyed on and the room seemed bleaker now.

And someone was seated across the desk, staring at him.

The severe slant of the ceiling behind the visitor created an initial illusion of great size. That dissipated along with the surprise of finding him there. The archbishop saw that the man was big, but hardly gigantic. Neither thin nor fat. In his forties. Casually dressed in grey slacks, foulard shirt, camel-hair jacket. His slightly receding brown hair, flecked with grey, was neatly combed. A thin mustache had been carefully cultivated in an effort to minimize a long upper lip.

His large dark eyes seemed to be staring through the man in black. The furrowed brow suggested a degree of discomfort.

"I envy you, sir," the man said. "The ability to just kick back and snooze like that is a goddamned gift. Oh, to have a mind that untroubled."

"It's less that than sheer exhaustion," the archbishop said. "I've had a rather . . . active morning."

The man continued to stare at him.

"Can I . . . help you with something?" the archbishop asked.

"You tell me."

"Who are you?"

"Trower Buckley."

The archbishop blinked. He could think of only one reason the creator of *Ogle* magazine would be sitting in his cramped quarters. His paramour—what was her name, Angel?—Angel had gone running to him about their ghastly encounter.

"You're familiar with the name, right?" Buckley asked.

"Oh yes, of course," the archbishop said.

"Then you're off to a good start, doctor."

The man didn't seem as hostile as he would be if he were there to wreak vengeance in Angel's name. Perhaps this was just a friendly welcome from the boss. "Actually, Mr. Buckley, though I have earned my DD, I've never been quite comfortable with the 'doctor' appellation."

"What the devil is a DD?" Buckley asked, his frown deepening.

"Doctor of Divinity."

"You're not a shrink? Dr. Magnus from Pasadena?"

"No. I'm Archbishop Hewitt from Buzz."

"Archbishop?" Buckley's eyes began to blink. "Then what are you doing here?"

"I gather from Mr. Grumbacher in Promotion I'm to be *Ogle*'s Religious Editor."

"When the devil did I . . . ?" Suddenly, Buckley's blinking ceased and he allowed himself a mere smile. "I don't recall any discussion about a Religious Editor, but damned if it isn't a class-one idea. Assuming you're the right man for the job. Are you the right man, sir?"

Not having a clue as to what the job would actually entail, the archbishop hesitated before answering. In spite of evidence to the contrary, he was no fool, merely a stranger to the non-ecumenical world. With the church no longer his buffer, might not *Ogle* serve as his new sanctum? Clearly it was capable of dealing with some of the immediate problems—starvation, homelessness, possibly even loneliness.

"Oh, yes, Mr. Buckley," he said. "I most assuredly am the right man."

"I think you are." Buckley extended a large but soft pale hand which the archbishop shook heartily. "I want you to call me Buck. What's your first name, archbishop?"

"Alphonse."

"Okay if I call you Al? Maybe Father Al?"

"Al is fine."

"This is great timing, your showing up now, Al, when I'm in the middle of writing my credo. The Promotion Department has been hacking away at it, but I'm relieving them of that duty. Daily I grow more convinced that I was placed on this earth to be something more than its sexual liberator. The *Ogle* Credo is too important a document to be cobbled together by common hand. Am I right?"

The archbishop nodded, playing it safe.

"Good. The kids out there may be saying God is dead, but you and I, Al, we know he is alive and well and has great plans for us. Let's talk about this."

A discussion of the Almighty was the last thing the archbishop had expected the day to bring. But he was nothing if not game. He gestured to the chair which Buckley had just vacated.

"Not here. This room is too small to discuss even petty ideas. Come with me. You can hang out in my office until they find a space more appropriate for my . . . new collaborator."

As they climbed the stairs to the top floor, the publisher said, "You know the quote in the Book of Common Prayer, about 'the world, the flesh and the devil'?"

"The three threats to man's immortal soul," the archbishop said.

"That's the general belief," Buckley said. "But we know that the world itself isn't necessarily a threat. I mean there's much good in the world. Albert Schweitzer, Martin Luther King, Pat

Boone, that whole crowd. And that leaves the flesh and the devil. Right?"

"Yes."

"It's obvious the devil is not anybody's idea of a positive role model. Would this not suggest that what the quote is really saying is that in this world, man can chose either evil, the devil, or its alternative? That would be the flesh, no? Otherwise it would be redundant. In other words, the way to nirvana, or heaven as Christian philosophies would have it, is through a celebration of the flesh."

The archbishop wished that the publisher were putting him on, but he could see that the man was in deadly earnest. "A very provocative notion," he said.

"Then you do think I'm on to something?" Buckley asked.

"Definitely something," the archbishop said, pleased with himself for how quickly he was getting the drift of the games secular people played.

Buckley paused at the doorway to the fifth floor. He turned and placed a hand on the archbishop's shoulder. "Al," he said, "I've got a feeling that together we're going to blow more minds than Owsley and his LSD."

Since the archbishop was not being terribly up to date on the drug scene, the reference to chemist Augustus Owsley Stanley III and his new lysergic acid factory was lost on him. But he got the drift of what Buckley was saying. "I'm here to help," he said.

"Yep. You're the man. I can feel it. You free to work with me the rest of the day?"

"I still have to claim my luggage and find a place to stay tonight."

"Don't worry about the luggage," Buckley said. "We'll send one of the editors for that. And as for lodging, my guest suite's empty. You'll love it. Round bed. Color TV. All the amenities.

That'll give us even more time to discuss my theories."

The archbishop was pleased with the way he'd maneuvered the publisher into putting him up. He wondered if he could extend that invitation indefinitely. He was surprised at how quickly he was adapting to worldliness. But with that adaptation came the understanding of the quid pro quo involved. By staying on the good side of this oddball God-loving semi-pornographer and philosopher-wannabe, he would definitely be earning his keep.

14.

In one of *Ogle*'s most cluttered and anxiety-ridden offices there worked a pair of publicity flacks named Lew Mitteer and Cholly Grandiose who had been in prior careers, respectively, "Radio's own Little Boy Lew, the silver-throated tiny tenor with the twinkle in his tonsil," and Charlie Blume, racetrack scribe for the *Valley News* and *Green Sheet* and self-styled "Boswell of the bangtails."

The reason Lew changed his billing was obvious: he now stood a good six-three and, having kissed his prepubescent twinkling tonsils good-bye some four decades ago, his silvery tenor had dropped to a basso so profundo it resembled pebbles rolling down a tin roof. The reason for Cholly's name change has gone unrecorded, though it seems to have taken place shortly after a rather abrupt removal of his byline from the *Green Sheet*.

Lew and Cholly, perhaps more than any other *Ogle* staffers, loved their jobs. The magazine was as much a part of their lives as the telephone which was their main source of contact with the outside world. For some mysterious reason, in an office where the average secretary had two telephone extensions, it was their fate to share not only the room but a single telephone line.

That afternoon, while Cholly was taking his post-luncheon stroll among the secretaries, Lew Mitteer grabbed for the idle instrument and dialed Larry Beagle. "Larry, baby," Lew whispered into the receiver, "this evening's HerEx. Ray Stooley's column. I planted the bit this a.m., sweetheart. Don't thank me now. Just drop a few nice words next time you're with Armstead or Buck. Later, pally."

Beagle had no sooner replaced his phone, when it sounded again. "Lar-ree, bay-bee," said the voice on the other end, barely heard above the background noises.

"Who is this?" Beagle asked curtly.

"Jolly Cholly, lover."

"Where the hell are you? It sounds like a tool and dye shop."

"I'm using the basement phone, goomba. They're workin' on the pipes down here."

"What do you want, Cholly?" Beagle said acidly. He was still in a foul mood from his last go-round with Armstead.

"So what should I want, but to tell you the news about Stooley's column. I don't suppose you've seen the bit I planted?"

"No, but I must admit my curiosity is piqued. Tell me about it."

"I doan wanna sperl it for ya. That Stooley, what a bastard of a lover-doll. Check it out."

"Cholly, do you know of anything happening in Des Moines that might have some bearing on the magazine?"

"Des Moines?" Cholly asked. "Zat in this country?"

Beagle slammed down the phone and buzzed for his secretary. When she did not reply, he dragged himself from his office and went in search of that day's *Herald Examiner.* He finally found one in Maurice Grumbacher's wastebasket and, with a curt nod to Grumbacher, retreated to his own office.

Beneath the column headline "THE STOOLEY SPEAKS" and a smiling picture of Ray Stooley himself, snapped many years ago when he had still been the assistant Society Editor and the wedding cake diet had not yet taken its toll, Beagle read the following:

"Sex and Violence Dept. Months ago, the coroner called it pure bad luck that *Ogle* mag exec Nick Hobard got his skull crushed by the frog statue guarding the entrance to the nudie rag's office building. But a person in the know has another take: Hobard made one too many enemies. Is somebody keeping homicidal secrets under their snap-brim hat?"

Beagle re-read the lines carefully, digesting every grim word. Then he summoned Lew and Cholly.

They both appeared at his door gulping for breath.

"What's up, lover?"

"What gives, sweetheart?"

Beagle pointed to Stooley's column. "You boys like this publicity, eh?" They both nodded, a trifle uneasily.

"Print is gold," Lew said.

"Fame is the game," Cholly added.

"Is the item legit?" Beagle asked. "Is there talk that Nick Hobart was murdered?"

Lew and Cholly looked at each other.

"Tell the man," Cholly said.

Lew gave Beagle a sickly grin.

"Are either of you morons really responsible for this?" Beagle asked.

"Hey, Larry boobie," Cholly got out quickly. "Simmer down. No sense putting Lew's bazoo on the chopping block just because he acted a little hasty."

"Me? Why you . . . you sheistkopf. Stooley's your stooge. Not mine."

"Let me understand this, gentlemen," Beagle said. "Both of you claimed that you delivered the item to Stooley. Now both of you disown it. Let's cut the crap, shall we?"

The two publicity men cast their eyes to the floor. "I lied about the scoop being mine," Lew Mitteer said in an amazingly small voice.

"Ditto," said Cholly Grandiose.

"Then who? And what the hell do I say to Milton when he—"

Beagle's phone began to ring. Without hesitation, he lifted it to his ear. "Hello, Milton," he said, eyes staring heavenward. "Yes, as a matter of fact I have a copy in front of me at this min—

"Right . . . well . . . but if . . . all right. Yes, Milton. That's what we'll do."

Beagle replaced the phone and in the same graceless motion picked a roiled handkerchief from his desk and mopped his brow. "Here's the party line, boys. Both of you get on the horn and deliver it to every reporter, columnist and bigmouth in town. There is no question but that Nick Hobart's death was accidental. The police have labeled it such. The coroner has labeled it such. Nick's life insurance company has paid the full policy amount to his sister in Coral Gables without a quibble. Stooley's squib is pure fiction."

"But Stooley's got a rep for straight items," Cholly said.

Beagle sighed. "Stooley also has a rep for booze. He must've been on the sauce when he wrote the squib. He even spelled Nick's last name wrong. If anyone asks, our lawyers are demanding an immediate retraction.

"Okay, let's get hopping."

"Just between us girls," Lew said, "is somebody sayin' Hobart was hit?"

"If they are, they're not saying it to me."

"Somebody fed the story to Stooley," Cholly said.

"I hope we never find out who," Beagle said.

15.

Harry was almost knocked over by the two publicity men scuttling from Beagle's office. He had been standing just outside the door where he'd overheard the conversation about the Stooley item.

It had been so intriguing, it took him a second to remember why he was there, carrying a large mailing piece under his arm.

He took it into Beagle's office and began unfolding it until it covered the promotion manager's desk.

Its main feature was a comic book–style, full-color drawing of the *Ogle* frog seated on its proverbial lily pad, high and dry, while competing magazines waving three-fingered white gloved hands, thrashed about in the water, sinking helplessly. A bold headline shouted: "BIG FROG IN A LITTLE POND."

The thrust of the copy, penned by Maurice Grumbacher, was that *Ogle* was the best advertising bargain in the free world and all other magazines, from *Time* to the *Atlantic Monthly*, were waterlogged dying creatures. It ended with an exhortation to big business to "Get with it. Find a seat on the lily pad. Get in the sun, the fun, the excitement of *Ogle* magazine."

"A seat on the lily pad?" Harry said. "The president of General Motors rushing to get a seat on the lily pad?"

Beagle stared at him and said nothing.

"What happened to the copy I wrote, Larry?"

"I . . . we decided it didn't quite cut it," Beagle said.

"What didn't cut it? Specifically?"

"I forget the main objection," Beagle said wearily. "As I recall, Maurice felt a lack of sprightliness. Now, if you don't mind, I've something import—"

"I worked for two weeks on my concept, Larry, which was a little more original than a frog and a lily pad."

Beagle chewed the inside of his cheek. "Maurice's copy has flair. It's fresh and . . . sprightly."

Harry faltered. He wanted to keep working for *Ogle,* at least until his book was finished. But he had to say something. "If Maurice feels that my stuff is bad, I wish he'd come to me and tell me what's wrong. That's the only way I'll know what he wants."

"Maurice should have done that. Why don't you discuss this with him? Right now I've—"

"You're really sold on Maurice's talent?"

"He's the best copywriter I've ever worked with. He's got experience, Harry. I hope you're not too headstrong to profit by it."

Harry's mouth dropped. "What experience?" he asked. "Maurice worked for a greeting card company for five years and he's been here for two. I was with an agency writing ad copy."

Beagle shifted his glance. "He's older and his writing is more mature. He turns a nice pun, too."

Beagle wheeled around until his back was to Harry, signifying the end of the conversation. He put the capper on it. "Maurice went to Stanford."

Harry left the office wondering, how in all the world of logic Maurice Grumbacher's ill-fated, failing semester at Stanford could have given him the edge in the Copy Department of *Ogle* magazine.

He muttered something about it to Weeks who, with characteristic sagacity, told him to stop rocking the boat.

"The guy keeps shit-canning my copy," Harry said. "How do

you like it when he tosses your stuff?"

"He never does," Weeks said. "And you know why? Because I never write anything. I go to Maurice and flatter him by asking him his ideas and he winds up writing the whole thing for me. Naturally he doesn't change any of it. Last week he put me in for a raise."

Harry slumped back in his chair. He stared at Weeks' balding head bobbing back and forth while he bent to some unnecessary task. Then he opened the bottom drawer of his desk and withdrew a folder of neatly typed manuscript: the first twenty-seven pages of *A Child of the Gap,* the semiautobiographical novel that he had been laboring over.

He was flipping though the pages, trying to figure out where he might inject the murder of his fictional magazine's circulation manager, when he caught a whiff of musk cologne.

Maurice Grumbacher was standing at his desk, holding out a stack of handwritten pages. "Those are my notes on the *Ogle* Credo," he said. "Larry tells me you want more work. Well, daddy-o, here it is and welcome to it."

Grumbacher turned to leave, but whirled back fast enough to catch Harry's face, twisted in a mimicking grimace. "And, Harry, Buck loved every concept on those pages, so don't even dream of improvising. Need I mention, you've gotta crash dive on it."

After checking to make sure Grumbacher was definitely gone, Weeks said, "What a maroon."

"Just look at this crap. I haven't seen writing like this since my kid brother was two years old. His 'k's are backwards. I can't believe he showed this to Buckley."

"He did. Buckley thought it was crap. He and that archbishop character have been huddling, working on another version."

"How do you know these things?" Harry asked.

"My new nutcracker," Weeks said. "Snoop and learn because

knowledge is power."

"If Buckley's really doing it himself, then Grumbacher is just screwing with me, wasting my time," Harry said.

"I don't think you have to worry about the big G. much longer," Weeks said. "They're saying he scragged Nick Hobart."

"Get serious."

"I am."

"First off, Hobart's death was an accident."

"Not according to Stooley's column in the *Examiner*. He says there's talk of a cover-up."

Harry was reminded of his conversation with Terry. "Stooley mentioned Maurice?"

Weeks shook his head. "No. I was making my rounds, like I do, and, just before her ice queen secretary chased me off, I heard Ida and the dancer, Bethune, yakking about some note that Grumbacher sent Hobart right before he kissed the frog. A threat."

"Yeah? That still doesn't mean murder or that Grumbacher did it."

"Max nix. Word about his involvement is gonna spread, which means the big G., guilty or not, is gonna have his mind on a lot more than putting ants in your pants."

Harry frowned. "Where do you suppose Stooley got that item, anyway?"

Weeks shrugged. "Maybe Bethune tipped him. Hell, it could've been anybody. Stooley hangs out in this neighborhood. Every morning, you can find him right across the street at Herkie's. It's where he drinks his breakfast."

Harry frowned, remembering where he'd left Terry. "I guess whoever talked to Stooley could lose their job," he said.

"Their job?" Weeks said. "Hell, if somebody really did bump off Hobart, whoever is stirring things up with Stooley could lose a lot more."

16.

Two days later, on the same bright, sunny afternoon that President Johnson's National Security Adviser Walt Whitman Rostow predicted that the Vietcong were "going to collapse within weeks, not months but weeks," Milton Zephyr Armstead instructed Beagle to summon his "so-called creative staff" to his office.

"Get that tanglefoot circulation guy, too," Armstead added. "Let's see what he's made of."

"What's up?" Beagle asked.

"You'll find out with the others. Why should I repeat myself?"

Beagle took his time, but was still the first to arrive at the meeting.

"So Larry-kins, what's the status on 'the Hobart murder case'?"

"You saw the paper's retraction," Beagle said.

"One line of type on page four hundred and twelve."

"That's an exaggeration," Beagle said.

"And you caught it. Bravo." Armstead leaned forward, glaring at Beagle. "I'm not talking about the goddamned retraction, you nitwit. I want to know where we stand on the frigging rumor."

"Where we stand?" Beagle said, hating the whine that had crept into his voice. "It's a nonissue."

"Really? That means you've discovered the identity of the disloyal piece of dung who gave Stooley his precious scoop?"

"I've been assuming that Stooley made up the item," Beagle said. "You telling me that isn't the case, that someone working here really has information that Nick's death wasn't accidental?"

Since Armstead believed himself to be a giant living among pigmies, he rarely felt the need to backtrack. But this was one of those times. "That isn't what I said at all. It's a given that Nick wasn't murdered. So the item is bullshit from the git-go. I never said it was anybody here that made it up."

"You used the word 'disloyal.' "

"Slip of the tongue," Armstead said. "Anyway, there are more important matters, like where the hell are your people?"

"They'll be he—"

"And what do we do about the son-of-a-bitch archbishop who's got Buck's ear?"

"Do about him?" Beagle asked.

"It's not bad enough I now have to go through him to get to Buck. I understand his salary—which Buck just doubled by the way—is coming out of our budget."

"I . . . what do you suggest we do about it?"

"Figure out a compelling reason for dumping the son-of-a-bitch."

"How would I do that?"

"*Dammit*, Beagle. Figure something out. Aren't you the cool hand who led a battalion of Army pukes to victory in the Big One."

"I was in the Marine Corps," Beagle said, stiffening.

"Oh? The Corps? Not the Army," Armstead said. "Like that's better?"

"Some would say so."

"The Corps, eh? Glory boys." He shook his head sadly. "You've got a family, right? Wife? Kids?"

"Yes," Beagle said. "Just one kid, though."

"So there you are with spouse and dependent and you frigging enlist in the frigging Marines, spend your prime years dodging bullets and bombs in some smelly foxhole or other. Am I right?" He shoved a pointed finger in Beagle's face.

"Well, you know what I did, Beagle? I saw the handwriting on the wall and got married, and the draft passed me by. When I heard they were thinking about calling up married guys, I knocked up the wife. Then, when the bullshit was over, and assholes like you came marching home, battered and bruised, I dumped that family baggage as fast as I could.

"And here I am today. And there you are. And if you can't see who's better off, you're even more pathetic than I think."

Beagle squirmed on the couch. Armstead's pointing finger neared his nose. Suddenly it was a fixed bayonet and the leering face took on an Oriental cast.

Beagle clenched his fists and started to rise.

And Maurice Grumbacher strolled into the office being trailed by his musky cologne and an apparently reticent Howard Bethune.

Breathing heavily but aware again of his surroundings, Beagle flopped back against the couch, thoughts of the old war resting precariously on a temporary shelf of his memory.

"What am I doing here, Milton?" Bethune asked. "There's work I should be doing."

"Well, Mister Dime-a-Dance, this meeting is crucial to the financial future of the magazine," Armstead said. "But if putting in couch time is higher up on your priority list, by all means waltz away."

Scowling, the circulation manager headed for a seat between Beagle and Grumbacher. He paused, gave Grumbacher a scowl, sniffed the air and moved on to a chair.

Armstead's attention shifted to Weeks and Trauble as they entered, carrying their yellow ledger pads. "Are those pads clean, men?" he asked.

"Yes, sir," came the unison reply.

"Well, you can cram them where the sun don't shine, boys, because there will be no notes taken at this meeting. If you can't remember it all, we don't need you. Fine staff you've got here, Beagle. Great little note takers."

"Could we please get started," Bethune asked.

"What's up, Howard? Got more snooping to do?"

Bethune's look—a mixture of surprise and alarm—warned Armstead that he'd let another cat out of the bag. Beagle and his people were staring at him with puzzled expressions.

John Bingham, the magazine's ad exec, was standing in the doorway, glaring at him.

Well, if they can't take a joke, screw 'em, Armstead thought. "Come on in, Johnny," he said. "Howard Bethune was about to lead us in a loyalty oath."

"What the hell is wrong with you, Armstead?" Bingham said.

"High on life," Armstead said. "Take a seat next to the ex-jarhead."

The ad man remained standing. "I'm not gonna be here that long."

"Sit, Johnny," Armstead said. "So I won't have to keep looking up."

Obviously amused, he watched the ad man fill the spare section of the couch. "Good. Now that we are all assembled . . . Buck has made the request, via his new religious crony, that we come up with some promotional assistance—an Image Campaign, as it were—for Johnny here and his band of sales slugs."

"We need something very hard sell," John Bingham said, "to help us pry some heavy advertising coin out of the Fortune 500."

"So, let the creativity flow, boys," Armstead said.

There was silence in the room.

"I can't hear you," Armstead said.

"Uh, well, we sell two million copies a month," Harry said, "with a pass-along average of five. That's ten million guys looking at each issue. I imagine that would put us up in *TV Guide* and *Reader's Digest* territory, if not beyond. That must mean something to advertisers."

"What's your name, son?"

"Harry Trauble."

"Well, gang," he said, "what do we think of Harry's idea, which I gather is to focus on comparative circulation figures?"

"How do we rank, Howard?" Beagle asked.

"If we stick to males between the age of eighteen to twenty-four," Bethune said, "we'd be in the top five. Of course, *Play*—"

"Enough!" Armstrong commanded. "I don't want to hear the name of that frigging rabbit rag mentioned again in my presence. I'm fed to the gills listening to how successful it is. That's defeatist talk. Especially when we're putting out a mag that's better and classier."

He wheeled suddenly on Roger Weeks. "Was that an eye roll, son?"

"No, sir," Weeks replied. "I've got a bum ocular muscle. Causes the eye to drift."

"What's your name?"

"Roger Weeks."

"You bullshitting me about your drifting eye, son? And before you answer, rest assured I'll be checking your medical chart in Personnel."

"No lie," Weeks said, causing his right eyelid to flutter.

Armstead glared at him, still suspicious but letting it go. "Okay. Where were we?"

"Discussing Harry's idea," Beagle said.

"Yeah. Well, it's a crappy idea. Facts and figures bore the shit out of me."

"They don't bore ad agencies," John Bingham said. "It's

what they live by."

"I'll keep that in mind. Now, do we have an idea we can use?"

"This is just off the top of the noggin, Milton," Grumbacher said. "But suppose we get a bunch of average Joes. You know—home-loving, wife-loving, kid-loving, churchgoing saps. Suppose we get them to say that they read *Ogle* and buy everything the magazine recommends. We can whip up a tasty ad campaign with them. Full page. Big picture, little type. Doyle-Danesy."

"Would you sit a little farther downwind, Maurice?" Armstead said. "Your musk oil is causing my breakfast to back up."

He waited until Grumbacher had moved closer to the door to continue.

"Well men, what do you think about Maurice's idea?"

"Testimonial ads," Harry said dismissively.

Armstead settled back in his chair. "In other words, you think the concept is idiotic, overworked, trite, and in general full of crap. Is that right, Weeks?"

"I'm Trauble, Mr. Armstead."

"Then who the hell is Weeks?"

"I'm Weeks, sir. Roger Weeks."

"Well, Trauble or whatever your name is—I agree with you. It's a crappy idea. It's a Grumbacher-type idea. One would think he could come up with some *killer* material."

John Bingham had evidently had enough. "Good luck with this, Milton," he said, rising to his feet. "I've got ads to sell."

"Behold the unhappy huckster," Armstead said when Bingham had left the room. "Too feeble to close a deal, so he asks for help. And when we try to give it, he walks off."

He hopped from his chair and began to pace about the office. After a few minutes, he turned to the others and said, "All right, gang, any other ideas?"

There was a long silence, broken by Grumbacher. "We've got

that booklet, 'The Frog and I,' about how Buckley started the magazine on just $900, and all sorts of interesting things, like the time they found a real live frog in—"

"Spare me the details," Armstead said. "I know them. I wrote 'The Frog and I.' "

"I thought Mr. Buckley wrote it. It has his name—"

"Are you for real, Maurice? Dammit, here's a supposed promotion man who believes everything he sees in print." He threw his cigarette holder down on his desk. "Well, you simpleton, what do you want to do with 'The Frog and I'?"

"We could . . . run clever little ads spotlighting some of the more interesting things that've happened around here."

"To what end?" Armstead asked.

Grumbacher was about to answer his question, but the phone rang and Armstead cut him off.

"Hello . . . yes, this is Milt. Hi, baby . . . I'm in a big important conference.

"Excuse me for a minute, men," he said, his hand covering the receiver. "Bat that idea around a bit. I won't be long." He winked at them and went back to the phone.

For a little less than half an hour he cuddled, caressed, twisted, twirled, waved, pressed and, in general, made love to the phone while Harry leafed through "The Frog and I," Beagle thought about the war, Weeks searched the office for objects worth boosting and Grumbacher fell asleep.

He was snoring when Armstead bent over him, holding his nose, and shouted in his ear, "We keeping you up?"

"Uh . . . Milton. Just dozed off for a minute. Sorry."

"You certainly are," Armstead said, returning to his chair. "Well men. Where were we?"

"The Image Campaign," Harry said.

"The Image Campaign, yes. Well, listen and you will hear the Image Campaign."

They all leaned forward.

"The idea came to me while I was on the phone. We get us an *Ogle* Guy. Affluent, single and swinging or married with house in the 'burbs. Member of the country club. Listens to Sinatra and the Stones. Church on Sunday morning, TV football in the afternoon. Like that. We get him to say he not only reads *Ogle,* he believes in it. The rabbit rag is . . . plastic to the *Ogle* Guy. *Ogle* is real. It's part of his life. He believes every frigging word we print. That includes our advertisements.

"The *Ogle* Guy is gonna be in our *Journal* ads. He'll be on TV. He'll be traveling around the country with three of four Eyefuls, visiting automobile showrooms, chain stores, hell, even supermarkets, any place there's a retailer who'll be calling the home office to demand that the magazine be added to the ad budget. That's our Image Campaign."

Grumbacher said, "But isn't that the same—?"

"Great concept, Milton," Beagle said, interrupting his assistant who'd been on the verge of talking himself into unemployment.

"You bet your ass it's great. Now, all we need to do is find the *Ogle* Guy. That's where you come in, Dancing Dan."

"Me?" Bethune asked.

"Dig into the big pile of subscribers and find the *Ogle* Guy for us. We want that man, and we want him this evening."

"That's ridiculous," Bethune said. "Even if it was possible to search through a list of more than four hundred thousand subscription forms in one evening, they don't contain the kind of personal information you're talking about."

Armstead had to admit this was true. He began pacing the floor, chin extended.

"There's the questionnaire," Beagle said.

"Right," Grumbacher said.

"I'm not reading you," Armstead said.

"It was something Nick Hobart requested," Beagle said. "He wanted to get a fix on the sort of people who were subscribing. So we prepared a card with a bunch of questions about age, income, marital status and so on."

"Why don't I know about this?" Armstead asked.

"It may have been when you were in Jamaica with the, ah, actress."

"Ah, yes." Armstead grinned at the memory. "My porno phase. So, what kind of a return did we get on the cards?"

"I'm not sure," Beagle said. "I don't recalling getting the returns back from Nick."

Armstead turned to Bethune. "Well? You seem to know where Hobart hid everything."

"I think I saw cards like that in one of the office cabinets," Bethune said, standing up. "I'll go through 'em first thing in the morning."

"You'll do it tonight, Bethune. We're not paying you to get powder on your ass."

"You don't tell me what to do, Armstead," Bethune said, starting to walk away. "I don't work for you."

"You may not be in my department. But make no mistake, I am a Vice frigging President of this company. And as such I can toss you out on your powdery keester anytime I want. Now get moving on that project, or just get moving. Frankly, I'd be happy to see you hit the road. And I'm not alone."

Bethune locked eyes with Armstead, but it was hardly an even contest.

Eventually, he said softly, "I'll take care of it."

"See," Armstead said to the remaining members of the Image Campaign meeting, "that's how we get things done."

17.

"But he razooed my idea," Grumbacher was complaining in Beagle's office later that evening.

"I know, Maurice," Beagle said. "But this is a team effort. The important thing is not whose idea it is. We now know what Milton wants, and we can get the damned campaign going."

"It's the prin-chi-pay, Larry."

"The what?"

"Prin-chi-pay. Isn't that Italian for principle?"

"I don't think so, but forget principles this once," Beagle said, amusing himself with the comment.

His smile slowly faded as he watched Grumbacher dragging himself away like a kicked dog.

Beagle walked to his closet for his hat and coat. He returned to the desk and stuffed a packet of papers into his briefcase.

He was heading toward the exit when he heard Armstead's unmistakable, nasal voice. The man was in his office on the phone, arguing with someone. "Tell Buck this may not be the best time for a party," he was saying. "Our parties have a way of making news and right now . . . What? Not open to negotiation? We'll just see about that."

Beagle heard the phone being slammed onto its cradle, accompanied by Armstead shouting, "That sanctimonious piece of shit."

The Promotion Manager was too weary to get involved in whatever that phone call was about. He just wanted to go home and forget *Ogle* for the rest of the evening. To avoid passing Armstead's open door, he had to circle the floor.

He was stopped by the sight of the desks in the center area, the bullpen, sitting still and silent and gleaming white in the reduced overhead lighting. He'd never realized before how reminiscent they were of the tombstones that dotted the countryside at Normandy.

This brief reverie was shattered by the rat-a-tat of an electric typewriter. It came from behind the closed door to the office used by Weeks and Trauble.

Beagle walked to the door and opened it.

Harry looked up, startled. "Uh, hi, Larry," he said sheepishly. "Midnight oil?"

"Yeah," Harry answered. "I'd appreciate your not mentioning it to Maurice. He doesn't like me working late."

Beagle was puzzled by the comment, but decided to let it go. "What do you think of our Image Campaign?" he asked.

"Suppose I said it sucked, would that make a difference?"

"I guess not."

"You okay, Larry?"

"Sure. Just trying to avoid Milton. I've had enough of him for today. Maybe I'll sit down for a minute, if it's not a bother."

"Oh, heck no," Harry said, pulling the sheet from his typewriter and hastily shoving it into a manila folder.

Beagle leaned back in Weeks' chair and smiled, at nothing at all that Harry could see. "What're you working on this late?" he asked.

"The credo," Harry lied.

"I thought Buck was working on that himself."

"Maurice asked me to stay with it, anyway. As backup, I guess."

From the other side of the bullpen, Armstead shouted Beagle's name.

The two men sat dead still.

Armstead shouted again.

They heard his footsteps approaching. And then continuing past Harry's closed door.

As the footsteps echoed away, Beagle stood up. "I'd better make my getaway while I can. See you tomorrow. And Harry, about Maurice's rewriting your copy. Don't worry about it. You've lots of time ahead of you. Your turn will come."

When the door shut behind Larry Beagle, Harry opened the folder and took out the sheet on which he had been typing. He slipped it back into the machine.

His turn would come all right, when his novel hit the best-seller lists.

But the combination of helplessness and weariness on Beagle's face had undercut the resentment Harry felt for the man's disregard for his talent. That resentment had been the main thing fueling his writing.

He removed the sheet from the typewriter and placed it on top of the thin stack in the folder. The manuscript sucked. Every page of it ate the big one. *A Child of the Gap.* Jesus, what was he thinking?

Okay, so his home life made him feel like the poster boy for The Generation Gap and the career boost he'd been expecting from *Ogle* was turning to dog shit. So what? Was that something worth writing a novel about?

Feeling sorry for himself, he reached for the phone.

Ogle had rules against its employees making personal long distance calls. But Weeks had shown him how to dial up the WATS Line, a direct phone line that left no record of calls made.

His mother answered on the second ring.

"Oh, Harry," she said. "Caught us right at dinnertime."

"Sorry, Mom, I was just wondering if there was any more news about Vaughan."

"He's out."

"Out of the Army?"

"No. Out of the hospital. Evidently, the wound was more like a scratch and your brother, as usual, was making a big production of it. He's so dramatic. He wouldn't tell us where they were sending him. Said it was a secret."

"But he's okay. That's good," Harry said.

"Your father says a man on the TV predicted the war would be over in just a few weeks."

"Who was that, Carnac the Magnificent?"

"I don't . . . oh, that's a joke. Your keen sense of humor. No, this was that Defense Department fellow."

"I hope he's right, for Vaughan's sake."

"I'd better go. You know how your dad is about eating all alone. Son . . . ?"

"Yes, Mom."

"Can't you do something more worthwhile with your life? I mean, you're an officer in the Coast Guard reserves. Don't they need Coast Guard officers in Vietnam?"

"If they do, they'll have to come and get me," Harry said. He'd read somewhere that Coast Guard officers over there wound up on unarmed small craft that navigated the finger lakes and served generally as targets for Cong snipers.

"Well, goodnight, son. Keep well and try not to catch any sexually transmitted diseases."

"I'll do my best, mom."

He hung up the phone feeling more depressed than ever. He thought about his mother's suggestion that he make an active duty request. Poor Vaughan, recovering from a bullet wound, would soon be sloughing through the slush and dodging even more bullets. And here he was, safe and secure and squandering his talent promoting a stroke book.

Larry Beagle, a soldier from another war, had been a survivor, a hero. He'd accomplished something.

Harry felt utterly useless. He'd achieved nothing and was achieving nothing, other than to waste his time writing a novel that had no purpose other than self-gratification. He collected the pages of "*Child of the Gap,* put them in their folder. For a moment, he considered dropping the folder into the wastebasket. But only for a moment.

Instead, he placed it at the far rear of his desk drawer.

Then he flicked off his office light and was about to step into the bullpen when he saw Ida Connor striding toward Armstead's office.

He waited until she'd passed, then made his exit.

Outside, at a safe distance from the new giant frog, he paused, trying to decide how to avoid another evening squinting at the little black-and-white TV in his apartment. He thought he'd head for The Grasshopper Lounge, a popular after-work hangout that was only a few blocks away.

Then his eye was caught by the blinking red neon sign in the window of Herkie's Wonder Bar and Grill across the street. In spite of its proximity, the neighborhood bar was usually avoided by the *Ogle* staffers, probably because its atmosphere was decidedly blue collar and the average age of its customers was somewhere between senility and death. But, as Harry recalled, at least one redheaded receptionist hung out there.

Maybe Terry O'Mara was in Herkie's now, on her second or third happy hour cocktail, wondering how to spend the rest of her evening.

He headed across the deserted street, not realizing that his quest for female companionship and maybe a little uncomplicated sex would change his life and the lives of everyone at *Ogle* forever.

18.

When Armstead heard high heels clicking toward his office, he quickly withdrew an icy bottle of Mumm's from a bucket on his desk and filled one of two fluted glasses. He leapt to his feet, dimmed the office lights until the room resembled, in his mind at least, sunset at the garden of the Hesperides, and moved to welcome his guest with the bubbly and a line he'd been working on, "A little something to launch the night."

"Why, thank you, Milton," Ida Connor said, taking the glass. "What are we celebrating?"

"Ida! I . . . was expecting someone else," he said.

"I imagine you were," Ida said. She sipped the wine. "Nice and dry. That someone must be on your A list."

Before Armstead could reply, John Bingham and Kevin Dobbs joined them.

"Gentlemen," he said, purposely glancing at his watch, "what's up?"

"You don't seem to be taking our situation seriously enough," Bingham said.

"What the hell are you talking about?"

"John says you blatantly mentioned our little secret in front of your staff," Ida said.

"When did I do that?" Armstead asked Bingham.

"When you accused Howard Bethune of snooping," the Advertising Vice President said.

"All that did was convince Howard something dark and devious is going on," Dobbs said. "He called me as soon as he got back to his office. Wanted to know if you and I were conspiring against him."

"Aren't we?"

"It's foolish to treat this matter cavalierly, Milton," Ida said. "We really can't have Howard running to the newspapers again about Nick Hobart."

"He swore he didn't talk to that reporter, Stooley," Dobbs said.

Ida frowned. "Someone else spreading stories?"

"Who cares? We put the kibosh on the Stooley thing," Armstead said.

"This is not the time for our company to be subject to negative publicity of any sort," Ida said. "Not while we're about to . . . expand the magazine's horizons. We can't have Howard or anyone else mouthing off to the press. We should be placating the man, Milton, not goading him."

"Bethune's a jackass," Armstead said.

"You're an arrogant jackass, Armstead," Bingham said.

"You're calling me arrogant? You pompous prick."

"Let's not bicker, gentlemen," Ida said. "We're at a crucial point in our endeavor, with Dr. Magnus about to arrive. Let's stay on track. Are we in agreement that it makes sense to assuage Howard's concerns?"

Armstead nodded reluctantly.

"Now, to an allied matter," Ida said, handing Armstead a folded letter. "This arrived at Trower's office this afternoon."

The promotion director scanned it quickly. "This Tobella cretin wants one hundred thou? For damage to his frigging reputation? What reputation?"

"Pay him," Bingham said.

"Don't go simple on us, John," Armstead said. "What happens if, a year from now, he decides to hit us up for another hundred thousand?"

"We'll have our lawyer create some sort of quit-claim document for Tobella to sign," Ida said.

Armstead nodded. "And if he refuses to sign it, we can always consider an alternative plan."

Bingham gawked at him. "Tell me you're not suggesting we murder—"

"Hell-o-o," a female voice sang out.

A beautiful brunette stood at the door, wearing a dress so short her body seemed to be 90% legs.

"Hi, baby," Armstead said. "That's some skirt you're not wearing."

"It's the latest thing in London; they call it a mini," she said. "I didn't mean to interrupt anything."

"We're all done here," Armstead said. "You and your mini come on in."

He introduced the young woman as Lenina.

"I use just the one name," she said.

"Are you in the entertainment field, Lenina?" Ida asked.

"Definitely no, thank you very much."

"Then . . . ?"

"I'm a poetess."

"Oh, really?" Dobbs asked with more than a hint of condescension. "And have you been published?"

"I've a short poem in the current *Moonbeam*."

The editor's mouth dropped. "*Moonbeam* published my first short story," he said. "That was a while back, of course. I'm very impressed, Lenina. I'll definitely look for your work."

"Why not go do that now, Kevin?" Armstead said. "I'm sure all of you have something better to do than to keep Lenina and me from making our own poetry."

With some reluctance, Dobbs allowed Bingham to lead him from the room. Ida wasn't as quick to depart. "A poetess, eh?

Did you two kids meet at a coffeehouse?"

"We met at the Treasures of the Coliseum exhibit at the Getty." Lenina smiled at Armstead.

"Poetry and art," Ida said, smiling, as she headed for the door. "Well, congratulations, Lenina, for finding depths to Milton no one else has had the courage to explore. You two enjoy yourselves."

When Armstead had closed the door after Ida, Lenina said, "What a sweet lady."

"A unique combination of Queen Elizabeth, Jane Mansfield and Lucretia Borgia," Armstead said, topping off the glass Ida had sipped. He handed it to Lenina. "A little something to launch the night," he said.

19.

Herkie's Wonder Bar and Grill was a larger establishment than its humble storefront indicated. Past the entryway, Harry found a restaurant of sorts, with approximately half of its twenty tables occupied by senior citizens, dining while listening to a recorded orchestra, probably led by Mantovani, play a sappy ballroom version of a painfully appropriate rock favorite, "Heartbreak Hotel."

Along one beige wall, two weary waitresses in rumpled blue uniforms sat behind a counter ladling out portions from several large warmer trays containing spaghetti and meatballs, chili and beans and breaded something, either veal or pork chops. Nearby was a salad bar that looked as though it hadn't been touched all night.

Past the dining room was a considerably noisier bar area where the mainly male customers sounded as if they were speaking in tongues—thick tongues. The large room's lighting depended primarily on the glow from several colorful illuminated beer signs and a 21-inch black-and-white TV above the long mahogany bar, currently displaying Ernest Borgnine engaged in a slightly more amusing war than Vietnam. It took Harry a few moments to realize Terry wasn't there, either.

He'd just about given up any hope of finding her when he saw a painted sign near a stairwell reading, "Billiards," with an arrow pointing up. As he reached the top of the stairs, he immediately spied Terry standing at a pool table, cue in hand, giving the position of the balls her full attention.

Nearby were two men, one holding a cue, the other a drink. The drinker was elderly, wearing a slightly battered grey felt hat and a sports jacket that he may have slept in. He was short, with merry blue eyes and a face full of white whiskers. The one fondling the cue had at least two inches on Harry's six-foot stature, a rangy guy with heavy-lidded eyes, a mound of oily black hair and sideburns down to his chin. The older man was studying the table; the younger was studying Terry's ass.

Harry waited by the entrance, not wanting to break her concentration or announce his presence until he had a clearer picture of the relationship between her and Sideburns.

She bent over the table and gave the cue a very light stroke.

The cue ball hit its mark and, a second or two later, the target ball plopped into a pocket.

Her pretty face betraying nothing, Terry began to prowl around the table, the men backing away to allow her room. She found her next shot, made it and moved on.

It took her less than seven minutes to clear the green.

She collected a couple of bills from the guy with sideburns, looked up and saw Harry. Without breaking eye contact, she handed her stick to the elderly man and crossed the room, moving into Harry's arms and kissing him full on the lips.

She tasted of whiskey and cigarettes, a surprisingly acceptable mixture, what with her tongue actively probing his mouth and her body pressed tightly against his.

When she finally broke the kiss, she said, "You did come here looking for me, right?"

"Oh, yeah," he said.

"Fine. I'll go get Colin."

Before he could question that, she was striding back to the table. There, she and the guy with sideburns began to talk, the latter staring Harry's way, scowling.

Harry thought the scowl was a good sign.

Terry took the cue stick from the older man's hand and gave it to Sideburns. Then she grabbed the old guy's arm and semi-dragged him to where Harry was standing.

"Uncle Colin, this is Harry Trouble, a friend of mine."

"I cert'ny hope so," the old man said, the words wobbling under a combination of booze and brogue, "considerin' the greetin' ya jist gave 'im."

"Hey," Sideburns yelled. "You can't quit on me now."

"Time to split," she said.

Hurrying, she led them down the stairs and through the bar area to a large kitchen where a big perspiring man in an apron and chef's hat was standing by while a short guy with a black pencil moustache and a wig that looked like a gorilla's pelt sampled the contents of a pot on the stove.

"Not enough salt," Mr. Bad Rug said.

"Damn soup start to taste like brine," the chef grumbled.

"Good. I like brine." Mr. Bad Rug spotted Terry and gave her a big smile. "There's my girl. Come for some zoop?"

"Come to tell you there's a hustler upstairs, Herkie."

"Besides you, doll?" Mr. Bad Rug asked. "You sure?"

"He's missing shots I could make when I was in braces. He's buying me booze and he's slurring when he talks, but all he's drinking is Coke, which he claims is rum and Coke—like I can't tell the difference with just one whiff."

"Describe him."

"A big guy, dressed like a rocker, mutton chops down to here. He said some very rude things to me when I told him I wasn't going to stick around to let him 'get even.' "

"I'll go take care of the bum," Herkie said. He headed from the room, shouting "More salt," over his shoulder to the chef.

Terry gestured toward an empty table at the rear. "We could eat here," she said.

"Up to you."

"Wilhelm, would you throw some steaks on the grill?"

"Grill close," the chef said. "All clean for the night."

"Oh, Willie. Just three little steaks, for me and my uncle and my friend?"

"No food for me, darlin'," the old man said, raising his nearly empty glass. "Interferes with m' drinkin'."

"You're getting too old for that nonsense, Colin," she said. "Three steaks, Willie."

"Achh," he said, shaking his head. "You pain in the ass, woman. But I cook. Fix you little salad, too. No soup. Too salty."

They'd barely taken seats at a table when Herkie returned with a tray containing two squat glasses filled with dark brown cocktails on ice. "The bum had lammed by the time I got up there," he said as he placed the drinks in front of Terry and Harry.

"None for the thirsty man?" Colin asked.

"You already got a drink," Herkie said.

"It's about empty."

"Do I look like a waiter to you, you reprobate? I believe you know the way to the bar."

As the old man rose, grumbling, to stagger off for a refill, Herkie asked Terry, "How much did you take off the hustler?"

"Forty bucks, plus the drinks," she said, grinning.

"That's my girl." He turned to Harry. "You gotta watch this one with both eyes."

"Thanks for the advice," Harry said. "And the drink. What is it?"

Herkie looked pained and turned to Terry. "Where'd you get this jamoke?"

"Harry's very pure," she said. "It's his only flaw, best I can see."

Herkie's eyebrows went up almost to his wig. "Yeah? Well, it

111

might do you some good if it rubs off."

"It's an old-fashioned, Harry," she said. "My favorite. I could drink 'em all day and all night."

"And she has," Herkie said.

"But only the way you make 'em," she said.

"The secret's in the bourbon," Herkie said. "We use two full ounces of Cabin Still, none of that Kentucky sippin' whiskey bullshit. The simple syrup isn't too thin or too thick. Toss in two dashes of Angostura and you just drag an orange slice through the booze. You don't crush it or squeeze it. Finally, you add one red cherry and voilà. A masterpiece."

Harry took a sip, tasted the hint of cherry and orange as the sweetened booze warmed his mouth and throat. "It's terrific," he said.

Herkie grinned. "Like they say in the white powder trade, the first one's free. Now, if you'll excuse me, I gotta go give Wilhelm hell. If I don't, he'll think I don't love him anymore."

Harry watched the little man heading toward the chef. "Quite a character," he said.

"Big heart."

"I get the idea he knows you pretty well," he said.

"I lived with him for nine years," she said.

He gawked at her. "Nine years? How young were you?"

"Eleven through twenty," she said between sips of her old-fashioned. "My dad's heart gave out when I was nine. A while later, Mom met Herkie. They kinda fell in love and we moved in. When she died, he and I decided it was probably a good idea for me to get my own place."

"So he's like your stepfather?"

"Very like that," she said.

They were in the middle of their meal when Colin joined them clutching a cocktail. He eyed his steak platter suspiciously, then took a sip of booze. Terry picked up his folded napkin, shook it out and tucked one corner into the neck of his shirt.

Withering under her glare, he sliced off a tip of the meat, seared on the outside and pink in the middle, forked it to his mouth and began to chew. "Not bad," he said, putting down his fork and taking another drink.

"Eat," Terry commanded.

"Like she's me flamin' mother," the old man said, trying to regain some of his Celtic pride. "Save yer concern for folks who need it. Like your loudmouth pal, Stooley, who just broke his nose in the barroom."

She started to rise, but the old man gestured for her to stay seated. "He's moved on, child. Shoved half the toilet paper in the lav up his schnoz, then sashayed off to do more damage to himself elsewhere."

"What happened?" Harry asked.

"Fell off the flamin' stool," Colin said, cutting another tiny piece of meat. "Bashed his honker on the bar."

"You know Stooley pretty well?" Harry asked Terry.

"I've never dated him, if that's what you're asking."

"No. I was just wondering if you were responsible for the item in his column about Nick Hobart's death not being an accident."

"God, no," she said. "I know better than to spill anything to Ray Stooley of all people. He's a reporter."

"I gave Stooley the real story on that Hobart murder," Colin said, "but the son of a bitch must not a been listenin'."

"You told him what real story?" Terry asked.

"Stooley was chattin' me up about your boss's death one night," Colin said, "and I was takin' full advantage of the rare occasion of him supplyin' the sauce. Tellin' the man all I knew."

"*Dammit*, Colin," she said. "That wasn't smart."

The old man didn't seem in the least chastised. "Yer missin' the point, lass," he said. "I told him who killed the bugger and he ignored it."

"You know who killed Nick Hobart?" Harry asked.

"I saw the whole thing. I was looking out the window upstairs, and I saw exactly what happened, and Stooley, the bloody fool, didn't print one flamin' word of it."

"You told him but you didn't tell me?" Terry asked. "What did you see?"

"Your boss, he was yellin' something up at the flamin' frog. And the frog got pissed and hopped to the edge of the overhang and jumped down on him."

"You're saying the statue came to life and killed Hobart?" Harry asked.

"I know. It sounds crazy as a waltzing titmouse, but I seen it, clear as night."

Terry reached out a hand and reeled in the old man's drink. "You've had enough," she said. "Now eat some food and Harry and I'll get you home."

"I'm not ready to go home, woman."

Terry leaned over to whisper something in Colin's ear and the old man's face seemed to close in on itself, like a pouting child's. He made a loud sniff and picked up his knife and fork. "Despairin' it is to come to the stage of life when you have to depend on the flamin' kindness of others."

He nibbled on a bite of steak.

Harry excused himself and ran up the stairs to the billiards room. He went directly to the window and looked out across the street. The section of the marquee behind the statue was in shadow. The light from Herkie's Wonder Bar cast a red neon glow over the new statue's upper torso.

He tried to imagine what Colin had actually seen, if he'd seen anything. Had the closing of the building's front doors or a truck driving by or an earth tremor caused the frog to wobble, tipping over onto Hobart? Or could someone have been standing behind the statue in the shadows, pushing it forward?

His contemplation was interrupted by a movement at street level. Howard Bethune was leaving *Ogle* at an uncharacteristically shuffling pace. He looked so depressed that if he'd been heading toward a large body of water, Harry would have felt compelled to rush out into the street to stop him from doing something foolish.

Instead, he simply returned to the table in the kitchen. And Terry.

20.

Only a few minutes earlier, Howard Bethune had been seated at his desk, considering his options.

After receiving the death threat shoved under his door, he had arrived at a few conclusions. The first, and most obvious, was that it must have come from either Ida Connor or Kevin Dobbs, the only two people he'd told about the note he'd found in Hobart's files.

This assuaged his fears a bit, since neither of them struck him as homicidal-maniac material. The threat, therefore, was a bit of melodrama. Either Ida or Kevin or both had wanted him to forget about the note, for reasons unknown. They'd tried a scare tactic. Fine. He'd have preferred their being straight with him, asking him to forget the note. But they'd gone for a more dramatic approach.

No big deal. Neither would be crushing any skulls.

But at the Image Campaign meeting, Armstead had alluded to his snooping through Hobart's files. Ida and Kevin may be incapable of murder but Milton Armstead was, in the words of Bethune's sainted mother, the sort of bloke who'd slit your throat for a penny.

Shivering at the thought, he focused on the box of questionnaires on his desk and was struck by another disturbing thought. When Armstead had demanded he stay until he found a candidate for *Ogle* Guy, had it been a set up for murder?

He stared at the closed office door. Was Armstead out there,

116

waiting? Or, if not he, someone he'd hired?

A chill running up his spine, Bethune stood and shoved his fist into the pile of questionnaires. He withdrew one submitted by . . . a Dr. Daryl Wunder of King of Prussia, Pennsylvania.

Bethune scanned Wunder's scrawl, noting that he was the product of a local college, a self-employed bachelor whose yearly income ran to a low six figures. He was a law-abiding, God-fearing man of medicine who spent from $3,000–$5,000 annually on clothing, smoked, imbibed socially, drove an American-made automobile less than three years old, and took time out from his busy schedule to lead a local church choir.

Good enough.

It was time to get the hell out of there.

He clicked off the desk light, throwing the room into almost total darkness. He didn't want to make himself a target when he opened the office door.

Trembling from both fear and eagerness to depart and pausing only to slip on his tasseled loafers and grab Daryl Wunder's reply card, he made his way through the darkness to the door.

Taking a deep breath, he threw it open and, quickly scanning the empty, shadowy desks, rushed from the office and away. In his haste, he did not see a new envelope that someone had slid under his door.

His plan was to deposit the card on Armstead's desk and head for the safety of his full-security apartment building on the Wilshire corridor. But Armstead's office door was shut.

He turned to the desk belonging to the vice president's secretary and placed the Wunder reply card on its pristine surface.

Job completed, he thought.

He'd taken a step toward the front door when he heard a female voice coming from inside Armstead's office. "You're a heartless bastard, Milton. You don't care if I go live on the farm or if I stay."

Curiosity replacing his fear, Bethune was drawn to the closed door.

"I told you when we met I was an absolutely selfish prick," Armstead said. "Is it my fault you didn't believe me?"

"But you say I give you more pleasure than any woman you've ever been with."

"Without exaggeration. But who's to say what the future will bring?"

"No wedding bells would be my guess," she said.

"I had my marriage experience," Armstead said. "It cost me half a million bucks and a black eye. It would have been cheaper to have her bumped off."

Bethune blinked and felt the chill return.

"What's with all this marriage talk, anyway?" Armstead said. "I thought you were supposed to be a free spirit."

"We humans don't always know what we want," she said.

"We immortals do. And now that that's settled, are you going to help me get rid of this, or not?"

Get rid of something? Bethune's mind conjured up a bloody knife, a telltale clue of some sort.

"Oh, Milton," the woman said. "It's so big and beautiful, I just can't resist."

There were noises: ooohs, ahhhs and a bit of grunting. Armstead and some bubblehead were getting it on. Nothing more sinister than that.

Feeling more than a little foolish, Bethune tiptoed away from the door.

"Evening, Howard," T.J., the night watchman at the reception desk said. "End of another perfect day, huh?"

Bethune frowned, then, realizing that the simple young man was being cordial and not cynical, nodded and wished him goodnight.

Outside the air was warm and still.

He looked up at the frog. Its lips seemed to be curled in a smirk directed at him. Damn. He'd given up the personalization of statues when he stopped going to Sunday mass.

Realizing it was this frog's predecessor that had done in his, he stepped back gingerly. Time to move on from what was seeming more and more like a murder scene.

His choice of relocation site was The Grasshopper Lounge, a few blocks down La Cienega, where a saucy waitress gave him a wink and pointed to an empty table in the rear.

Bethune noticed a few familiar faces reflected in the bar mirror, the leftovers from the happy hour throng. The freeway commute home had taken its toll. Likewise the inevitable pairing off. Those still holding up the bar were die-hard regulars who had no better place to go.

The waitress brought him an icy cold gin martini, straight up with one pimento-filled olive skewered on a plastic grasshopper green toothpick. Sipping the perfect cocktail while simultaneously savoring the olive's brine, he experienced the first really relaxing moment of his day.

An FM sound system floated a Sinatra ballad past the low mumble of the bar contingent. Bethune closed his eyes for a moment and floated along with "Change Partners."

This pleasant state was interrupted by an annoying nasal voice shouting orders to the waitress.

Bethune opened his eyes to a sight that caused his heart to leap. At the table directly across from him was a stunning brunette with fair skin and such flowing grace of motion that, as her hand moved to flick the ashes from her cigarette, it seemed to be in complete unison with the music.

Her eyes were large, semi-sad, outlined by lashes as black and long as a raven's pinfeathers. Her divinely sculpted features were as harmoniously designed as any Lester Lanin arrangement. She was the girl who had haunted his dreams, the lovely nimbus to whom his heart and soul had gone out so freely and so frequently in his fantasies. Before him now, in warm, living flesh.

"What's your problem, Bethune?" he heard her date, Milton Zephyr Armstead, ask loudly. "Never seen a broad with big knockers before?"

Bethune mumbled something gibberishy, unable to take his eyes from the girl's face.

"What're you doing here, anyway?" Armstead said. "I thought I told you to keep working until you found the ideal man for our campaign."

"I f-f-found him."

"Oh?" Armstead slipped his arm around the girl's shoulders, fingertips brushing the swell of her breast. "Well, reel in your eyeballs and get the hell out of here. You're making me nervous."

Bethune knocked back his martini and paid the waitress. But he didn't leave. Couldn't. He slunk to a stool at the bar where he could observe his dream goddess in the mirror, unnoticed.

Sinatra, gliding his way through Irving Berlin's tricky lyrics, sang about watching some ring-a-ding babe on a dance floor and thinking that maybe he should get the waiter to tell her partner he was wanted on the phone . . .

Bethune took a five spot from the change of a twenty on the bar in front of him and waved it to the waitress, who raised an eyebrow. "You rang?"

"I'd like you to tell Mr. Armstead over there that he's wanted on the phone."

She looked at the table where Armstead was kissing and fondling the beautiful brunette. "Last time I interrupted something like that, I got a knife pulled on me."

"He doesn't carry a knife," Bethune said, uncertain if that were true.

The waitress shrugged and snatched the five spot. She took one step toward Armstead's table when he pulled back from the brunette, rose and said in a voice loud enough for the whole room to hear, "Time to go sluice the goose."

As he veered toward the rest rooms, the waitress said, "I'll tell him about the phone when he's through pissing."

Bethune couldn't have cared less what she told Armstead.

Lenina saw him heading toward her, the guy Milton had told to buzz off. "My name is Howard Bethune," he said, "and I've been dreaming about you most of my adult life."

"Not a bad opener, Howard," she said, pushing the other chair out with her foot. "I'm Lenina. Sit down and tell me more about this dream. Is there a water bed in it?"

"I'm serious," he said. "Don't you have a dream that keeps coming back, one that's so wonderful you hate yourself for waking up?"

She gave him a crooked smile. "How many of those martinis did you eat?"

"I'm not drunk," Bethune said. "I'm sober and I'm serious. Don't you have a dream, too?"

"Uh huh. But I hate to tell you, Howard, I don't recall you being in it."

"How can you be sure? You were interested enough to notice I was drinking a martini."

She did find him attractive, in a weird so-ugly-he's-handsome way, like the TV actor who played Paladin. And he wasn't some guy off the street, exactly. Milton had talked to him. Nice suit, even if it did have flecks of white powder on it. From a girlfriend? Was she jealous? How crazy would that be?

"Tell me your dream," he said.

"It's about Nirvana."

"Most dreams are."

"No," she said. "I mean the real Nirvana. Up the coast past Malibu. It's a community of creative people. Poets, writers, painters. They farm the lands, raise crops. Completely self-sufficient. I dream of living there one of these days."

"As what? Poet, writer, painter? Farmer?"

"Poetess."

"Beautiful. Intelligent. Sensitive. Is there music on the farm?" he asked.

"How could anyone live without music?" she said.

She was surprised when his eyes started to moisten. Jesus, he was for real. And she found that very, very appealing.

He took her hand. "Let's get out of here," he said.

"And leave poor Milton?"

"Poor Milton is a Grade-A swine. You deserve better."

"You?"

He smiled. "Sure me. Anywhere you look in this room, you'll find a better man. Including the guy who just fell off the bar stool."

"Do you work with Milton at *Ogle*?"

He nodded.

"That hardly qualifies you for sensitive good guy of the year," she said.

"I'll quit," he said. "We'll go to this Nirvana and live both our dreams."

"Oh, brother," she said. "I thought Milton was trouble. But you . . ."

He stood up. "Come on," he said. "Before he gets back and causes a scene."

She had done a lot of impetuous things in her life. But this went way beyond impetuosity. Still . . . what the hell!

Armstead returned to his table in time to see them making their exit on the run. He was annoyed that the bitch had ditched him for a subscription manager, especially one that he was convinced was a little wispy in the Weejuns.

Well, in point of fact, he'd taken some of the edge off by slipping her one back at the office. And, although she was an extraordinary piece, a guy could get tired of even filet mignon if he had it every night.

He tossed down his stinger with such cavalier abandon the ice cubes nearly crushed his upper lip. The thing to do was to find another broad and take her to dinner. Hell, he might even take her dancing. That was Lenina's one failing: the bitch had two left feet.

Whom to call? He was struck by the memory of a luscious platinum-haired bimbo who could tie a knot in a cherry stem with her tongue. Anybody who could do that certainly would be able to follow his twist moves. What the hell was her name? He couldn't recall, but that was no problem. She'd been spectacular enough that he'd written it down.

He patted his suit jacket, searching for his little black book and remembered he'd left it at the office. He drank Lenina's stinger, tossed a few bucks on the table and, feeling just a tad tipsy, headed back to the *Ogle* Building.

21.

Getting Colin out of Herkie's had been no simple task.

Reacting to the old man's plea for help, his bar pals had grabbed one of his arms, engaging Harry and Terry in a tug-of-war that required the intervention of a gentleman named Skat, whose job it was to keep some semblance of order in the bar and grill.

"Thass enough, now," Skat said to the involved parties. Weighing in at two hundred and thirty-eight pounds, much of it hard muscle evenly spread over a jet-black, six-feet-two-inch frame, he did not have to raise his voice or repeat himself.

He hoisted the still truculent Colin over his shoulder and carried him like a burping baby to the front door. "Whea's yo' caw, Ter'?" he asked.

Three minutes later, Harry was driving Terry and the old man to an apartment off LaBrea Boulevard. Colin was snoring on the small rear seat, bent like a pretzel.

"You think he really saw the frog fall on Nick Hobart?" Harry asked.

"Hard to tell what he sees and what he thinks he sees," Terry said.

"Huh?" Colin asked, his eyes fluttering as he struggled toward consciousness. "Show me some respeck, lass. I bloody well saw the bloody am-fobian jump that fella."

"Go back to sleep, uncle."

" 's why I never mentioned it to ya at the time. Ya flamin' disbeliever. Saw the frog an' the frog handler up there on the ledge."

Even in the dark cab, Harry saw Terry's eyes flash.

"You saw somebody on the marquee with the frog?" Harry asked.

"Oooo. Marquee. Got y'self a fancy boyo here, don't you?"

"Never mind that, you old goat," Terry said. "Did you really see somebody besides the frog?"

"Up on the marquee?" He closed his eyes. " 'zactly . . . s'what . . . I . . . sa . . ."

And he was out, snoring loudly and wetly.

"He's not gonna throw up, is he?" Harry asked. "I just got this car."

At the apartment on Willow, Harry carried the comatose Colin up two flights of stairs to where Terry's Aunt Louise waited, a tall, gaunt woman in robe and hair curlers. "Just toss that bag o' bones on the couch," she said.

"Thanks, baby, for bringin' him home," she added, kissing her niece's cheek. "But you shoulda just left him in a sewer someplace, teach him a lesson. Have I met this fella before?"

"He's brand new, Weezie," Terry said. "His name's Harry Trauble. Harry, my aunt Louise."

He shook the woman's hard, callused hand.

"You don't look Irish," the woman said.

"I don't think I am," he said.

"Take it from me, a hard-headed kraut. You sleep with the Irish, this is the price you pay." She pointed to the snoring Colin.

"Thanks for the vote of confidence, Weezie," Terry said.

"Like I never saw you on that same couch, in that same condition, makin' them same noises."

Terry rolled her eyes. "This is what they mean by no good

turn going unpunished," she said. "Night, Weezie. See you in church."

Her aunt winked at Harry. "Be nice to her, you hear. She may hit the sauce, but she's a sweetheart."

Back in the Mustang, Harry said, "To our building, now?"

"Let's make a stop first. On Staysail."

"Where the heck's that?"

She explained that it was in Venice, near the ocean, two blocks east of Muscle Beach.

He didn't much care for Venice. Even during the day, there was something vaguely disquieting about the seaside community with its man-made canals and oddball inhabitants. It was where you might find snake charmers or religious zealots or drug peddlers strolling in the relentless sun.

At night, the streets were dark and deserted, and, if the news media were to be believed, very dangerous.

"What's on Staysail?" he asked.

"Joe's."

"A coffeehouse?"

"No. And not a bar, either. In spite of my aunt's comments, I can actually control my drinking."

"Then Joe is . . . another of your friends?"

"Right," she said. Something in her smile suggested she was having fun with him, delighting in his jealousy.

The air turned cool as they reached the end of Venice Boulevard. The roads had been traffic free, but as the Mustang turned south onto Neilson Way, a black Mercedes sports car suddenly appeared traveling north, heading straight for them.

Harry jerked the steering wheel, sending the Mustang sharply to the right. The Mercedes roared past, missing them by inches.

Harry pulled to the curb and stopped. He had to force his fingers to release the wheel. He turned to Terry, who had shifted in her seat to gawk at the retreating sports car.

"You okay?" he asked.

"Banged my head a little on the side window," she said. "But I'm okay."

"That looked like Armstead who nearly ran us down," he said.

"I recognized the car."

"He oughta take driving lessons," Harry said. "Jesus."

He moved them onward again, asking, "How much further?"

She gave him simple directions that took them to Staysail, but when he started to turn down that street, she said, "No. Go to the next block."

"Why?"

She gave him an odd smile. "We don't want to be seen going into Joe's building."

"Why not?"

"Tell you later," she said.

"This has turned into a very strange evening," he said.

"Strange . . . and kinda exciting, right? Park here."

He did as he was told. She turned the key, killing the engine, and slipped it from its slot. She dangled it over the backseat and when he turned his body to grab it, she moved forward, working herself around the gear shift into his arms, pushing him against the side door, kissing him as passionately and unexpectedly as she had on first seeing him upstairs at Herkie's.

This time she added a little body shimmy to the sensation, moaning deep in her throat while her tongue ringed his lips before sliding through them.

Without much conscious effort, his hands moved over her body, thighs, stomach, breasts. He was nearly overwhelmed by passion.

She pulled back from him without warning, and he gasped for air like a swimmer who'd waited underwater almost too long.

"I'm going to drive you crazy and you're going to love every minute of it," she said.

Then, she was out of the car.

When he tried to join her, he discovered that his legs were unsteady. Had the kiss done that, too?

She was marching down the street. "Wait up," he said, wobbling after her. "What's the hurry?"

"Faster I talk to Joe, the faster we get to my bedroom."

"Why didn't you just phone him?"

"He's sure his phone is bugged."

None of it made any sense to Harry, except for the "faster we get to my bedroom" comment.

Just before they reached Staysail, she led him into an alley, a poorly paved, dimly lit passage separating rows of dark two-story structures. Bins overflowed with garbage and packing material, narrowing the passage enough for Harry to wonder how vehicles were able to roll through it unscathed.

"What are these buildings?" he asked.

"Used to be warehouses," she said. "But lately artists and photographers have been moving in."

She paused at a grimy brick structure with an imposing metal back door. In the moonlight, the door seemed to be painted a deep purple color that for some reason, possibly having to do with his Catholic upbringing, reminded Harry of sins and suffering.

A dim light outlined the door.

"It's open," Terry said. She pushed it inward, exposing what seemed to be a gutted building.

"Your friend Joe has got more faith in this neighborhood than I do," he said.

"Actually, he's a raving paranoid. This isn't good." She stepped past the door. "Joe?" she called out.

No answer.

Harry saw the evidence of Joe's paranoia: the door was lined with bolts, locks and chains, all intact and undamaged.

"Watch out for the cactus," Terry said.

A soft, wavering light spilled down an open circular wrought iron stairwell. There was enough of it for Harry to see four ceramic pots containing assorted forms of cacti, placed near the walls of what appeared to be a sculptor's studio. At its center were statues in various stages of completion.

Nearest was a stone centaur, several feet taller than he. Most of its nether horsy parts were still to be sculpted, so that the creature seemed to be emerging from a hunk of granite.

"Joe? Orlando? Anybody here?" Terry called up the stairwell.

Past the centaur, a voluptuous naked giantess in bronze stood, arms akimbo, legs parted wide. She reminded Harry of Wonder Woman caught without her red, white and blue outfit and magic lasso.

He took one long and admiring look and followed Terry up the circular stairs.

"Oh," he heard her say as she emerged from the stairwell several steps ahead of him, her movement causing the light to flutter. "Ohhhh," she said again as she disappeared, dragging it out this time as if in pain. "Jesus, Mary and Joseph."

He climbed the stairs quickly and was momentarily distracted by a gathering of larger-than-life men and women in robes and capes, their expressions changing from sorrow to demonic glee to sorrow again. Taking a deep breath, he assured himself that the terrifying figures were statues. Their facial animation was caused by the flickering lights from several dozen votive candles to his and the statues' left, nestled in wine red glass holders that formed a U around a king-plus size bed on a raised platform.

Terry stood beside the bed, eyes tearing, making a sound like the mewing of a cat. Following her gaze, he saw two men lying side by side on the bed, a carelessly tossed purple silk sheet covering some of their nakedness.

It took a few seconds for the impact of what he was seeing to register. When it did, he issued an involuntary "Ho!" and looked away. The sight and smell of blood alone was enough to make him woozy.

He'd recognized the men as the same pair who'd been on the *Ogle* Building marquee taking pictures. Joseph Tobella, the sculptor, and his assistant Orlando Royale. Now lying silent and still as the statues.

Harry shook his head, trying to dislodge the image of the garrote sunk into the torn and bloody flesh of Orlando's neck. "Jesus," he said.

Tobella's body had not been quite as ghastly. Except for the open eyes staring at the closed skylight high above the bed. And the metal rod buried in his bare chest. "Holy crap!"

Harry's nostrils were full of the sickly sweet iron smell of the blood. His stomach was gurgling. He suspected he was on the cusp of hyperventilation. Forcing himself to open his eyes and take measured breaths, he saw Terry leaning over the bed, reaching out a hand toward Tobella's body.

"Don't," he said.

She paused, staring at him with a vacant look.

"He's dead," Harry said. "Th-they both are."

"Have to . . . make sure," she said and returned to her task, pressing fingers against the sculptor's neck.

She withdrew her hand slowly and stepped back. "What in . . . God's name . . . happened here?" she asked between sobs.

Harry had regained control enough to put his arm around her. He turned her from the corpses. "Somebody killed 'em," he said.

"You think?" she said sarcastically.

"I think we'd better call the police."

"I hope you're kidding," she said, sniffling now. "Poor Joe's flesh was still warm. The blood is wet. This didn't happen very long ago. What we'd better do is get the heck out of here, right now."

"But we didn't do anything wrong."

"I grew up in this town," she said. "I know how things work. The cops don't have much imagination. Our being here will make us the most likely suspects, unless you've got some kind of clout you haven't mentioned."

"No clout," he said. "But what reason would we have—"

"It's called motive, Harry. And they can probably come up with half a dozen. One example: I posed for Joe in the nude. You saw the bronze statue down there."

"That's you?"

"Uh huh. Anyway, they'll say it made you insanely jealous and you came here and . . . did this."

"But Joe was queer, right?"

"They'll say he swung both ways. Or you were too crazy to notice. Or maybe I was jealous of Orlando and I killed 'em, with your help. We can talk about this somewhere else."

She removed her blouse.

He blinked at her beautiful bare breasts. In spite of the situation, he was aroused. And totally confused.

Not giving him the chance to react, she headed for the stairwell. There, she began her descent, using the blouse to wipe both handrails.

"You're getting rid of the killer's prints, too," he said as he followed her, careful not to undo her work.

"Can't be helped."

On the main floor, she asked, "You touch anything else down here?"

"Maybe the back door."

She wiped areas of the rear door they may have come in contact with and then, grumbling about the dirt on the blouse, put it back on. She looked up and down the dark alley and said, "All clear. Let's boogie."

"Gimme a minute," he said. "I'm a little shaky. I don't see dead bodies every day."

She studied him briefly, then hugged him and kissed his cheek. "I'm so sorry I got you into this."

"What is it we're in?" he asked as they moved along the dark alley. "Besides failing to report two murders, I mean?"

"I . . . I think it's all about what happened to Nick Hobart."

"What?"

"Like I said, I did some modeling for Joe a year ago. He was the one who suggested I apply for a job at *Ogle*. Anyway, after Nick's death, when they sued Joe, he asked me to snoop around for anything that might help his case. That's why I wanted to talk to Joe tonight, to tell him what Colin said about seeing somebody near the frog."

"I'm not sure your uncle would be what they call a reliable witness," Harry said as they got into the Mustang, "even if they could pry him away from the bar long enough. What other kind of stuff have you been telling Joe?"

"Not a lot. About Nick's shady past. And the other day I happened to overhear Delray—the maintenance guy—say something about the building shifting and shaking every time a truck rolls by."

"Is that why Joe was up on the marquee?"

She nodded, then looked suddenly stricken. "Maybe he found something up there. Damn. If I hadn't . . ."

"Terry, don't start guilt-tripping yourself," he said, eyes on the nearly empty street. "We don't know why somebody decided to kill those two guys. I just don't see it having anything to do with Hobart or *Ogle*."

"Then what was Milton Armstead doing in this neighborhood?"

He'd been wondering that himself. But it wasn't the time to add to her concern by admitting it. "Maybe he was just driving through. Or he has a girlfriend in Venice. I mean, he's probably capable of murder. But it'd be with a gun or a knife. I don't see him arming himself with a wire strangler."

"It's a clay cutter," she said. "Joe uses 'em. Milton could have had one of his temper tantrums and grabbed the first thing he could find."

"So you think what? That Tobella opened the door and Armstead walked in, found two guys in the nude, went bizarro, stuck a spike in Tobella's chest, while Orlando cooled his heels waiting to be next?"

"Maybe Milton snuck in . . . oh, heck, it does seem impossible. But Joe was convinced his phone was tapped and that he was being followed. That's why I thought we should use the rear entrance to the studio. Joe was sure Trower Buckley had put a private eye on him."

"Why would Buckley do that?" Harry asked.

"The magazine was suing Joe," she said. "Maybe it wasn't Buckley. Maybe it was the lawyers hired a detective." Her pale forehead wrinkled and tears formed in her eyes. "But no detective did what we just saw."

"You don't honestly believe Armstead or Buckley could have done it?"

She shook her head.

They were paused at a red light on Lincoln Boulevard. Terry studied the twenty-four-hour supermarket to their right. "There's a phone," she said. "Pull into the lot."

He parked beside the pay telephone.

"Got a dime?"

He rooted in his pocket, found a quarter. She grabbed it and hopped from the car.

Harry watched in amazement as she pulled herself together

and reported the murders to the police in a crisp, efficient manner, using a British accent that to his ears sounded remarkably authentic.

Back in the car, she said, "I could really use a drink. You have anything at your place?"

"A jug of vodka," he said.

"Works for me."

He preceded her into his apartment, doing a quick cleanup, shoving magazines and newspapers and piles of used clothes into a closet. Then, apologizing for his lack of bourbon and other old-fashioned ingredients, he cracked the cap on a 1.75-liter jug of vodka that claimed to be imported from Russia but tasted like it had been distilled in Idaho.

Terry didn't seem to mind either the harshness of the booze or the condition of the apartment. As they huddled together on his oatmeal-colored couch in the living room, listening to Bob Dylan singing "Like a Rolling Stone" on a drugstore FM radio, he saw that there were tears in her eyes.

He put his arm around her and drew her closer.

She cried for a while. Then she said, "It wasn't premeditated."

"Huh?"

"The killer didn't have a weapon," she said. "He used Joe's clay cutter and chisel, things that happened to be at hand. So he didn't go there to murder anybody. But something happened."

The memory of the two dead men had been keeping Harry's libido from operating at full tilt. This continuing discussion of the murders was closing it down entirely. But that didn't seem to matter. He liked being with her. He clearly wasn't wild about being involved in a grisly double homicide. But, if he had to be, he couldn't think of anybody with whom he'd rather share the experience.

Now she was toughing it out—trying to get past her grief by analyzing the crime. The least he could do was go along with that. "I don't remember seeing any evidence of a fight," he said.

"No. But Joe and Orlando had been stoned," she said. "There was enough smoke in the room for a contact high. You noticed that, right?"

"Sure," he lied. The only smell he'd noticed was the blood.

"So maybe they were too out of it to fight," she said. "The killer rings the bell. They're upstairs in bed, goofed. Joe comes down, opens the door. Maybe naked. Angry. He could be pretty bitchy. He got under the caller's skin and freaked him into murder."

"Then the killer heard Orlando coming downstairs," Harry said, running with that scenario. "Grabbed the clay cutter and, when Orlando stood gawking at his lover's body, came up behind him and . . ."

Terry drained her glass and held it out. "Why'd he carry them upstairs and put them in bed?" she asked, while Harry shifted his weight to lift the jug.

"The candles," he said, pouring shots for them both.

"I don't follow," she said.

"Killer goes upstairs, checking to make sure there's not somebody else in the building. Or maybe he's looking for something . . ."

"The thing that brought him there in the first place," she said eagerly.

"Anyway, he sees the burning candles. Figures it'll blow the cops' minds and confuse things if the two bodies are in bed, like a ritual sacrifice, or maybe a homo murder-suicide."

"But I didn't see blood downstairs or anywhere in the place except the bed." She yawned.

Harry checked his watch. A little after ten. Not very late. But the vodka had just about put him under and Terry's green eyes were at half-mast. "We'd better get some sleep," he said.

She nodded and rose from the couch. "Let's see. This apartment is the reverse of mine, so the bathroom should be . . . there."

He went to the unmade bed and did his best to smooth out the sheets and plump up the pillows. "Your turn," she said, emerging from the bathroom and staggering past him to sit on the edge of the bed.

Dutifully, he relieved himself, brushed his teeth and returned to find her sprawled across the bed, asleep. He took two light blankets from the closet, covered her with one and took the other into the living room where, after stripping down to his shorts, he fell asleep on the couch, listening to the radio.

The last thing he remembered was Barry McGuire singing "Eve of Destruction."

22.

"Don't worry about Milton, Al," Trower Buckley said as he and Hewitt sipped after-dinner Remys in the publisher's book-lined study. "He can be a pain in the prat, but when the chips are down, he delivers. It'll be a gala to end all galas."

Elsewhere in the spacious penthouse apartment at the top of the *Ogle* Building, Buckley's mistress, Angel, was keeping herself busy, probably making sure the cook-housekeeper—a long-suffering if well-paid black woman in her forties named Henrietta—cleaned the dinner dishes before heading for home.

"I don't think he'd be as obstinate if the party request had come directly from you," Hewitt said. "He resents my acting as your buffer."

"Well, of course, he does," Buckley said. "And that's too bad, because it's my magazine and I make the rules. I like your style, Al. By the way, earlier tonight you said something to Angel that's been vexing me."

"Oh?" Hewitt asked, feeling just the tickle of apprehension whenever Buckley brought Angel into their conversations.

"She made a reference to 'the whore of Babylon'?"

Hewitt nodded that he recalled the comment. Buckley had been going on and on about the photo editor's unsuccessful attempts to cajole the pouty actress Joey Heatherton into posing for the magazine. "Did you see *Twilight of Honor?* The babe looks and acts like she'd go down on you at the tip of a hat, but apparently she thinks it's a sin to show off the goods," he'd said, and Angel, miffed as always by his discussion of other women, had replied waspishly, "What does that make me, the whore of Babylon?"

"You told her she didn't look large enough or Italian enough," Buckley said. "What was that all about?"

"Just a bit of dry, academic humor," Hewitt said.

"I'm always up for a joke," Buckley said, opening the humidor on a table beside his leather chair and withdrawing two genuine Havana panatelas.

Accepting the offered cigar, Hewitt settled back in the comfort of his chair. Savoring the aftertaste of the cognac, ever more amused at how remarkably pleasant his new life was becoming, he said, "Nearly everybody misquotes the apostle John. What he wrote was not 'whore of Babylon' but 'whore named Babylon.' "

Buckley paused in the midst of lighting his cigar to look at him blankly. "If that's the punch line, I don't get it."

"It's not ha-ha funny," Hewitt said. "Religious scholars have come to assume that John was speaking in code. The 'whore named Babylon' was a reference to the city of Rome, not to a woman."

"Hummm," Buckley said. He started puffing to bring an even glow to the tip of his cigar, filling the area with smoke. "Tell me more about this Babylon business. Anything I can use in the *Ogle* Credo?"

"Well, let's see," Hewitt said. "There was a time I could have given you chapter and verse, but not after that excellent dinner wine. As I recall, John said there were blasphemous names written on the whore named Babylon's forehead. He was talking about the titles——'almighty,' 'omniscient' and so on—that he believed belonged to God but were being bestowed instead on the emperor of Rome."

"I love this biblical stuff," Buckley said, leaning forward to add another inch or so to the liquid in Hewitt's snifter. "Continue."

"John goes on about the whore being drunk on the blood of the just. Here, he's referring to Rome's abuse of power."

Buckley sat up straight. He was bristling, as if his chair had sent a sudden electric charge through his body. "Drunk on the blood of the just," he said. "Get me a pen, something to write with."

Hewitt hesitated, wondering why he didn't get his own pen.

"I said: get me a fucking pen!" Buckley ordered.

Hewitt felt the sour taste of anger dissolve the headiness of the cognac. He arose and walked across the room to an ornate desk. "I suppose you want something to write on, too?" he said testily.

"Of course. Quick, quick, quick. Before I lose the train of thought."

That train has left the station, Hewitt told himself as he presented the publisher with pen and lined yellow notepad.

Buckley began to scribble, mumbling, "And these so-called protectors of public morality are . . . hmmmm . . . nothing more than . . . hmmm . . . vampiric . . . is that a word? well it is now . . . vampiric defilers of the First Amendment . . . drunk on the blood of the just."

Hewitt had been witness to similar "creative spurts" during the brief time he'd been living in Buckley's guest suite and spending much of the time in the man's company. If this one ran true to form, the publisher would be bent over the notepad for the next several hours, oblivious to anything but the act of composition.

Hewitt slid his unlit cigar into the pocket of his smart new black velvet sports coat, downed the remains of his cognac and left the study, unnoticed.

Angel was on the couch in the living room, semi-wrapped in

a black peignoir, squinting myopically at the continuing story of *Peyton Place* on a large color console. Next to her on a tiny emerald green velvet pillow was a frog of slightly lighter hue wearing a jeweled collar.

"You and Raymond enjoying the show?" Hewitt asked.

Continuing to focus on a troubled Mia Farrow, Angel said, "Raymond fucking loves this show. Just like his mommy."

The camera zoomed in on Mia just as a tear formed at the corner of one eye. There was a musical sting, a fade to black and a commercial for Alka-Seltzer began. Angel turned to him. "Buck ready for me now?"

"He's working on the *Ogle* Credo."

"There goes the rest of the night," she said. "Wanna watch some TV? I can move Raymond's pillow to the coffee table."

"Don't disturb him. He looks so comfortable. I've been meaning to ask: why'd you call him Raymond?"

"Doesn't he look like a Raymond?"

"I guess he does," Hewitt said, enjoying the secret game he was playing which he'd labeled Appease the Lunatics.

She looked him up and down, appraisingly. "You've changed, mister. And it's more than just the new clothes."

"Changed how?"

"Listen to him fish for compliments, Raymond. He wants me to tell him how handsome he looks."

The peignoir was not designed to hide its contents. Hewitt's eyes drifted involuntarily to her formidable body, the same body that had repulsed him only a short while ago. Now it produced quite the opposite effect.

She was aware of it. Smiling, she patted the couch next to her. "Come on. Allison and Rodney are about to go to a pool party. Lots of beautiful kids getting hot and heavy in tiny swimsuits."

It was a tempting invitation, but he was not about to let his penis vault him off the gravy train. He took the cigar from his coat pocket. "I think I'll go outside for a smoke and walk off some of that fine dinner."

She shrugged. "It's a lousy neighborhood to be walking around at night. But it's your funeral."

He could think of nothing outside to match the danger on that couch.

"Man doesn't like us, Raymond," Angel said, pouting.

"Man's afraid he likes you too much," Hewitt said and was amused to see her grin. Appease the Lunatics.

" 'Night, Al," the uniformed night watchman said as Hewitt headed toward the stairs descending to the front door. "Checking out the town?"

"Just going for a walk, T.J."

"Well, be careful out there."

Hewitt thanked T.J. for his concern. There was something comforting about being on a first-name basis with his co-workers. The whole time he'd spent in the religious life, he'd felt separate, and, to be honest, a bit aloof from the congregation. Now he relished being part of a team, especially since he was held in such high regard by the team leader. Most of the time.

Outside, the night was a perfect temperature. Not too hot; not too cool. The stars stood out crisply against the cloudless, dark blue sky. The moon was wearing its benign, smiling face. The music crossing the street from Herkie's was unusually melodic. An Irish lullaby? He paused to light his cigar, thinking that the whole universe seemed in perfect alignment.

He drew in a nice, unhealthy mouthful of aromatic smoke and, taking his time allowing it to escape his lips, considered his situation. He was working for a company that produced a totally inconsequential and generally worthless periodical. His fellow employees, as far as he could tell, were all self-involved hedonists. He was spending most of his waking hours in the company of a very odd duck who had total control of his, Hewitt's, fate and absolutely zero control of his own emotions.

And yet, as he strolled down the dark street away from the traffic and bustle of La Cienega Boulevard, he had never felt so free, so self-confident. So, dare he say, happy.

Then he saw the man stretched out on the pavement, lying on his side, his right arm covering his face. Was he dead?

Hewitt bent over the figure, heard a rasp of breath and smelled the booze it carried. "Are you all right, sir?" he asked.

Getting no reply, he shook the man's shoulder. "Are you hurt?"

"Huhhh?" The man flopped onto his back and Hewitt was somewhat surprised to see that it was a barely conscious Milton Armstead.

"Are you hurt?"

"Who the fug a' you? Mi' Wallace?" Milton Armstead said, wincing as he opened his eyes. Even in the usually complimentary light of the moon, he looked like death on a cracker.

"Can you move?" Hewitt asked.

"Why the fug shoo' I move? Wha' the fug you doin' in my beh'room?"

"This isn't your bedroom, Armstead," Hewitt said. "You're lying on the sidewalk."

"Aw shi'," Armstead said, closing his eyes again. "No, no, no."

"Should I call an ambulance?" Hewitt said.

"No." Armstead's long fingers grabbed his arm. He struggled to rise. "He' me yup."

Hewitt managed to get the drunken man to his feet.

Armstead looked around with bleary eyes, puzzled. He relaxed slightly at the sight of the frog statue on the *Ogle* marquee. "He' me to Oga. Pay you."

"You don't have to pay me," Hewitt said. He put his arm around the drunken man and staggered with him to the *Ogle* Building. There, he banged on the glass door until T.J. pulled his nose out of his paperback and ran down the stairs to help.

Together they marched an alternately cursing and moaning Armstead up and into his office and deposited him on the couch. "You hurt yourself," T.J. said, pointing to the bloodstains on Armstead's shirt.

" 'Mokay," Armstead said. "Can take it from here."

Hewitt saw that there was dried blood on the man's hands, too. "Maybe a doctor," he said.

"No. Gimme phone. Gotta call Manfred."

The name meant nothing to Hewitt. He watched T.J. locate the Trimline phone under a stack of papers on the desk.

"Gimme," Armstead said, anxiously grabbing the instrument, cradle and all, from T.J.'s hand. He punched a few buttons, listened briefly and grunted into the receiver, "At office. Need pain pills an' fresh clothes, pronto." He handed T.J. the phone. "Put it back," he said and rolled over on the couch, facing away from them in ungracious dismissal.

T.J.'s hand whitened as he squeezed the phone.

For a brief moment, Al Hewitt thought the young man might hit Armstead with it. Instead, he opened his fist, letting the instrument fall to the carpet. He adjusted his green policeman's hat, shot the bird to Armstead's back and marched toward the door.

" 'Scuse my French, Al," he said, as he and Hewitt made their exit, "but fuckheads get my goat and that guy's one ungrateful Grade-A fuckhead."

The fuckhead was not resting comfortably.

Key-rist, he was thinking. Why did I drink that swill? Granted,

143

one has to do something to dull the senses after an experience like that. But it's no time to be non compis. I've still got their blood on me. Have to clean up.

He rolled off the couch onto the carpet where he stayed briefly, contemplating the enormity of getting to his feet unaided. Had he ever been this drunk before? He thought not. Surely he'd never had better reason for blitzing out.

Using the edge of the desk, he pulled himself to his feet. He stood unaided for about as long as a ballet dancer can defy gravity, then caved. He fell against the couch and stayed there motionless until a lean black man in black slacks, black T-shirt and white windbreaker entered the office carrying clothes on a hanger.

"You all fucked up, daddy," Manfred DeLemoy said.

"The unner'stamen o' th' year."

Manfred put down the clothes, lifted Armstead as if he were a small child and placed him on the couch in a sitting position. "Get you some water for the med-i-ca-shun," Manfred said and glided from the room.

Armstead sat there, staring down at his blood-crusted hands. "Kee-rist," he said aloud. "If on'y that bitch hadn't run out on me."

But Lenina had run, and he'd wound up paying a surprise visit to Joseph Tobella. And nothing would ever be the same.

"Manfred," he shouted. "I nee' those fuckin' pills."

23.

The following day, Harry and Terry called in sick, separately, from his apartment.

It wasn't just because of their hangovers, or the fact that, at around four in the morning, she'd moved beside him on the couch, wearing only white panties that were quickly removed—though these were certainly considerations.

The main problem had been the news reports.

Starting with the seven a.m. *Good Day, L.A.* show, the drugstore radio in the living room—which he'd forgotten to turn off the previous night—had lured them from their post-coital slumber by a breathless announcement of the "grisly deaths of two young men in a Venice loft."

By eight o'clock, he and Terry had actually managed to move from the couch to the bedroom, the radio losing out to a little black-and-white TV that rested atop Harry's Coast Guard footlocker in a corner.

Lying in bed, they watched the *Today Show*, which was filled with bad news from Vietnam, courtesy of granite-faced news-man Frank Blair. The Southern California murders had not merited a mention. But on a brief local insert, an animated but clueless young woman with a blonde poodle-cut hairdo made a basic statement that "the bodies of two men, apparent murder victims, were discovered last night in a loft in the Venice area. Identification is being withheld until family members are located and notified." She promised that more information and film footage would be available on the noon news broadcast.

At eight-fifty, Terry asked if he had any coffee in the apartment. Or tea. Or eggs. Or bread. Or . . . anything other than the vodka.

He told her they were out of vodka, too.

She suggested they raid her larder, but he insisted on making a quick drive to the nearest Lucky's that resulted in two big brown bags filled with food and drink that he hoped would get them through the day. By ten-thirty, they'd had coffee and bagels with lox and Philadelphia cream cheese and were back in bed, Terry sipping from a can of beer, while on the little TV screen, *Concentration* had given way to a local press conference featuring a representative from the District Attorney's office.

Squinting and perspiring under the bright lights, Edna Philbo, a pie-faced public relations representative of the LAPD told the gathered media that "Chief of Police Maurice Dreeson says that an arrest is imminent."

"Any truth to the rumor that the victims were . . . homosexuals?" It took a few seconds for the camera operator to pan the crowd and locate the speaker, an owlish crime reporter.

The camera swung back in time to catch Edna Philbo's, "I've no comment on that."

"What about the crime scene resembling a ritual sacrifice?" The camera shifted to a plump man with blackened eyes and a strip of white plaster on his broken nose.

"That's Ray Stooley," Terry said.

"Again, no comment," the press rep croaked. "Thank you for your attention."

"Did the killer leave any clues?" Stooley would not be denied. You could almost sense the cameraman's frustration as, once again, he shifted gears.

"Cigarette butts?" Stooley asked. "Tie clasp?" The camera caught a wicked grin. "Maybe a . . . cuff link?"

Back to the press rep, who was glaring at the reporter as if she wished Stooley had been in the bed with Joseph Tobella. "No . . . comment," she said between clenched teeth.

Edna Philbo was edging away from the camera when Stooley stopped her with a final question. "Aren't the cops out there right now, beating the bushes for a British fag?"

Choosing her words very carefully, Philbo replied, "There are substantial leads that the police are following diligently. Thank you."

"They bought your accent," Harry said to Terry, "but they think you're a fag."

"Well, I am queer for men," she said, pinching him on the butt. Then she sobered. "You didn't leave a cuff link at Joe's?"

"Never wear 'em," he said, holding up a bare arm.

"Then the item belongs to you?" Homicide Detective Steve Cardona asked casually enough to suggest that Larry Beagle's answer would be of minimal consequence.

Cardona and his partner, Detective Emmett Oskar, were blue-bearded, rawboned lawmen who seemed to blot out the overhead light as they towered over Beagle's desk. The Promotion Manager tried to keep his nerves in check, but his hand was shaking as he examined the cuff link.

Ignoring the golden *Ogle* frog in bas-relief on the link's surface, he turned the object over and saw the initials "L. B." under the wing-back fastener.

"Th-those are my initials," he said. "But mine is right in . . ."

He nervously opened the center drawer of his desk and began rooting around in its clutter.

"I . . . It's been months since I've seen the damn things," he said, throwing items aside. "Never wore 'em. A little too flashy."

If he'd looked up, he would have seen Detective Oskar rolling his eyes and Detective Cardona shaking his head sadly.

After a few minutes, he gave up and eased the drawer shut. "S-s-someone must've . . ."

"Taken them?" Cardona finished for him.

Beagle nodded. The two men seemed to be crowding him.

"Missing anything else?" Cardona asked.

"I . . . I don't know. Little things disappear from time to time. Once some checks were taken from my—"

"You don't lock your desk?" Oskar asked.

They were leaning toward him. Threateningly, he thought. He was breathing heavily as an old feeling of panic began to sweep through his mind and body.

"I, ah, don't . . . No. Don't lock my desk."

"Pretty trusting," Cardona said.

He frowned. Were they speaking German? It sounded like they were speaking German. He blinked. He couldn't see their faces clearly, couldn't tell if they were armed with bayonets. His eyes dropped to the top of his desk, scanning it for some kind of defense weapon.

The detectives picked up on his anxiety, exchanged glances and separated, moving quickly around the desk where they could subdue him if they had to. "Take it easy there, Mr. Beagle," Oskar said.

"We're just talking here, sir," Cardona said.

Beagle's head swiveled from one to the other.

"I . . . I . . ." Beagle fell back in his chair, gasping for breath.

"Bastard's having a heart attack," Cardona said.

"Faking it?" Oskar asked, then saw foam at the corner of Beagle's mouth. He grabbed the phone. "I'll order up some medics."

"Medic," Beagle yelled and pushed back against his chair shuddering.

24.

"Larry didn't do it," Weeks said to Harry the following morning. He was sitting on a large white sofa, a new addition that forced Harry to either climb over its cushions or slide across their desktops to get to his side of their office.

"Somebody ought to tell Channel 4," Harry said. "They were still calling him the 'suspected killer' about an hour ago."

Weeks shrugged. "My sources are better than theirs, what can I say?" He went back to what he'd been doing before Harry arrived: cutting full-page ads from library copies of *Ogle* and sliding them into plastic covers.

"He may have been a big war hero and all," Harry said, "but I can't see him killing anybody like that."

"He didn't. He never left his place in Pasadena that night." Weeks dropped a library copy of a June, 1962 issue into the trash and picked up a May, 1962 issue, a collector's item with the frog winking at a flirty Bettie Page on the cover. "Wife and kids confirmed it to the cops; also two old broads who live on his block, who were having dinner at the Beagles' around the time the fruiters were buying the boutique."

Harry was distracted by a centerfold that was on the floor. He picked it up and gave it a brief study.

The nude model was brunette and myopic and looked vaguely familiar, probably because he'd fantasized about her in his early teens. He held the centerfold up to Weeks. "She look familiar to you?" he asked.

"They all look familiar to me," Weeks said. "Before I came to work here, I used to think they kept using the same model over and over again with wigs and touchups."

Harry refolded the centerfold and dropped it back on the floor. "How is it you know so much about Larry?" he asked.

"Ears unplugged, eyes wide open," Weeks said.

"Your unplugged ears pick up anything on how Larry's doing in the hospital?"

"Not at the hospital," Weeks said, sliding an ad for a 14k-gold pen into a clear sheet protector. "Wasn't a heart attack. Just hyperventilation. He's home, taking it easy."

"Good," Harry said. "You want to tell me about the couch, now?"

"What about it?"

"What's it doing here?"

"It's an executive couch. A status symbol. I slipped a guy in the mail room a fiver to help me get it down here from Bethune's office."

"Won't Bethune be missing it?"

"I doubt it," Weeks said.

"Roger, dear, I think it would be a smart idea . . ." Ida Connor had entered their office and was staring at Harry in mild surprise. "I didn't expect to see you at work so soon, young man. I understood you had the flu."

"No. Just a little . . ." Harry made a vague gesture toward his stomach, ". . . intestinal thing."

"Ah. Well, I'm happy for you. Unfortunately, Milton's maladies are continuing. Since he won't be coming in today, either, once more we've cancelled the ten o'clock meeting. I'll keep you boys posted on the reschedule.

"Meanwhile, Harry, since you're here, let me see when I can put you and Dr. Magnus together."

"Dr. Magnus?" Harry asked.

"The new efficiency expert," Weeks said.

"Precisely," Ida said. "He wants to get a fix on all the executives. Junior as well as senior. Roger had his session yesterday."

Weeks raised an index finger and made whoop-de-do circles in the air.

Ida flashed a smile at the gesture. "The maintenance men will be here shortly to take the couch back. Dr. Magnus needs it more than you two," she said and departed.

"Gottdammitt," Weeks said. "I love this couch."

"What's Magnus like?" Harry asked.

"A dickweed," Weeks said.

"And the session?"

"He asks a bunch of dumb fucking questions and you provide a bunch of dumb fucking answers."

"Like?"

"Do you love your mother and father? Do they love you? Did you cheat in college? Do you take drugs? Do you respect your immediate supervisor? Do you love your immediate supervisor? Do you respect your secretary? Would you like to slip the sausage to your secretary?"

"We don't have a secretary," Harry said.

"That's what I told him and he said to make believe. So I said that if I made believe she was beautiful, I'd want to slip her the sausage. But if she was a dog, my office mate could have her."

"Thanks for thinking of me," Harry said. "He didn't want to know about how you spent your day? The amount of jobs you completed?"

"Well, sure," Weeks said. "That's what I'm doing now, putting together a collection of the ads I've done."

"You didn't do any of those."

"Like he'll know the difference? The guy's a dickweed."

Something bothered Harry, but he couldn't put his finger on

it. The discussion about Larry Beagle? No. The Dr. Magnus stuff? That was disturbing, but it wasn't what was causing that niggling sensation.

He leaned back in his chair, closed his eyes. And, surprisingly, it came to him. "Why did Ida come down here just now?" he asked.

Weeks looked up from his chore, his unlined baby face registering only unconcern. "To tell us the meeting was off? Or to piss me off about the couch?"

"It sounded as if she was going to ask you to do something."

"Like what?"

"I don't know," Harry said.

"Maybe she wanted me to call you at home," Weeks said. "Find out how you were doing. How were you doing, by the way?"

Harry flashed on the day and two nights he'd just spent with Terry. Lovemaking punctuated by TV news updates on the murders.

"What'd you say?" Weeks asked.

Harry wasn't aware that he'd said anything.

"Did you say 'sex and violence'?"

"Sick-y virus," Harry said, standing and readying for a slide across the desks. It was time for him to take a walk, before he inadvertently told Weeks anything else.

Terry was at her reception desk, guarding the closed door to the third floor, looking none the worse for their previous night together. Quite the contrary. It was as if a lack of sleep combined with several beers and a fifth of Jim Beam had had the effect of a beauty tonic.

"Can I help you, sir?" she asked brightly.

"How're you feeling?"

"Like Snow White just after the prince planted one on her,"

she said, giving him a sweet smile. She added, "I hear Larry Beagle's been cleared."

"So they say."

"Now they've got the hounds out for Howard," she told him.

"What?"

"Howard Bethune. He's gone missing. Didn't make it in to work yesterday or today. Cleaned out his apartment. The police think it looks pretty suspicious."

"Doesn't it?"

"Howard didn't even come to work here until after Nick's death. Why would he have killed Joe and Orlando?"

"We don't know that the murders have anything to do with Nick Hobart or *Ogle*," Harry said.

"If there's no connection to *Ogle*, why would the police be looking here, first at Larry Beagle and now Howard?" she asked.

"Maybe they know of some other link between Beth—"

The third-floor door was opened quietly by a blissfully grinning Maurice Grumbacher. The bliss diminished only slightly at the sight of Harry standing next to Terry's desk. "I hope you're not bothering this lovely broad," he said.

"Actually, I was—"

"Mr. Trauble has an appointment with Dr. Magnus, Mr. Grumbacher," Terry said.

Grumbacher raised his eyebrows. "Really?" he said. "I wasn't aware that staffers were meeting with him, too."

"Junior executive," Harry said.

"Yeah, sure. Well, I've just spent an hour with the guy and I don't see how he's gonna get his job done." He adjusted the knot of his tie, straightened his shiny black coat and headed down the stairs. Over his shoulder, he added, "Not that he isn't one hell of a good listener."

Grumbacher began to hum a tune that could barely be recognized as the theme from *What's New Pussycat?*

When the last "Wooo wooo wooo" and nearly all of his musk cologne had faded away, Harry said, "I've never seen the jerk so happy. Whatever he's on, I want some."

"Maybe he's in love," she said.

"With himself, maybe," Harry said. "That was quick thinking, telling him I had an appointment with the efficiency guy."

"Actually, you do, in half an hour." She held up a clipboard with a typewritten schedule. "And there's another appointment, tonight. With a beautiful Irish expert on things more entertaining than efficiency."

The maintenance men were de-couching his office when he returned. Weeks was off somewhere, probably ferreting out company secrets, but he'd stuck a note behind the platen of Harry's typewriter. "Ida called—you and Dr. Dickweed at 10:30."

Harry had a few minutes to kill. He looked at the stack of tear sheets in their plastic protectors on Weeks' desktop. Idly, he began flipping through them, pausing from time to time to appreciate a tasty full page for the MG Sports Sedan or Ballantine Ale, a double-page spread touting Manhattan shirts and featuring champion race driver Stirling Moss.

Could Dr. Ivor Magnus be dickweed enough to believe a copywriter for *Ogle* might actually have turned out those agency ads? Harry didn't think so.

Twenty-five minutes later, he wasn't quite so sure of the efficiency expert's acumen. Dr. Magnus did not make a terribly good first impression.

His closely shaved face was pink and boyish. Premature balding had left him with a shiny dark mink-like strip across the back of his scalp from sideburn to sideburn. He was a small man, looking rather doll-like seated on Bethune's chair, much of him hidden by the desk. What showed was wearing a tight black suit coat, a stiff white shirt and a very unusual silk tie

154

with a pattern of bloodshot eyeballs against a dark blue background.

Magnus' real eyes, magnified by round purple-tinted lenses, studied Harry intently as he sat hunched on the reclaimed couch. "You look nervous, Mr. Trauble," he said, his precise locution offering just a hint of a Prussian accent. "This is not—how do they say—rocket science? Just casual conversation. I do not want you to feel ill at ease."

"Could be the room," Harry said. "The last man to sit in your chair hasn't been seen in a while. He's wanted by the cops."

"Alas, I know about Mr. Bethune. Yesterday morning I had to wait for the police to, ah, poke about in here before I could begin my work."

"Before Bethune, this office belonged to a guy who was crushed to death by the *Ogle* statue out front."

Dr. Magnus responded to that news with a quick, mirthless smile. "Why should this be of concern to you?"

"I guess it shouldn't. It's not me sitting in their chair."

That earned him another unnatural grin. "Precisely."

"Dr. Magnus, what sort of doctor are you?"

"I'm a psychologist," the little man said. "But our meetings will be of an informal nature. You may call me Ivor. May I call you Harry?"

"Sure."

"Well, tell me a little about Harry. Are you native to Los Angeles?"

"Actually, I was born in Memphis, Tennessee."

"Your childhood was there?"

"I was two when we moved to Cleveland."

"Ohio?"

"Right," Harry said, trying to think of another Cleveland. "That's where the Sleepy Traveler motel chain has its main office. My dad worked for STI."

"In what capacity?"

Harry couldn't imagine what that had to do with increasing *Ogle*'s efficiency, but there didn't seem to be any reason not to tell Dr. Magnus that his dad had traveled the U.S., making sure the franchisees were maintaining the standards established by Sleepy Traveler, Inc.

In fact, Harry found it strangely calming to talk about his very conservative parents and his overly protected early life in Cleveland and his love–hate relationship with Vaughan.

By responding to Dr. Magnus' seemingly pointless questions, particularly the one about his father's retirement, he actually began to understand the reason for his current ambivalence toward his parents. He resented their pulling up stakes in Cleveland the month after he left their bed and board. As part of a retirement package, his dad had been given the opportunity to purchase a Sleepy Traveler franchise in Hot Springs, Arkansas, complete with live-in manager. The senior Traubles were now residing in a very comfortable ranch-style home on Lake Hamilton.

"It would've been nice to spend a few years with all of us together—him not on the road all week," Harry said. "Getting to know one another a little better. Living on a lake. Dad had been eligible for retirement for at least five years. It was like they waited until I was out of the way to become a real family."

"Hmmm. Another way of looking at it would be that your father was only thinking of you, that he wanted to make sure you no longer needed his help, that you were standing on your own two feet. That you were a man. It was a compliment to you, no?"

Maybe, Harry thought. Maybe they really did love him after all. Why else would they be so concerned about him working at *Ogle*? They saw it as a backward step; he hadn't been able to convey the message that it was going to be his springboard to better things—better jobs, the bestseller lists.

"Ach. I'm sorry, Harry, but I see by my watch that our time is up," Dr. Magnus said. "I think we've made a little progress here. No?"

"Absolutely," Harry said, though, in truth, he couldn't see where they'd accomplished a thing that would add to the magazine's efficiency. But he was feeling one hell of a lot closer to his parents than he had in years.

"Well, look at that smile," Terry said. "Is it Dr. Magnus or are you just glad to see me?"

"Gotta be you," he said.

"Hold that thought until tonight. At my apartment."

"What time?"

"We'll eat around eight-thirty," she said. "But I want you to appreciate how good a cook I am, so please be there by seven-thirty. Then, once we get the sex stuff out of the way, you'll be ready to pay full attention to the meal."

"I'll be there at seven. That way we won't have to rush."

She gave him one of her beautiful smiles. "Harry, this isn't just . . . ?" She shook her head. "Never mind. See you at seven."

"Till seven," he said. "And no, it definitely isn't just . . ."

25.

That evening, when Ida, Kevin Dobbs and John Bingham arrived at Milton Armstead's flamingo-pink, two-story beachfront home in Malibu, they were informed by Manfred DeLemoy that his master was in the sauna.

"Tell him we're here," Bingham ordered.

Manfred's lips twitched in what may have been a smile. "Mistah Ahm-stead suggests that you folks join him."

"In the sauna?" Dobbs asked.

Manfred nodded. "I've laid out towels."

Bingham turned to Ida. "I knew this was a waste of time," he said. "I'm heading home."

"Milton assured me this was important," she said. "About the Tobella murders and their impact on the company."

"What could he possibly know about the Tobella murders?" Dobbs asked.

"That's what he wants to tell us."

"Then let him put some clothes on and pretend he's a civilized human being," Bingham said.

"Mistah Ahm-stead very ill, suh," Manfred said. "Doctor say he need heat to ward off new-mo-ni-ah."

"No way will I share a steamy, confined area with his licentious, naked, skinny ass," Bingham said.

"I . . . I'm with John on this," Dobbs said.

"Mistah Ahm-stead too ill for sex-u-al ack-tivity," Manfred said.

"Mistah Ahm-stead is ill, all right," Bingham said, heading for the door.

"If whatever he has to say really is important, Ida," Dobbs said, "you have my home number."

She watched Manfred accompany the two *Ogle* executives to the front door and see them out. When he returned, she said, "That's a lovely accent you put on."

"Stole it from my gran'daddy," he said. "C'mon, Ida. I'll show you to the hot box."

"How sick is he, really?" she asked as they descended a stairwell to the basement.

"It's a two-day hangover. Man drank a gallon of hooch and now he's payin' the price." He led her to a room with a flagstone floor and forest green walls, one of which was broken by a large floor-to-ceiling mirror. At the far end of the room were two doors. One hung open, leading to a spacious black-and-white-tiled shower. The other was closed and opaque with steam.

Three bathmat-size white towels had been laid out on a teak-wood bench, along with three sets of clogs. A pitcher of water and glasses were on a teakwood table.

"How much longer will he be in there?" Ida asked.

"Another twenty minutes."

She looked at her watch. Sighing, she said, "Well, what the hell?"

"You need anything, lemme know," Manfred said, pointing to a button on the wall near the steamy door.

Alone, Ida began to undress.

This wasn't a wonderful idea, she knew. Not just because, half-dead or otherwise, Armstead would feel compelled to try to seduce her. Rather, it was because she was mildly intrigued by that possibility.

It had been several months since she'd been with a man and though masturbation had its own rewards, it did not quite measure up to the real deal. Armstead had his weak points, but, if the ladies of the office were to be believed, sexual prowess was not one of them.

A good roll in the hay with no strings attached might be just the pick-me-up she needed.

In silk bra and panties now, she considered her figure in the mirror. Not bad for an old gal. Maybe a few pounds more than when she was in her nubile teens. Motherhood at twenty had given her fuller breasts. More curves.

She unhooked the bra and was proud of the way her breasts held firm. The nipples were hard. Because of Milton? Could be.

She wondered if she shouldn't keep the panties on. She didn't want to seem like she was throwing herself at him. Ridiculous. A woman with a grown son and she was behaving like a schoolgirl.

She peeled off the panties and placed them next to her bra and neatly folded clothes. Then she slid her feet into the clogs, picked up one of the towels and started for the door.

She hesitated, struck by two disturbing thoughts. She had no doubt that this would be a one-night stand; Armstead would be in agreement with her on that. But it could cause some shift in their working relationship, an unwanted one no doubt. Even more disquieting, the great lecher was used to young women. Suppose he simply wasn't interested.

Better play safe, she thought. The towel was big enough to serve as a makeshift sarong.

The heat nearly took her breath away as she stepped into the room.

The door closed behind her with a click that Armstead evidently heard. "About time," he called out through the steam cloud.

She walked toward the sound of his voice and saw him sitting on a wooden bench, squinting her way. His moist body was thin and hairy. He reminded her of the hapless cartoon character Wile E. Coyote. With one notable difference that, even at half mast, would not have been appropriate to a family cartoon.

"Ida," he said. "Where are the others?"

"Gone home," she said, sitting beside him. "They weren't in a sauna mood."

He raised an eyebrow. "But you were, eh?"

"It was your idea to meet here," she said. "Something you wanted to discuss?"

"You look a little warm," he said. "That towel must be pretty uncomfortable."

"It is. I feel as overdressed as Mandrake at the beach."

"So?"

With a shrug, she loosened the towel and let it fall.

"Ho-lee Hannah!" Armstead said. "You've been hiding that bod from me all these years?"

She was fascinated by the speed of his priapic response. Not to mention its growth potential.

"Well, look what just woke up," he said and began to caress himself.

If he had reached out to her instead, she would have followed him down whatever sexual corridor he chose, light, dark or in between. But the sight of him lying back passively against the sweating wall, stroking himself and grinning at her, pushed her increasing ambivalence into the negative zone.

"If you want to get rid of that," she said, "I'll step outside for a minute."

"I'm just prepping for you," he said, sliding toward her now, reaching out his free hand to touch her breast.

She didn't stop him. Actually, his touch felt rather thrilling, a fact she could not hide from his fingers as they caressed her nipples.

"Your body is stunning, Ida. As smooth and firm as a flower child's."

She moved away from him on the bench. "Don't be silly, Milton. I'm old enough to be your ex-wife."

"Au contraire," he said, sliding against her, hand on her thigh now. "You should be a centerfold."

She thought about reminding him that she had been, once upon a time, when her breasts were even firmer than they were at present, but his fingers were doing some marvelous things to her now.

Still, this wouldn't do. As aroused as she was, she'd decided it would be an horrendous mistake to surrender to him. When he slipped to his knees and began kissing the inside of her thighs, she bent down and whispered in his ear, "Focus, Milton. You asked me here to discuss the newly dead Mr. Tobella."

"Jesus, Ida," he yelled, stumbling back, nearly falling onto the hot rocks in the center of the room. "Talk about inappropriate . . . Why not a discourse on leprosy or V.D.?"

She saw, with some surprise, that his penis had done an instant reverse telescope. A shudder went through him as he sat down on the bench again, huddled in the corner. "I've been trying to put it out of my mind," he said, "but it was too fucking horrible. The sight of 'em, lying in their own blood."

"You were there?"

He nodded, then, seeing her frown, added quickly, "It wasn't me killed 'em."

"I'd hardly be sitting here still if I considered that a possibility."

"And you are sitting here." His eyes widened as they traveled over her glistening body. "Damn, you're sexy."

"What were you doing at Tobella's?"

"That's a complicated story. I could explain it better if we took a little of the edge off." He slid toward her. "Here's a deal:

162

I'll even do you first."

"How generous. And romantic. I think I'll pass."

"C'mon. You know damn well you want it."

"Not as much as you seem to think." She stood, wrapped the towel around her waist and walked toward the door.

"Ida, I . . . don't go, please."

The contrite tone surprised her. She turned to find him slumped on the bench. "Don't be pissed at me. You know how I am. Sex now, reality later."

"It's not you I'm pissed at, Milton. I should never have led you on and then turned you off. I wasn't being malicious; I just changed my mind."

"I caught that. I know I killed the deal. Came on too strong. Okay, no sex. Please stick around and have dinner with me. Manfred's one hell of a chef. I'll behave like a gentleman. A eunuch gentleman, if you so desire. I really do want your take on what I should do about Tobella."

"Why do anything?"

"I know who killed him," he said.

"Oh?"

"I'll tell you everything at dinner. If you stay."

"A lady must dine," she said.

The image of her beautiful pink womanly body kept him in a state of erection while he shaved, showered and dressed in slacks, black turtleneck and claret-colored velvet smoking jacket. He cursed himself for taking so long to realize that she was ball-able material. What must that fabulous body have been like ten years ago? Or twenty-five, when she and Trower had met at UCLA?

Well, that was then and this was now and she'd agreed to stay for dinner, giving him another chance at bat.

She was seated at a table on the balcony off the formal dining room, staring at the dark ocean just a sandy beach away. Her fair hair was damp and slightly curled and smelled of the forest pine soap Manfred kept in the shower next to the sauna. The top buttons of her silk blouse were undone, giving him a sneak preview of unfettered breasts. Had she purposely gone braless? Might her panties be in her purse, too? He preferred to think so.

He topped off her fluted glass with champagne and filled his own. "To fortune," he said.

She took one sip and said, "Well. Who done it?"

"Let's have a bite to eat first," he said.

He kept her glass filled and by the end of dinner—Manfred's special coq au vin—she seemed a little woozy. And still very curious. "This was all quite lovely, but it's nearly eleven," she said. "Are you going to tell me?"

"Who killed Tobella and his pansy partner? Let me give you the full story." He tried to pour her the final couple of inches from their second bottle, but she covered the top of her glass.

"No more wine," she said. "Just talk."

He emptied the bottle into his own glass. "You remember Lenina?"

"The poetess?"

"Hippy-dip. The little bitch ran off with Bethune," Armstead said, as if he still couldn't quite believe it. "Left me sitting alone in a fucking bar."

"Well, at least it was a fucking bar," Ida said.

Armstead ignored the comment. "That was the start of the worst night of my life," he said. "Naturally, I was . . . upset. At her fecklessness, I mean. Not to mention her display of such ridiculous taste in men. I got a little squiffed and went back to the office to check my Rolodex for a likely substitute.

"Well, you know how childish I can be, Ida. Particularly when I've been hitting the ragu. Once I got there, I decided to pay

Bethune's office a visit to . . . powder his couch or do something else equally jejune."

"I don't imagine you were hoping to catch them there, making like bunnies?" she said.

"That thought may have occurred to me," he said, downing the champagne. "But the dancer's office was empty and dark. I switched on the lights and noticed an envelope on the carpet. It had Bethune's name on it."

"And you opened it."

"Hell, yes. It was from Joe Tobella. He'd heard Bethune was concerned about Hobart's death."

"Heard from whom, I wonder?"

Armstead shrugged. "All the note said was if Bethune wanted proof that Hobart had been murdered, he was to meet Tobella at an address in Venice that night."

"You went to the address?" she asked.

He nodded.

"And you found the two bodies?"

"When I got there, the front door was ajar. I stuck my head in and called Tobella's name. No reply, so I went in and poked around. They were upstairs in bed, dead as doorknobs. It must've just happened. The blood was still flowing."

"And their murderer . . . ?"

"The fucker was still in the room with the stiffs," Armstead said.

"You saw him?"

"No. Shit. I was gawking at the dead guys when the bastard pushed me from behind. I fell onto their bloody corpses and by the time I recovered, he'd made it down the stairwell. I heard him running and then a door slamming."

"You chased him?"

"Ke-rist, no. Do I look like the kind of idiot who chases kill-ers? I waited till I was sure he was gone and did a fast, fast fade."

"If you didn't see him, how do you know who he is?"

"It's gotta be Bethune."

"What makes you think so?"

"Not just me. He's numero uno on the cop's list of suspects. Innocent people don't run. And the note puts him at the scene of the crime."

"I'm having trouble tracking all this, Milton. First, Howard seduces your little playmate. Do you suppose he then went back to the office, saw the note, read it, left it there and raced off with a girl he'd just met to rendezvous with a man he'd planned to kill?"

"I don't have all the fine points worked out. He could have dropped the note on his way out."

"My guess is he and the little minx are probably holed up in a motel along the ocean, screwing their brains out, totally unaware he's a wanted man. Still . . . you have the note?"

"I left it where I found it," Armstead said. "I imagine it's in some LAPD evidence locker."

She shook her head. "I've an inventory of everything they removed from Howard's office. No mysterious envelope. Which is probably a blessing since your fingerprints would have been all over it."

"What the hell could have happened to it?" Armstead asked. "Who would . . . ? Jesus, it could be the killer took it. We should check the log to see who was in the building."

"Don't get ahead of yourself, Milton," Ida said. She placed a calming hand on his. "The cleaning lady probably tossed it with the trash."

"Yeah," he said, his interest wavering from thoughts of murder to the circular pattern her fingers were tracing on his hand.

"It's all a mishmash," she said. "The only person the note would incriminate would be Howard. And I can't see him killing those boys, then returning to the office to get the note. But enough morbidity."

She brought his hand to her breast. "As a wise man once said," she told him with a smile, ". . . sex now, reality later."

26.

Earlier that evening, when Harry arrived at Terry's apartment carrying a bouquet of flowers he'd plucked from the building's garden, he heard the murmur of conversation on the other side of the door. Nothing distinct, but enough to tell him she was not alone.

He knocked.

The door was opened by a large man in a rumpled suit. Past him, Harry saw Terry on a white sofa, wearing a black silk kimono. Another large man sat on a chair facing her.

He caught a whiff of something cooking but he was too distracted to pin it down.

"Hi, Harry," Terry said. "Come on in. That's Detective . . . Oskar by the door. And this is Detective Cardona."

The two men stared at him with blank faces. Detective Oskar did not step back to allow him entry.

"And this is . . . ?" Cardona asked.

"Harry Trauble," Terry said. "My boyfriend."

"We're just winding up, here, Mr. Trauble," Cardona said. "Be another ten minutes. Think you could maybe walk around the block or something?"

"What's going on?" Harry asked.

Cardona gave him the dead eye. "Ms. O'Mara can fill you in, if she wants. In ten minutes."

The other detective, Oskar, shut the door in his face.

Harry stood there, the flowers wilting in his fist, feeling like a jackass but also worried about why the police had dropped in on Terry.

He strained his ears, but all was silent in the apartment. They were probably waiting for him to go. His eyes went to the peephole in the door. It was dark. He imagined Detective Oskar's eyeball glaring at him.

He went down to his apartment and had a beer and did some more worrying.

When he returned, twenty minutes later, Terry greeted him at the door with a kiss. As he'd suspected from that previous glance past Detective Oskar, she wore nothing under the kimono.

"Dressed kinda skimpy for the cops," he said.

"Just shows 'em I have nothing to hide. It was you I dressed for, goof."

The room smelled of dinner. She smelled of talcum and shampoo and tasted of bourbon.

The kiss made his toes curl but he still felt compelled to pull away long enough to ask, "What did they want?"

"They asked me questions about Joe," she said. "What was our relationship? When I'd last seen him."

"Why you?"

She shrugged. "They didn't say, but I imagine they found my name in his address book. Something like that."

"Then they're talking to a lot of people?"

"I suppose." She smiled. "Don't worry so much." She took his hand and led him to the sofa. She'd made drinks for them—Herkie old-fashioneds, by the look of them, his fresh and hers slightly depleted—and prepared a plate of brie and wheat thins.

"You are the hostess with the mostest," he said. "What's cooking?"

"Pot roast," she said. "It's my never-fail. Ready in about an hour."

The sofa was soft and comfortable.

He looked around the room. She'd decorated it so skillfully it took him a minute to realize it was a mirror image of his own living room. She hadn't any more furniture than he—the sofa, a coffee table, a couple of chairs and a nice wall unit housing books, plants, a small television, a stereo and a neat row of record albums.

"The place looks great," he said. "Like an adult lives here. Mine screams prolonged adolescence. I haven't even gotten around to putting up a brick and board bookcase. You have a real stereo."

"Might as well put it to use," she said.

She found an FM station that was working its way through Elvis' "It Feels So Right."

"I think I could use a hug and kiss about now," she said, when she'd returned to the sofa. She moved into his arms. Their kiss was only an inch away when there was a knock on the door.

Terry drew back and put a finger to her lips.

After a brief silence, the distinctive voice of Detective Cardona came through the door. "Miz O'Mara, it's us again."

She slid from the sofa and padded across the carpet to open the door.

"Sorry to bug you one more time," Cardona said, entering the room, "but we just realized Mr. Trouble was on our list, too. Is he . . . yeah, I see he is."

Harry tried to keep the apprehension off his face as the detective smiled at him. "Think we could have a few minutes of your time, sir?"

"Now?"

Cardona's eyes went from the cocktails to Terry and back to Harry. "If it wouldn't be too inconvenient. You wanna come with us?"

"Come with you where?"

"Your apartment or our vehicle," Cardona said. "Your choice. We just have a few questions."

"Why don't I go into the bedroom," Terry said, "and you can talk to Harry here?"

Cardona looked back at his partner who was standing near the door. Detective Oskar shrugged and Cardona said, "Sure."

Terry flashed him an insincere smile, picked up her old-fashioned and retired to the bedroom.

"Okay if I join you on the couch?" Cardona said.

"I guess."

Oskar sauntered into the room, pulling a pen and small spiral notepad from his coat pocket. He took the nearest chair.

"You've been at *Ogle* for what . . . three months? Four?"

"Three," Harry said.

"And you've known Miz O'Mara that length of time?"

"No. We just met a few days ago," Harry said.

"Live in the same building. Work at the same place. But you just met?"

"This is a big building," Harry said, conscious of Oskar scribbling away and wondering why any of this would be of interest to them.

"Ever have any dealings with Joseph Tobella?" Cardona asked.

"Nope. Never met the man."

"Know what he looked like?"

Harry nodded. "He was at the magazine a while ago."

"When was that, exactly?" Cardona asked.

Harry's mouth was dry but the only liquid available was the cocktail and he didn't think it was a great time to be dulling his senses with booze. "A few days before the murders."

"Can you elaborate on that for us, Mr. Trauble?"

"Four days, I think."

"And where did you see him on that day?"

Harry described his arrival at the *Ogle* Building that morning, seeing the sculptor and his assistant on the marquee taking pictures.

"Did you exchange words with Mr. Tobella?"

"No."

"Did anybody?"

Harry hesitated before answering. As much as he despised Maurice Grumbacher, he felt creepy about throwing him to these lions. "I guess some people were there who wanted to know what they were doing up on the marquee," he said.

"What people?" Cardona asked.

"I'm not sure—"

"Maurice Grumbacher?" Cardona asked.

"Yeah. He was there."

"Could you describe his mood? Was he just mildly curious? Maybe annoyed?"

"Closer to annoyed, I guess."

"More than annoyed? Maybe . . . furious?"

"Angry."

"Why?"

"He didn't like them climbing up there without permission. Something to do with insurance."

"Was that all that ticked him off?" Cardona asked.

"Tobella said it was his fault that the statue fell."

Cardona's eyes widened. Not a lot, but noticeable on an otherwise stone face. "Grumbacher's fault?"

"Tobella claimed he'd warned Grumbacher the marquee might not support the frog statue for very long and Maurice said that was okay."

"Maurice Grumbacher had been Tobella's contact at *Ogle*?"

Harry shrugged. "I don't know," he said.

"Were you still there when Mr. Tobella and his associate got down from the marquee?"

"Un huh."

"Describe that scene for us."

"Scene? They got down, folded the ladder and left."

"Was Grumbacher still there?"

"Yep."

"Still angry?"

"Annoyed, I guess."

"We understand he attacked Mr. Tobella."

"Attack? No. Tobella insulted Maurice and Maurice raised a fist. Tobella challenged him to use it and Maurice backed down."

The detectives exchanged a glance.

"How's about this version, Mr. Trauble? Maurice Grumbacher grabbed Mr. Tobella and demanded he turn over the film from his camera. Mr. Tobella twisted free, blew him off and walked away while Grumbacher yelled threats of bodily harm."

"As best I recall, it was the way I described it."

"You work for Grumbacher, right?"

"He . . . supervises my copy."

"You friends?"

"No."

"He an okay guy to work for?"

"Not really," Harry said.

Cardona smiled for the first time. "So you're not shading the truth about the threats out of friendship or to make points with your boss?"

Harry frowned at the word. "No. I'm telling you the truth. And he's not my boss, exactly."

Cardona cocked his head and studied Harry with hard brown eyes, as if trying to stare past the words into the young man's head.

"Remember what you were up to on the night of the murders?"

The question caught Harry off guard. "Uh, sure. I . . . we

had dinner at a place called Herkie's Wonder Bar. Across the street from the magazine."

"By 'we' you mean you and . . . ?"

"Ter . . . Miz O'Mara."

"And after dinner?"

"We drove back here."

"Came here straight from the bar?" Cardona asked.

"Well, no," Harry said. "We took Miz O'Mara's uncle home first. Then we came here."

"To this apartment?"

"Actually, to mine."

The detective gave him another searching look. "Thanks for your cooperation, Mr. Trauble," he said.

He stood, a signal to Oskar to cap his pen and close his note-pad. "You didn't happen to see any of the photos that Tobella took of the marquee, did you?" he asked, as if it were of little importance.

"No. Where would I have seen 'em?"

The detective shrugged. "Around the office. Maybe on somebody's desk."

Harry shook his head. "How would they have . . . oh, I see. They weren't at Tobella's?"

Cardona didn't reply. "Well, that wraps it up," he said, moving toward the door with Oskar two paces behind. "You and Miz O'Mara have a nice evening."

Harry shut the door behind them, then consulted the peep hole to make sure they weren't lurking in the hall.

When he turned, Terry was standing less than a foot away, naked as a grape. She moved into his arms. "We're running late," she whispered in his ear.

A little less than an hour later, with one hunger temporarily ap-peased, they addressed another, Terry wearing her kimono,

Harry wrapped in a much-too-small tattered pink bathrobe.

As he dug into the roast, carrots and potatoes, Terry said, "I'm glad you corrected yourself about taking Colin home. That way our stories matched."

"I got a little rattled," he said.

"That's what trips up the guilty," she said. "Not that we're guilty of anything."

"Except disturbing the scene of a crime, leaving the scene of a crime and a few other little odds and ends. This is great pot roast, by the way."

"It's my big-winner meal," she said. "Part of my heritage. Don't expect French or even Italian."

"So I guess you listened in on everything?" he said.

"Water glass to the wall," she said.

"Then you know the killer took the photos Tobella shot at *Ogle*."

She cocked her head. "That may not be true."

"What do you mean?"

She left the table and went into the bedroom. Less than a minute later, she returned with a white 8 × 10" envelope. She opened it and slid its contents onto the table—a contact sheet containing inch-high prints of forty numbered photographs, a guide in selecting which pictures to develop, and the negatives of the shots in long strips.

Harry stared at them. "Tell me these aren't—"

"Of course they are," she said. "Joe may have had another set developed, but he sent the originals to me."

"Why?"

"He called and asked if I'd mind holding them for him. He said they were crucial to his case and he was concerned the people who were watching him might try to get rid of them."

"Why not put 'em in a bank box?" Harry asked.

"Joe didn't trust banks."

"But he trusted you?"

She nodded. "Don't you?"

"Sure," he said, a little too emphatically.

"Joe told me he saw me in one of the pictures and that gave him the idea to let me keep 'em."

Harry squinted at the contact sheet, then placed it back on the table and finished off the few remaining morsels of dinner on his plate. "What's the big deal about the photos?" he asked.

"Joe said they were proof that the marquee wasn't properly attached to the building."

"But if somebody did get rid of these, couldn't Tobella have just taken some more?"

Terry shrugged and began bussing the table. "I guess he was afraid the marquee would be fixed."

Harry looked at the contact sheet again. Even in the tiny format he could see close-ups on bolts that had pulled an inch or so from the wall, earthquake cracks in the wall, fissures in the surface of the marquee. The thought of having to walk under that marquee made Harry a little queasy.

"I don't see your picture," he said.

"It's in there," she said, returning to the table with pecan crunch ice cream. "I'm in the background. We both are. You can barely see us."

Harry finally found the shot. Orlando had been facing away from the wall, photographing the crumbling tip of the marquee. He and Terry were standing across the street.

"You look great," he said, wondering how she could possibly have known about his thing for pecan crunch. "I look like I've just been hit by lightning."

"I have that effect on men," she said.

"Why didn't you turn this stuff over to Cardona?"

"And tell him what? That I'd lied about barely knowing Joe? Then there'd be the: 'You sure you don't know who might have had reason . . . ?' type of follow-ups. Screw that noise."

"What are you going to do with these?"

"Well," she said, licking the dregs of pecan crunch from her spoon, "most of 'em will go to the safest place I know. The one of us, I'm going to have some copies made with the marquee cropped out. Years from now, I'll be able to say, 'See, that's the morning your grandpa and I first met.' "

He liked the way she looked without the dark lipstick and the eye liner. Softer. Younger. Sweeter. "I think I'm ready for seconds," he said.

"Tell me you're not talking about the pecan crunch."

"I'm not talking about the pecan crunch," he said.

27.

"The gent perched like a well-garbed bird of prey near the door is our new Associate Publisher, Al Hewitt," Armstead announced to the crowd assembled in the conference room the following morning. "I imagine some of you have met him; he's become damn near ubiquitous in the rather short amount of time he's been here."

"I'm happy to see you've regained your health," the ex-archbishop said.

"I owe my recuperative powers to Russian cigarettes and sexual excess," Armstead said.

Harry had to look twice at Hewitt before realizing who he was. The man had gone through quite a makeover since their meeting in front of the magazine building. The black cleric's garb had been traded in on a charcoal grey British-cut hacking jacket, pale pink shirt, black knit tie and light gray slacks. His highly polished black shoes sported tassels. Some proficient barber had shaped and blown-dry his formerly lank and lifeless hair into a fashionable curly coif. And, unless Harry was mistaken, the ex-archbishop had had a few sessions with a sunlamp.

Hewitt saw him gawking and nodded in recognition.

The room was filled with the usual suspects from the promotion department, along with John Bingham, Ida Connor and the "efficiency expert" Dr. Ivor Magnus. The latter was clearly the most attentive person present, filling his notebook's pages with scribbled hieroglyphics.

"So," Armstead said, "here we are again to discuss the ever-popular Image Campaign. You may remember when last we met, it had been decided that we find a guy from among our subscribers who would exemplify the *Ogle* reader in all his affluent, acquisitive majesty.

"Before he boogalooed off to parts still unknown, our former subscription manager-slash-dance instructor Howard Bethune managed to come up with a strong candidate for *Ogle* Guy, one Dr. Daryl Wunder from King of Prussia, Pennsylvania."

He turned to Beagle. "So, Larry, the floor is yours."

The promotion manager looked tired and stressed out. "We've made some progress," he said. "Here's the first in a series of 'Who's Eyeing *Ogle*?' ads." He handed Armstead an art board that had been resting beside his chair.

Bingham and some of the others inched closer to get a look at the mock-up. Harry didn't bother. He'd seen it: a photo of a handsome, casually but expensively dressed guy in his late twenties seated at a terrace restaurant somewhere in Europe, with snowcapped mountains glistening against a sapphire sky in the background. Sharing his table was a beautiful, fresh-faced young woman staring at him adoringly. At another table two other beauties were being awestruck by him. Seemingly oblivious to the stunning ladies and the stunning scenery, the man was reading a copy of *Ogle* magazine. The caption announced, "Who's Eyeing *Ogle*? A Man Who Travels."

Harry's tag line had been "Who's Reading *Ogle*?" The "Eyeing" update had been Grumbacher's. Harry had argued that "reading" meant that the man was actually paying attention to *Ogle*. "Eyeing" had a more superficial implication that supported the negative notion that most people purchased the magazine primarily to look at pictures of naked women.

Grumbacher had dismissed Harry's criticism with an airy

wave of his hand. "Copy should rock and roll," he had announced. "The line now rocks." Larry Beagle had sided with Grumbacher. Not only about the copy but about the photograph which, per Grumbacher's demand, would show the man actually looking at the magazine, rather than merely having it on the table.

Again, Harry had argued that it made the man look foolish to have traveled all the way to Europe only to stick his nose in a magazine. "Poor Harry," Grumbacher had said to Beagle. "He just doesn't understand the concept of modern advertising, doesn't know why that woman goes to the Metropolitan Museum in her Maidenform bra, doesn't know what that little yachtsman is doing floating in a toilet." He had added rather nastily to Harry, "In ad circles we call it a visual grabber. Lesson over."

Armstead stared at the ad for a while, then dropped it onto the desk. "The guy goes all the way to Switzerland. He brings the dame with him. They go out to a restaurant that's got to be costing him the price of a right leg, and what's he doing? He's reading a frigging magazine?"

Harry turned to smile at Grumbacher. "What did you call it, Maurice?" he asked. "A visual grabber?"

Armstead glared at Grumbacher. "This is your doing?" he asked.

"The department worked on it," Beagle said. "And you've got to admit, it is an attention getter."

Armstead looked at the ad again and smiled. "It's as silly as a tree full of owls and it makes us look like assholes, but it's a close enough rip-off of the rabbit rag's 'What Sort of Man . . . ?' ads for Buck to go for it. What do you say, o assistant to the Great One?"

Hewitt didn't seem at all intimidated. "My impression is that Buck's main focus at present is on his party. I wouldn't bother him with anything else until that's nailed down."

"By the way," Bingham asked, "is there gonna be nudity at the party?"

"Most assuredly," Armstead said.

"Then I don't want any invites going out to the advertisers."

"Don't worry about that," Armstead said. "This is gonna be one of Buck's 'private' parties."

"Private?" Beagle said. "I thought its purpose was to boost company morale. The staff will be invited, right?"

"Some of the staff," Armstead said. "The better-looking secretaries, of course. And the Eyefuls. And any of their female friends. The magazine executives, the department heads and their associates are all invited. But the majority of the company, the riffraff, will have to find their fun somewhere else."

"T-that hardly seems equitable," Beagle said.

"Who wants equitable?" Armstead said. "Our parties have five broads for every guy and that's a ratio we've come to love. If you don't like it, stay home with the family jewels. More broads for the rest of us.

"So, are we done with this fercockta meeting?"

"What's the copy gonna say in the ads?" Bingham asked.

"Serious statistics," Beagle said. "We have some fairly impressive figures on reader travel."

"Really?" Armstead asked. "I always thought our readers just stay home, pulling their pud."

"On a cost per thousand basis," Beagle said, warming to a subject that he actually seemed to enjoy, "an advertiser will be getting more bang for his buck with *Ogle* than with such circulation champs as *TV Guide* or the *Digest.*"

"And the male in the picture will be our guy, Daryl Wunder?" Bingham asked.

Beagle nodded. "The girls will be models, of course. Other ads will find Wunder buying a new car, enjoying the hell out of a smoke, relaxing with a glass of wine and his stereo."

"It's acceptable," Armstead said, almost begrudgingly. "Not terribly imaginative. But it should fill the bill. When do we get a look at Wunder?"

"He's flying in late tomorrow night," Beagle said. "One of the ladies will greet him at the airport with a photographer. He's booked into the Beverly Wilshire. Maurice and I will be having breakfast with him. We'll bring him back here for a meeting at ten and—"

"Make it eleven," Armstead said. "My brain doesn't wake up until ten."

"Eleven, then. I've got his afternoon filled with a meeting with Sy Sylvestre—"

"Make sure our fabulous fashion fairy does not put the moves on him," Armstead said. "None of those soulful observations of the guy's crotch or questions about which side he dresses on."

Beagle sighed and continued doggedly, "Anyway, Sy will fix him up with some wardrobe items and Carlos will take some test shots. After that, if you want to have dinner with him, he'll be available. Or we can just send him back to Pennsylvania."

"Definitely the latter," Armstead said. "Well, this isn't exactly the fireworks display I'd hoped for. But it'll do. Okay, that's it, assuming nobody else has anything more to say."

"Uh, actually, I've got an idea," Roger Weeks said.

Maurice Grumbacher, who was standing next to Weeks, took a step away, distancing himself.

Armstead studied the young man. "Give, kid."

"I . . . The basic concept for the campaign is on target. But I don't think we've taken it far enough. The opening ad, for example, should be something a little more dramatic than just a cool guy at a restaurant in Switzerland with his lady. If we want to show that we reach the traveling man, we should go all out."

Armstead's eyes glittered. "How do we do that, exactly?"

Weeks removed the current issue of *Newsweek* from underneath his notepad and tossed it onto Armstead's desk. He pointed to the cover—a scene of American fighting men in action. "That's where we send our *Ogle* reader for that first travel ad. Vietnam."

The others gawked at the magazine, a bit stunned. But Armstead was grinning. "Yeah," he said. "Yeah, yeah, yeah. Only we don't just send our man, a model and a photographer. We do it up right. We send a whole *Ogle* troop over there. A bunch of Eyefuls, singers and dancers and let's throw in an over-the-hill blue comic. And a couple thousand copies of the magazine to hand out and remind those soldiers what they're fighting for."

"This isn't funny, Milton," Beagle said.

"Funny? Who's talking funny? A guy reading a magazine in a restaurant is funny. This is deadly serious. This is *Ogle* becoming a magazine of significance, a magazine willing to do its share in aiding the war effort. Believe me, bub, this is promo at its finest."

Beagle seemed shaken. "But it's . . . There's a real war going on. People dying. It's not something you use to sell magazines."

"What the hell are you talking about?" Armstead said, rising now, face reddening. "The war is the ball game. Look at the goddamn news every night. We send some broads over there in bikinis and little frog outfits and we'll get more press than Cassius Clay. When our broads get there, Bob Hope can just hang up his jock."

"It's a war zone," Beagle said.

"We're not gonna send anybody to the front lines. We'll stick to the big cities. It'll be safe."

"Paris is a big city. Dresden is a big city. How safe were they?"

"Keep your memoirs to yourself, Beagle," Armstead said. "I let you talk me out of trying to sneak copies of the magazine on the Mars rocket. But this one is gonna fly. And you know what?

You're gonna fly with it. You're going to Vietnam to oversee the whole deal."

Beagle paled. He opened his mouth but no sound came out.

"I thought you'd be happy to get back to where the action is. We can tog you out in a tailor-made set of khakis. Maybe they'll let you wear your old battle ribbons."

"D-don't do this, Milton," Beagle said imploringly.

Harry was shocked by the whiteness of Beagle's skin, by the palsied shaking of his hands.

"Consider it done, soldier," Armstead said. "I want an itinerary on my desk by the end of the week. Now get to work. And you, whatever the fuck your name is, this was one swinging good idea."

Beagle seemed so dazed as they left the conference room that Harry asked if he could be of some help.

"Huh? Oh, no, thank you, Harry," the promotion manager said. "I'm just a little . . . Probably coming down with something. I'll be fine."

In their office, Weeks was more animated than Harry had ever seen him. "That's how you sell an idea, my man. That's how you get the big guys like Armstead to sit up and take notice."

"A travel ad set in Vietnam?" Harry asked. "How about a booze ad in a drunk ward?"

"Do I smell the ugly aroma of sour grapes?" Weeks asked. "Oh, man, did you dig the way Armstead took the idea and ran with it? This is gonna be big time. And little old Roger Weeks is the man behind the plan."

"Maybe you should go to Saigon instead of Larry," Harry said.

"Hey, Roger Weeks doesn't go anywhere that bullets fly."

"Larry looked like he'd been kicked in the stomach," Harry said.

"You would, too, if you'd been told you were gonna have to relive your worst nightmare," Weeks said.

"What are you talking about?"

"Beagle. He got shell-shocked in the Big One. Came out a basket case. Got a Bronze Star or something, but he was a real veg for a couple of years in a psycho ward."

Harry started for the door.

"Where're you going?" Weeks asked.

"To tell Armstead about Larry. He'll have to send somebody else."

"Hold on, compadre," Weeks said. "Armstead knows Beagle's medical history. It's in his personnel jacket. That's how I found out."

"C'mon. Not even he is that big a prick."

"You're cute, Harry. Naive and cute. Armstead is the biggest prick you or I is likely to come across in our lifetime. Unless we're very, very unlucky."

"Why's he so hard on Larry?"

"Timing. Buckley and Ida hired Beagle while Armstead was in Germany overseeing the kraut edition of the magazine. When the big A returned, he was sincerely pissed that they hadn't bothered to wait for his input before hiring his second in command. He's been trying to break Beagle ever since."

"What a world," Harry said.

"It's beautiful when you're in love," Weeks told him.

28.

Because it was his habit to work on his novel after business hours, Harry rarely joined the other *Ogle* staffers who would wander down the block to sample the Happy Hour doubles at the Grasshopper Lounge. But that evening, he accepted Weeks' offer of a drink to celebrate his success at the image meeting.

It was early enough for the bar's territorial boundaries to still be in play. The subscription and accounting people, the "drones" as Armstead called them, were gathered where they would have a clear view of the actual cash register total when tab-paying time rolled 'round. The editorial guys with a few of the better-looking secretaries and the odd attractive non-*Ogle* woman congregated at tables on a raised platform against a far wall that allowed them to look down on the rest of the boozers.

There the older, burnt-out editors spoke gruffly of Hemingway and "Bill" Faulkner and "that lucky sonofabitch, the James Bond guy," and knocked back double scotches with a fierce determination that usually had them walking on their knees by eight o'clock. The younger editors, "man"-ing and "like wow"-ing one another about The Stones and The Animals and that new West Coast group, The Grateful Dead, sucked domestic beer from bottles and made frequent trips to the john where they puffed weed and pretended they were dangerous.

The middle of the bar belonged to the art and photo departments, though, in truth, not too many artists showed up, since they preferred a cavern on La Cienega that catered to a more bohemian clientele.

The promotion department had no designated area, so Harry and Weeks ignored all borders to take a table near the entrance. They sat there drinking double martinis on the rocks from thick tumblers and lied about how much they liked the taste of gin and ice water.

It had been Weeks' idea to sit close to the front door. He was planning an early getaway. He had a date later with some mystery woman.

"Is it serious?" Harry asked.

"It may even be . . . it."

"Wow. Does she work for the magazine?"

"You want me to talk about her in some goddamned bar," Weeks said. "Maybe I should go scrawl her phone number in the head. 'For a great blowjob, call . . .' You save that kind of stuff for after they've fucked you over."

"Just making conversation," Harry said.

"Okay, then let's converse about me," Weeks said. "It's my time. I realized that in the meeting. I'm like a gambler on a streak. I've got to keep pushing and pushing until I win it all."

"Or your luck runs out," Harry said.

"Don't bring me down, Trauble," Weeks said. "This is my night."

They clinked glasses.

By the third round, Harry was feeling no pain. Weeks bought him a fourth and then split the scene. Harry didn't even realize he was alone until a feminine voice asked, "Saving this empty seat for somebody?"

"Hi, baby," he said as Terry took the chair vacated by Weeks. "How'd ya know I was here?"

"You weren't at home and you weren't at Herkie's, so . . . I took a wild guess."

"Been drinkin' with my fren' Rog."

She picked up his nearly full glass and drained it. "Nasty," she said. "How many of these did you have?"

"No more than flix," he said.

"Time to go beddy-by," she said.

As they were making their exit, Larry Beagle was heading in. The promotion manager looked exhausted, nervous, his eyes darting around the room. "Is Milton here?" Beagle asked.

"Have 'n seen him," Harry said.

"He told me to meet him here," Beagle said.

"Uh, Larry," Harry said, " 'bout this Vietnam thing—"

"I don't want to talk about it," Beagle replied with uncharacteristic venom. "It's an insane idea."

"Tha's wha' I was goin' to say," Harry replied. But Beagle had already moved past them toward the bar.

"What's the Vietnam thing?" Terry asked as they walked toward his Mustang.

" 'Nother o' Armstead's nutso ideas."

"Milton's ideas aren't really nutso," she said. "Self-serving. Mean-spirited. Evil, maybe. But they usually get the results he wants."

"This one can get Beagle really fucked up," he said. "Maybe killed."

"Like I've been saying all along, Milton is capable of murder. I'm driving, by the way."

Harry had no memory of the trip to the apartment, but he did recall the kiss in the elevator. And the groping and stumbling down the corridor to her apartment. And the rending of clothes as they made their way across the dark living room, past the picture window overlooking the Pacific.

He remembered her velvety but firm flesh, the smell of magnolias kept in a dish beside her bed. He remembered her mouth moving along his body.

He remembered her bringing him almost to climax, then leaving him briefly only to return and straddle him, positioning him inside her, doing all the work, her round breasts swinging in front of his face like softballs of love.

Then, nothing, until he awoke at a little after three in the darkened bedroom. Terry was asleep on her side, facing away from him. The magnolias on a plate near his nose smelled sickly sweet and decadent. Someone seemed to have driven a railroad tie into the center of his skull.

Trying not to moan, he eased himself upright. Terry stirred, turned and opened one eye. "You okay?"

"Hung over," he managed to croak.

She gave him a bright smile and slipped out of bed gracefully. Even in pain he was able to appreciate the beauty of her body. "Where you going?" he asked.

"You just stay there and look pathetic," she said.

He lowered his head carefully until it again rested on the pillow.

She was back within seconds with a cool damp washcloth that she folded and placed over his eyes. He heard her bare feet pad away across the carpet. "Where you going now?"

"To brew a magic potion."

Before he could drift off again, she was beside him, removing the washcloth.

She'd replaced the aging magnolias with a lighted candle that smelled of piney forest. She held out a small fruit juice glass filled with a cloudy green liquid. "Drink this," she commanded.

"What is it?"

"A feel-good thing. Great for hangovers."

Harry took the glass and drained it. It tasted of licorice, powerful, pungent licorice.

Suddenly, his headache disappeared. Then the weirdness

started. His brain seemed to be dissolving, draining into his throat.

He sat upright. His skeletal frame was dissolving, too. Except for one part of his anatomy which seemed to be the repository of all the other parts, hardening, lengthening. Terry took the glass from his fingers and placed it on the table near the candle.

Harry had never before felt sexual desire quite that acute.

She smiled and circled the bed slowly, drawing the coverlet with her until his body was exposed to the cool night air.

The change in temperature did nothing to calm his passion. Especially not with Terry joining him on the bed, rolling over until her body was pressed against his.

"Good medicine, no?" she purred.

"What . . . what the hell is it?" he heard himself asking.

"A liqueur that's illegal in this country," she said. "I stole it from Herkie's private stock."

"Bad girl," he said.

"You'd better believe it," she said and kissed him hard.

There was licorice inside her mouth, too. His senses were filled by the taste and smell of it. She pulled him atop her. His heart thudded against his chest but it was nothing compared to the exquisite sensation of their bodies mingling.

He awoke the next morning well after nine. Her leg was across the lower part of his body and he couldn't move. He didn't want to. He was relaxed, drowsy and in no mood for the foolishness at *Ogle*. That could wait another day. All he wanted to do was to stay there and hope that Terry would awake soon so that they could make love again.

He was thinking that he had definitely been born at the right time. Bless you, Gregory Pincus and Enovid and Conovid and F. D. Searle for making life so much goddamned fun. Birth control pills! What must it have been like for the past generations. Withdrawal. Rubbers. Stone Age stuff!

It was clear sailing ahead. He closed his eyes and smiled, comforted by the knowledge that, like movies and television and books and, well, life in general, sex in the Seventies and Eighties was only going to get better and better.

As if sensing his thoughts, she snuggled against him and he could feel the magic of the moment. Or maybe it was Herkie's special liqueur still doing its thing.

29.

Armstead leaned back in his chair, his face even more sallow than usual. The black cigarette had fallen from his lips to the desktop, where it was burning a hole in a hillock of little blue memo pads.

Like the rest of the people in the first-floor conference room, Harry sat staring in silence. Even Ivor Magnus was looking up from his notes.

Armstead and Beagle were at center stage, the entire cast of a two-person drama.

"You're too good a man for this, Larry," Armstead was saying in an ultra-friendly voice that Harry found totally unconvincing. "Put down the gun."

Beagle shoved the weapon forward until it almost touched Armstead's carrion nose. "Say goodnight, Gracie," he said quietly.

When the meeting to introduce Dr. Daryl Wunder had convened a few minutes earlier, none of the participants had noticed the glazed look in Larry Beagle's red-rimmed eyes, or his unshaved beard stubble or the bulge in his rumpled coat pocket. They'd been too busy being surprised by the man who had been selected to be the focus of the big image campaign.

Dr. Wunder was a black man. While unexpected, that of itself would not have caused undue concern. The country was growing up. Earlier that year, segregationist Lester Maddox had been forced to shutter his all-white Pickrick Restaurant in

Georgia. Sidney Poitier had won an Academy Award. White people were admitting that they listened to the blues. It would have been difficult, and probably illegal, for *Ogle* to try to find out how large a segment of its readers were Negro, but surely a good many were.

Still, Dr. Wunder wasn't exactly a stand-in for Poitier. Or even for Chuck Berry, if it came to that. It was mainly the clothes—huge wide-brimmed pearl grey felt hat, grey knee-length suit coat with wide lapels and shoulders so padded they barely made it through the conference room door, matching trousers billowing down to narrow cuffs that kissed his two-tone shoes. And there was jewelry—elaborate rings on most of his fingers, gold chains around his spindly neck, a tiny gold ball decorating his right ear lobe.

His first words to the crowd were, "Hey, how y'all doin'?"

When Armstead walked into the conference room and got his first look at Daryl Wunder, he paused, raised an eyebrow and said, "It's a mite early in the day for us to be needing the services of a pimp."

"Never too early, never too late," the apparition replied. "Ah'm Daryl Wunder, Doctor of Luuuuv. Or as you would have it, the *Ogle* Guy."

Armstead ignored the extended bejeweled hand and said, "Beagle, you stupid fucking son of a bitch, do something about this."

"What would you suggest, Milton?" Beagle asked in an abnormally high-pitched voice.

Armstead rolled his eyes and turned back to the doctor. "Mister . . . Doctor Wunder, I'm afraid there's been a mistake . . ."

"Mistake?" Wunder's eyes narrowed and he took a step toward Armstead. "I sure as hell hope not, broth-a, 'cause each hour I am away from mah patch in King of P. is costin' me heavy coin, unnerstan'.""

Armstead turned to Beagle and glared at him. "What the hell were you think . . . ?" He didn't bother to finish the sentence. Instead, he chuckled and said, "From what I hear about Vietnam, sending this mack daddy over there would be like sending coals to Newcastle."

"It was your idea," Beagle said tonelessly, but he was drowned out by an exclamation from Wunder.

"Vietnam? No fuckin' way the Wunderman goin' to Vietnam," he shouted.

"You got that right, doctor," Armstead said. He turned to Beagle. "I give you a concept. I outline the plan. I do everything but hold your palsied hand on the follow-through and still you drop the ball."

Dr. Wunder cocked his head and winked at Armstead. "You got some sass on you, brutha," he said.

Armstead did not accept this compliment gracefully. "There's your ideal *Ogle* reader, Beagle. There's your prize, average, all-around grade-A, number-one example of . . ."

Wunder turned to follow Armstead's line of sight to whatever had caused him to stop speaking. Larry Beagle was pointing a gun at the man.

Unlike the others in the room who were frozen in their tracks, the luuuv doctor was preconditioned to react to such a situation. His gravity knife had just cleared his trouser pocket when Beagle smashed the barrel of his weapon against his hand, popping a knuckle, shattering the stones in two of his rings and sending the knife flying into the corner of the room.

Wunder let out a yelp and raised his damaged hand to his mouth where he sucked the swelling knuckle.

Al Hewitt's lips were moving, probably in silent prayer. Ida Connor took a backward step toward the door. The others stood riveted as Beagle shifted the gun back on Armstead.

"Concentrate, Mr. Beagle," Dr. Magnus said soothingly. "Free your mind and let it dissolve the anger that—"

"Bla bla bla," Beagle said. "Clam up, or you're next."

"Larry, for Christ's sake, put down the gun," Harry finally managed to get out.

Beagle ignored him. "Why don't you beg, Milton? You'll die anyway, but I could use a laugh."

Beagle's finger tightened on the trigger.

"No," Harry shouted.

"Too late, buddy-boy. It's us or them."

As Beagle pulled the trigger, he was attacked by two men rushing into the room. One pushed his gun arm up, sending the bullet into the acoustic tile ceiling. The other pushed him forward onto the conference table, slamming his face against the hard wood.

While they busied themselves disarming the squirming man, Armstead, as pale and brittle as chalk, staggered back and flopped onto a chair, staring at his saviors.

"You got this old boy under control, Steve?" Detective Emmett Oskar asked his partner.

Detective Steve Cardona grunted an affirmative as he cuffed Beagle's wrists behind his back.

Oskar spotted the love doctor and frowned. "What's been going on here, anyway?"

"Just another ordinary day at *Ogle*," Harry said.

"That pathetic psycho tried to kill me," Armstead said.

"Gee, I wonder why," Cardona said. "Well, we'll take care of him."

"The man needs therapy," Dr. Magnus said.

"Yeah?" Cardona said. He jerked Beagle to an upright position and studied his prisoner's puffy face. "Looks like his cheekbone might need some of that therapy. The rest of him, I don't know. It'll all come out in the wash."

Beagle looked both ossified and perplexed, like a zombie who'd just been struck by an idle thought.

"Put that fucker under the jail," Armstead yelled.

"Thanks for the suggestion," Cardona said, "but we like to go through our boring little legal protocols first."

"Take his pimp friend with him," Armstead said.

"Hole on now," the love doctor said. "Ah'm jus' a visitor to this fair city."

"Relax, asshole," Oskar said, "we're homicide, not vice. Just be missing before we pass 'em the word."

As Wunder slid from the room, Cardona shook his head and grinned. "With all this nonsense, I almost forgot why we came. Maurice Grumbacher, you're under arrest for the murders of Joseph Tobella and Orlando Royale. Hands behind your back, please."

He looked at his partner. "Em. You got some cuffs for Grumbacher?"

"I didn't do it," Grumbacher whined.

"Are you guys demented?" Armstead said. "You've already cuffed the most likely suspect."

"Mr. Beagle has an alibi for those crimes," Cardona said. "Our bets are on Grumbacher."

"You can't believe this bowl of jelly could kill anybody?" Armstead said.

"Thanks for the vote of confidence, Milton," Grumbacher said before yelping as the cuffs bit into his wrists.

"Just protecting and serving," Oskar said as he and Cardona dragged the promotion manager and his assistant from the room.

"Sorry to have interrupted your meeting," Cardona said to Armstead, "and saved your life and all."

They could hear Grumbacher repeating that he didn't do it all the way to the front door and out.

"One of this company's executives tries to kill you, Milton,"

Bingham said, "while another knocks off a couple of fags. This place is like a breeding ground for Murder, Incorporated."

"It's all bullshit. Beagle's been a ticking time bomb from day one. I don't know how you could have hired the crazy bastard, Ida."

"What do you think, doctor?" she said.

Magnus cleared his throat. "You know what they say about the line separating sanity from insanity."

"Yeah yeah," Armstead said. "It's as thin as a razor's edge."

"You seem to have erased Mr. Beagle's line. As for the apparently homicidal Mr. Grumbacher—"

"Grumbacher didn't murder anybody," Armstead said.

"What makes you so sure?" Bingham asked.

"The guy bathes in that musk shit," Armstead said. "If he'd been at Tobella's, he'd have stunk up the place." Even before the words left his mouth, he knew he'd made a serious mistake.

They were all staring at him. Ida was shaking her head sadly.

"What?" Armstead said, trying to bluff it out with a show of annoyance. "It stands to reason that if there had been some kind of identifying odor the cops would have been on him long before this."

"I thought they were looking for Bethune," Bingham said.

"No," Weeks said. "They ruled him out."

Once again Harry was amazed by his office-mate's fund of knowledge.

Al Hewitt got to his feet. "I'd better inform Buck we'll be putting the image campaign and the party on hold for a while."

"What are you talking about?" Armstead said.

"What he's talking about is the big picture," Bingham said, standing also. "There is a world beyond *Ogle*, Milton, and it's full of normal people with sensible priorities who understand that if two of our executives go on trial for murder and attempted murder, we have an image problem that'll need more than some *Ogle* Guy to get rid of."

"I'd better head back upstairs," Hewitt said. "Buck doesn't like to wait for news, good or bad."

There was a general exodus. Harry took his time leaving, because he was curious as to why Weeks was still seated. He was able to overhear the beginning of a conversation.

"It looks like you're going to need a new promotion manager, Milton," Weeks said.

"You're a cold-hearted little bastard, aren't you?" Armstead said. "Well, I like that in a man. So, I'll think about it. But remember, kid, whoever gets the job is gonna be Saigon-bound."

Harry wasn't able to hear Weeks' reply, if there was one.

As he moved past a line of empty secretarial desks, his mind shifted from Weeks' ambition to Grumbacher's innocence. Milton had been right. There'd been no musk smell at Tobella's on the night of the murder. And given that Milton knew this and given that he and Terry had seen Milton driving away from the crime scene, the V.P. had to have been in Tobella's loft very near to the time the two men were being murdered.

30.

Kevin Dobbs was with Trower Buckley in the publisher's fifth-floor office, discussing the approaching party, when Al Hewitt interrupted them with news that two of the magazine's directors had just been arrested.

Dobbs groaned and ran a hand through his crew cut, but Buckley, seated behind a massive Teutonic desk atop a chair with a high, carved back and large oak arm rests, merely raised an eyebrow and said, "Get the ACLU on the phone, pronto. This is nothing but another bloody attack on the First Amendment rights of—"

"It's got nothing to do with censorship," Hewitt said. "Your Promotion Manager, Beagle, tried to kill Armstead."

"But he didn't succeed?" Buckley asked.

"No," Hewitt said, noting the look of disappointment on Dobbs' face. "Two homicide detectives subdued and disarmed him. They were here to arrest the Assistant Promotion Manager, Maurice Grumbacher, for killing the sculptor—I think Tobella was the name—and his friend."

Buckley frowned. He looked down at his left hand and, as an afterthought, removed the signet ring from his fourth finger and screwed it onto his index finger. He tapped both ring and finger on the wooden arm rest and was quite satisfied with the effect. "Better get a shrink for this Beagle and a lawyer for . . . the other fella. You suppose he did kill Tobella?"

"Armstead doesn't think so."

"Well then," Buckley said. "Now, to return to the party . . ."

"The party?" Dobbs asked. "With all this murder in the air?"

"Haven't you ever wanted to kill Milton?"

"Well, yes, but—"

"So, the only real problem is this . . . other fella," Buckley said. "And Milton says he didn't do it. Even if he were guilty as Oswald, what would that have to do with my party?"

Dobbs looked to Hewitt for help, but, since the editor had been treating him like a pariah, the ex-archbishop was disinclined to offer any. He merely stood there smiling bemusedly.

"It's just that . . . a party, a celebration as it were, seems a little inappropriate with murder on our doorstep," the editor said.

"No, Kevin. Inappropriate is when you cancel a gala because you harbor a doubt that an *Ogle* executive would be capable of murder. Inappropriate is when you lose faith in your home team. Get me?"

Dobbs nodded, but he clearly wasn't happy.

"So, Al, here's an idea I have," Buckley said, turning to Hewitt. "Ever see that album cover of Noel Coward standing on the desert outside of Las Vegas with a tea cup in his hand?"

"I may have," Hewitt said. "He was appearing at a casino?"

"Exactly," Buckley said. "The juxtaposition of this limey fruiter in a tuxedo, dapper as hell, sipping tea in swinging Vegas, it spells Class with a capital 'C.' So here's my take on it. I'll be going formal in a dinner jacket, standing in the center of a swimming pool, water up to my cummerbund, holding a glass of champagne and, here's the kicker, I'll be surrounded by naked Eyefuls. What do you think?"

"Class with a capital 'C,' " Hewitt said.

"You're a . . . respected captain of industry, Buck," Dobbs protested. "This is the wrong image for—"

"Bullshit!" Buckley said. "It fits the magazine's image perfectly."

"The magazine's image, yes," Dobbs agreed. "I was thinking of your personal image. And the message it may convey to potential stockholders when *Ogle* goes on the Big Board."

"I have created one of the most successful magazines in America, Kevin, built solely on the image and likeness of me. *Ogle* and I are one. It is based on a dream I had way back when I was attending Stanford."

This was, Hewitt had discovered during a long, fruitful search through assorted newspaper articles, a revisionist account of the magazine's creation. Trower J. Buckley had been born into the quietly successful West Coast law firm of Buckley and Buckley, the only son of Algernon Buckley, Junior, the sole grandson of irascible Algernon Buckley, Senior, who'd announced to the family when the boy had barely struggled through UCLA (not Stanford) that his grandson would have to be written off as an income tax deduction for the rest of his life.

World War II delayed that prophecy. During the years of young draftee Trower's tour, he'd been lucky enough to be assigned to the *Stars and Stripes* newspaper in Europe, where, while fulfilling the approximate duties of a copy boy, he got his first whiff of fresh newsprint.

Post V-J Day, Algy, Senior's appraisal seemed to be dead on. Trower had served only one week with the family law firm, in the most junior position one might imagine, when he'd fallen asleep with a lit cigarette, prompting a conflagration that destroyed most of the books in the firm's library and the library itself. To his grandfather's further dismay, young Trower had escaped with little more than an inflamed throat from smoke inhalation.

His father, acting on Trower's vague fondness for literature, secured an editorial position for him with the West Coast office of a leading Manhattan publishing house. That had ended quite abruptly with a one-million-dollar lawsuit over a seemingly innocent misquote that he had let slip in an unauthorized biography of a great, if litigious, lady of the silver screen. The lawsuit had been initiated and won by the firm of Buckley and Buckley. It was the only time old Algy had looked on his grandson with kindness.

Finally there was *Ogle,* created on a whim fueled by the enthusiasm of a friend from college, Ida Connor, and two Lake Shore Country Club chums who contributed money to the start-up, Milton Armstead and the late Remy Laggerloff.

Trower's father had put up his end of the funding in the belief that the magazine would resemble *The Atlantic Monthly,* a periodical that he treated with the same respect as the King James version of the Good Book. Trower had outlined the basic format—strong contemporary fiction, proper social commentary, reviews.

When the first issue of *Ogle* hit the stalls, with its cover photo of Diane Webber frolicking in the surf at Malibu, naked as a melon and brown as a berry, Trower's dad took down the family shingle that had been hanging in Los Angeles for almost a hundred years and moved to Santa Barbara to spend his remaining years in relative seclusion. Trower's grandfather, mercifully, had died two months prior to the magazine's debut.

Against Algy Buckley's fondest wishes, *Ogle* had caught on, following in the frothy wake of the pacemaker, the Big Rabbit in Chicago. Trower was so pleased with his success that any trace of previous failures had been completely scrubbed from his mind if not from the permanent record. Furthermore, he was convinced that *Ogle*'s amazing readership had nothing at all to do with the great American fondness for voyeuristic sex, but rather was based on his uncanny knack for knowing the precise elements in proper combination that made for magazine greatness. It was all relative to his undeniable taste.

"In the swim, with a bunch of nude women, Buck?" Dobbs said. "At a time we're trying to take the magazine public?"

Buckley's brow furrowed. "I've yet to make a decision about going public with *Ogle.*"

"I know that," Dobbs said.

"I'm not sure I want a bunch of Babbits thinking that their single share of *Ogle* stock gives them the right to tell me how to run my magazine. In case the point was lost on you, Kevin, let me underline it. I don't like anyone telling me how to run my magazine."

"Got it," Dobbs said.

"Al, would you put Carlos to work selecting the Eyefuls? I want to look them over first."

Hewitt already had a little notepad in hand. Jotting down the assignment, he said, "I'll talk to Ida about legal and mental assistance for the two men in custody, too."

"Fine, but talk to Carlos first," Buckley said, returning his attention to Dobbs. "Now, where can we find a location for our little party?"

"We have a small kidney-sha—" Dobbs began.

"Didn't you tell me you and your wife had gone swimming at your friend, ex-Governor Moody's? Big, sprawling place in the Palisades?"

Dobbs paled. "You know how politicians are when it comes to even the mildest form of controversy. A lot of naked girls in his pool . . ."

"Get it for me, Dobbs."

"Why don't Al and I see what other pools are out there?" he said. "Maybe we can get Sinatra's? I hear Andy Williams has a beautiful—"

"Frank and Andy are great guys, and they can sing the hell out of a song, but I'm the star of this show," Buckley said.

"I bet we can find some really exotic pool. Maybe with a waterfall or a black sand bottom."

"Kevin, you know that ridiculous little piece of avant-garde trash you're always raving about? Poetry. Enigmatic fiction. Back to the womb bullshit. Interviews with pretentious assholes."

"*Moonbeam?*"

"*Moonbeam.* How would you like to edit *Moonbeam*, Kevin?"

"Well . . . ha . . . as if I'd give up my job here . . . ha, ha."

"*Moonbeam*'s publisher has run out of chips," Buckley said. "The rag's on the block with a hefty backlog of manuscripts and poetry and art. I might just reel it in."

"But . . . you don't even like it."

"It has a certain cachet. And we can always use a tax write-off. But we weren't talking about *Moonbeam*, were we? What were we . . . oh, yes. You were saying you'd do me a personal favor and get the ex-governor's house and pool for our party. Right?"

Dobbs gulped and nodded.

"Of course, I'll want a tour of the place. Check out the lay of the la—"

"Buck?" Angel stood at the door, teary-eyed, wringing her hands. "We gotta talk, right now."

"Come on over here, baby," the publisher said, taking her into his arms. "These boys are going to get to work on my party, while you tell the old Buckaroo what the problem is."

Angel broke down into sobs as the two men left the room. She was just starting to interrupt the sobs with words when Dobbs pulled the door shut.

"There's no way I can ask George Moody to host a party with nude women," he whined.

"The worst he can say is 'no.' " Hewitt was still wondering about the cause of Angel's distress.

"The man's my friend. Do you think you might ask him . . . ?"

"I never even heard of Moody until five minutes ago," Hewitt said. "He's much more likely to respond positively to a friend's request. He knows you work here, right?"

Dobbs nodded.

"Just bring up the subject casually. Feel him out."

"I don't know if I can do it," Dobbs said.

"I guess it depends on how much you want to edit the little magazine," Hewitt said, heading down the hall to the stairwell.

Dobbs dragged himself past the suddenly busy editors and into his office. There, he paused before a bookshelf that held every issue of *Moonbeam* since its inception. It was in that twenty-year-old debut issue that the first published fiction of a hopeful young writer named Kevin Dobbs had appeared.

He sighed, crossed to his desk and dialed the ex-governor's number.

After a bit of badinage, he managed to stumble through the request.

To his surprise, the middle-aged pol was delighted with the idea.

"Won't Hilda—?" Dobbs began.

"Hilda? Well, I think I'll just have to send Hilda and the girl away to our place in the Springs. Wouldn't want them getting in the way of . . . the photographers."

Dobbs replaced the phone, a bit saddened that his friend seemed so eager for the party. His mood lifted as he cast his eyes again on the shelved copies of *Moonbeam*. He, Kevin Dobbs, was going to be the new editor of the nation's most avant-garde literary quarterly.

In *Ogle*'s photo studio, the ex-archbishop was experiencing a slightly different mood swing. He'd approached the high-ceilinged area, vividly recalling the trauma of his last visit. That had been only a short while ago, but he was a different man now, with an understanding of how the game was played. If Carlos tried something like that on him today, the sleazy photographer might not be so pleased with the result.

He strode through the studio's swinging doors to find Carlos and Florence Proneswagger, frantically digging through a large file cabinet, tossing glossies and contact sheets onto a growing pile at their feet.

"What's up?" he asked.

Miss Proneswagger barely gave the ex-archbishop a glance, but Carlos whirled around, startled. Seeing it was only Hewitt, he exhaled and went back to his work.

"Buck must've just called down here, huh?" Hewitt said.

They both froze.

"W-w-what you mean?" Carlos asked.

"Aren't you looking for Eyefuls for the party?" Hewitt asked.

Carlos blinked and said, "Shit!"

Miss Proneswagger said, "Eyefuls?"

"Right. He'd like a list of . . . what the heck is going on here?"

"Shit," Carlos said.

Miss Proneswagger, her chin quivering, said, "We have a little problem."

"Gee, that's too bad," Hewitt said, rather enjoying their obvious panic. "Anything I can do to help."

"Shit," Carlos said, returning to his search.

"It's your problem, too," Miss Proneswagger said. "It seems as though someone has broken into the file cabinet and stolen all of Carlos' special photos."

"The ones with Angel and male employees?"

"You got it," Miss Proneswagger said.

"They're not just misplaced?"

"Apparently not," Miss Proneswagger said, gesturing to the now-empty cabinet.

"Shit," the ex-archbishop said.

"Amen," Carlos said.

31.

"So you think what? That Armstead offed the two queers?" Roger Weeks was asking Harry in their office.

"Well, he all but admitted he was there."

"So, let's assume we're working for a homicidal maniac," Weeks said. "How can we use this information?"

"Use it? Jesus. In the first place, we don't know for certain he's a homicidal maniac. Well, a maniac, maybe. But—"

He was interrupted by the co-publicist Lew Mitteer bursting into their office. "Okay?" he asked, pointing to the phone on Weeks' desk.

At Weeks' nod, he held the receiver to his chest as though it were a chalice and said, almost apologetically, "Cholly's got mine tied up, and this is really a burner. I gotta buzz my dentist."

They watched the tall, sad-faced man while he dialed a string of numbers.

"Dr. Spleen, please," he said into the receiver. "Yeah, I'm a patient." He gave his name and asked if the results of his test had come in.

Evidently they had because his brow furled even further. "What's that, honey? Oh, yeah, your pictures. I showed 'em to Mr. Buckley himself. He said you got the most soigné set of knockers he'd seen this year. Praise from Caesar . . . Oh, hello, doc, I didn't know you were on the line . . . Huh? Oh, sure, if she says it's okay we'd be glad to show you the pictures . . . Right, we're like doctors ourselves, all day long looking at naked broads, uh, ladies . . . Right. But actually, you asked me to phone about my tests . . ."

Lew shut up for nearly half a minute, then, in apparent re-action to Dr. Spleen's report, his mouth dropped open like Tchaikovsky's Nutcracker. "Oh, sweet Jesus," he exclaimed. He paused, squeezed his eyes shut and caught his breath. "No, I'm okay, doc. But you hit me pretty hard. There's no other way? . . . Well, if you say so, I wanna get started on it right away."

Lew hung up the phone. He looked as if he was about to pass out.

"What's up?" Roger Weeks asked, more curious than empa-thetic.

"My choppers," Lew said, showing them as unattractive a set of teeth as one might find their side of the Atlantic. "Unless I get in there today to have eleven of 'em yanked, they all are gonna go."

"Why?" Harry asked.

"A, uh, condition called pie-something. Some Dago name. Like the old joke: the teeth are fine but the gums have gotta go."

"Hey, Lew," Cholly said, poking his big head into the room. "You think you could stick around your desk, huh? I'm busy fielding all the goddamn calls about Beagle and Grumbacher. Got no time to be your goddamn errand boy, for Cri' Pete. You got a call."

"Who?"

"Buckley. He wants you up there."

Lew Mitteer darted away, leaving just a hint of oral decay in his wake.

Buckley was in the den with Angel. They were stretched out on a sofa before a dark television set. The young woman was lean-ing forward, sobbing, and the publisher was trying to calm her by massaging her temples with his fingers.

"Uh. Hi guys," Lew said to let them know he was there. "What's the . . . ?"

His sentence trailed off with the discovery of an object on the coffee table. Raymond, Angel's pet frog, was lying on a tiny foam rubber pillow, flat on his back.

Lew thought the little critter was dead but one of its long, skinny legs gave a sudden twitch.

"What's up with Raymond?" Lew asked.

Angel began to weep afresh, her gown parting with each wracking sob. Lew tried to keep his eyes from exploring that impossibly perfect body but . . .

"You're not here to gawk, Lew," Buckley said in a cold fury. "Raymond's got intestinal problems, *dammit.* Some sort of disorder. I've already sent for the vet, the best in the city."

Lew ran a hand over the bottom of his face. The skin felt warm. From the diseased gums? "Uh, how can I help?"

"Angel is very upset. I have to . . . administer to her in the bedroom and I want you to keep your eye peeled on Raymond until the vet arrives."

"Right," Lew said. "Uh, isn't your new assistant—?"

"My assistant is busy handling little matters like the party and getting our guys freed from the hoosegow. Is this more than you can handle, Lew?"

"It's just that my dentist tells me unless I get in to see him today, chances are I'll lose all my choppers and wind up gum—"

"Where's your sensitivity, man? Raymond is sick. Can you help us on this or not?"

"Sure," Lew said. "No problem."

When they departed for the privacy of the bedroom, Lew removed his coat, pulled down his tie and snapped the button off his collar. Then he phoned Dr. Spleen and told him the periodontal surgery would have to be postponed.

"I understand," Lew said in reply to the doctor's warning that time was not on his side. "I'll get it done soon as I can."

He replaced the receiver and parked on a nearby ottoman to poke a finger at his sore, swollen gums and listen to the music of the day—the lovers mating and Raymond belching.

He was awakened from a reverie of sorts by the arrival of Al Hewitt, who seemed surprised to find him there.

"Hi," he said, looking around the living room. A bit nervously, Lew thought. "Everything . . . okay?"

"I guess. If you don't count my teeth getting yanked and the frog dying."

"I, ah, was thinking more of Buck. Is he okay?"

"Sure. That's him you hear, making like Flynn in the bedroom."

"With Angel?"

"Who else?" Lew said.

"Good. He's not upset about anything? Besides the frog?"

Lew frowned, a little suspicious now. "Like what?"

"Nothing. Nothing." Hewitt gave him a brief, unconvincing smile. "I'll just . . . go to my room."

Lew watched the man make an awkward exit, wondering what was twisting his knickers, but not enough to give it any serious thought.

It wasn't much later that the vet made his house call.

Dr. Christian Phillipe was a thin, pale man with dandruff and a habit of sniffling. He took one look at Raymond, sniffed mightily and shook his head. "Your frog is on his last leg," he told Lew.

"Point of fact, doc, it's not my frog."

"Then I must speak to the owner immediately."

"He's a little, uh, engaged right now," Lew said, but the rest of the apartment was now mercifully silent.

"Not too engaged to save this little fellow's life, I hope?"

Lew shrugged and dragged himself in the direction of Buckley's bedroom. He gave a half-hearted knock.

No answer.

Another knock. Harder this time.

Again, no answer.

He was about to knock again when the door was thrown open and Buckley was facing him, clad only in flaming red silk jockeys and black socks.

"What's so bloody important?" he wanted to know.

"The . . . vet . . . he wants to speak with you."

"Me?"

"Raymond's owner."

"Raymond belongs to Angel. *Dammit,* Lew, you should know that. I curse the day I let you talk me into buying the damn frog. He's been nothing but trouble from the jump."

After the door was slammed in his face, Lew went back to the sniffling Dr. Phillipe and Raymond. The little frog was breathing heavily. Lew moved closer to look at him.

"Stay back, man, for God's sake," the vet ordered. "You're breathing toxic fumes on the patient."

Lew retreated quickly, hand over his mouth, trying unsuccessfully to tell if his breath was really that bad.

"What the devil have they been feeding this poor guy?" the vet asked.

"I dunno? Flies?"

"Common houseflies?"

"I guess. I dunno."

"Flies? I must speak with the owner right away."

"She's on her way," Lew said.

It was fifteen minutes before Angel waltzed into the room trailing a lacy peignoir and smelling of Chanel.

The vet took one look at her and leapt to his feet. "What a prize bitch!" he exclaimed.

Lew frowned at the guy. "That kinda crude shit don't float here, doc."

Dr. Phillipe used a wet dog–like body shake to bring himself out of the trance. "Sorry if I offended," he mumbled. "I spend so much time in the animal kingdom."

He refocused his attention on the little frog.

A robed and slippered Buckley shuffled into the room. "What's the word, doc?"

The vet dropped to his knees beside the coffee table, his face just a few inches from the infirmed frog. He removed a jeweler's loupe from his pocket and gave the critter a closer look, muttering something indecipherable.

"W-what's wrong with him?" Angel asked.

Keeping his eyes averted from her, Dr. Phillipe said, "There is a surgeon in Boston, Dr. Garson Zoach. You've probably heard of him. He was on Johnny Carson. He's done miraculous things with ill frogs. In the *Lancet*—"

"Never mind all that," Buckley said. "Lew, get this Zoach here on the next plane."

"Nononono," the vet said. "Dr. Zoach never flies, not even in cases of emergency. Perhaps he would travel here by train . . . but that would take too long. This frog needs immediate—"

"Lew," Buckley ordered, "throw some dough at this Loach and get him here tonight."

"He won't come," the vet said.

Buckley looked at the man as though he wasn't quite sure he believed him. Then he shrugged. "I can respect a man's idiosyncrasies." He turned to Lew. "Get on the horn to the airlines. Reserve a seat for Raymond and Angel. First class."

"A trained professional should be in attendance on the flight, also," Dr. Phillipe said.

"Make that three tickets, Lew," Buckley said.

Angel looked at the publisher with shining eyes. "You're some sweet son-of-a-bitch," she said.

This Buckley did not deny. Instead, he shouted to Mitteer, "And be sure to notify Zoach that little Raymond is on his way. Tell him anything happens to that frog and we expose him and his clinic to four million American men in the pages of *Ogle*."

Lew Mitteer left the apartment in a cold sweat, his pulsating gums no longer his main concern.

Securing passage for Raymond aboard a plane posed no real problem. The travel agent pointed out that airline rules allowed for only one animal or creature in first class per departure. Luckily, no other amphibians were seeking transport on the desired flight.

Next came the call to Dr. Zoach. The doctor was anxious to see Raymond. He cautioned, however, that the case sounded extremely serious, and there was the possibility that Raymond might be left paralyzed, never to hop again, or worse yet, he could wind up on that great lily pad in the sky.

"Doc, lemme tell ya," Lew said. "You fix the goddamned frog and there's an extra grand in it for you." Personally, Lew felt that frogs were only good for two things—catching flies and providing legs for a meal. But he definitely did not need the tsuris that a dead Raymond would cause and accounting wouldn't even blink at a request for a thou to save the life of Buckley's pet.

Later, at the airport, Angel very realistically faced facts. Dressed in a smart white pantsuit, white pillbox hat and no sign of underwear, and trying to keep the sniffling vet from brushing against her "accidentally," she cradled a small, cotton-lined box in which Raymond rested. Her eyes were moist with tears as she called Lew's name.

"Yeah," he answered.

"Suppose, Raymond d-i-e-z?"

The box gave a little twitch. Lew wasn't sure what to tell her.

"Oh, dear and gentle Jesus," she offered, eyes skyward, "you must have other frogs to keep you company in heaven. Please don't take my little Raymond."

"Look, kid," Lew said. "He's gonna pull through. Right, doc?"

Dr. Phillipe stared down Angel's blouse and said, "If not, I am poised to provide comfort."

A garbled voice informed them that their flight was ready for boarding.

Just before entering the little portable tunnel leading to the plane's belly, Angel paused. "Lew?" she asked in an anxious voice.

"Yeah, honey?" Lew responded, fearing the worst.

"Lew? Can they stuff frogs?"

"Stuff?"

"You know. With cotton or sawdust or whatever? For the mantel?"

Lew looked at her for a long minute before he said, "I'll check it out."

32.

At a little after eight that night, Harry was feverishly typing at his desk when he was distracted by a strangely appealing combination of odors. Camellias and *whiskey*.

Terry O'Mara was sitting in Roger Weeks' chair, an old-fashioned in one hand, smiling at him. "Hi," she said. "I come bearing gifts."

She pointed at a twin of her cocktail resting on his desk.

"This is gift, singular," he said, picking up the drink.

"What am I, chopped liver?"

"Is there an Irish version of chopped liver?" he asked.

"What am I, corned beef and cabbage?" she said.

He leaned forward to clink his glass against hers.

"Do you resent my interrupting your work?"

"Of course not," he lied.

"Then let me push it a little. Come with me to Herkie's."

"Right this minute?"

She nodded. "Stooley's over there. I think he knows where Howard Bethune is and he may be drunk enough to tell us. If we get there before he passes out."

"Remind me why we want to know Bethune's whereabouts," Harry said, carefully removing the page from his typewriter.

"Clearly he's the link between Nick's murder and Joe's," she said.

"Nobody but you is saying Hobart was murdered."

"Then humor me. Nick was my friend and so were Joe and Orlando."

There wasn't much argument wiggle room in that. He placed his manuscript pages back into a folder and slipped the folder into a drawer.

"It seems obvious to me," she said. "Joe's statue mysteriously falls on Nick. And then, on the same night that he and Orlando are murdered, Howard, Nick's successor, runs away somewhere? That's some coincidence."

"The two homicide cops must have talked to Bethune by now," Harry said.

"Maybe they have; maybe they haven't. I say we find out where Howard is and if he's within driving distance, we go see him. If not, we try to reach him by phone and . . ."

She stood up suddenly and went to the door, looking out into the darkened outer office.

"What?" he asked.

"I thought I heard somebody. Guess not. You coming, or do I start trolling for some other great-looking guy to while away the midnight hours?"

"Some choice." He took a gulp of cocktail and carried the glass from the office, following her.

She paused at the reception desk, distracting the night watchman from his paperback. "Anybody in the building tonight besides us, T.J.?" she asked.

T.J. frowned, putting his mind to it. "Well, Mr. Armstead's in his office. I think Carlos is in photography. Mr. Dobbs hasn't checked out yet. Probably working late up in Editorial. Mr. Buckley and the new fella, Al—Mr. Hewitt—must be up in the penthouse. That's about it. There a problem?"

"Not at all," Terry said.

Stooley was at a table in the kitchen. His blackened eyes had healed to a yellowish smudge and there was a strip of plaster on his nose. Seated with him were Terry's uncle Colin and another crony, a whiskery codger new to Harry.

Willem the chef stopped glaring at the trio long enough to give Terry a half smile. "The boss gone to movies," he said.

"The new Francoise Dorleac?" Terry asked.

"Of course."

"Good hunk o' cow, chef," Stooley shouted their way.

The compliment was lost on Willem. He glared at the reporter and mumbled, "Man so busy talking he don't know if he eats prime beef or suet."

The reporter was momentarily silent while he chewed the steak and stared at them. The unknown crony took that opportunity to rest his head on the table and go to sleep. Colin, who'd been doing more drinking than eating, judging by his nearly untouched plate, waved them over.

"Who's that with you, Red?" Stooley asked Terry, studying Harry.

"Th' new boyfren'," Colin said. "Harry Somethin' not Irish."

"Harry Trauble," Harry said.

"I know that name," Stooley used his knife to indicate empty chairs. "Join us," he said around a mouthful of steak.

They squeezed in between Colin and the old duffer asleep on the table. "If you don't mind, Red," Stooley said, "check Fannon every now and then to see if he's still breathin'."

The reporter turned his ice blue eyes on Harry. They were surprisingly clear and bright. "Trauble. You work over at the Frog House, eh?"

"You know the names of all the *Ogle* employees?" Harry asked.

"Just the ones the cops visit in connection with the Tobella case. What did Cardona and Oskar want with you, anyway?"

"What makes you think they wanted anything?"

Stooley smiled. "I buy a lot of hats for guys at Robbery Homicide. They keep me up to date. Your turn. What'd the dicks want?"

"They asked me if I knew the victims. I told 'em I'd never met 'em."

"That it?"

Harry could see no reason not to mention what Cardona had been after. "They'd heard I was at a shouting match between Tobella and Maurice Grumbacher. Grumbacher is a—"

"I know who he is," Stooley said. His interest seemed to have shifted from Harry back to the remains of his dinner.

Harry wanted to keep the conversation going. "They arrested Grumbacher today," he said.

Stooley paused with the forkful of steak on its way to his mouth. "And kicked him loose about three hours ago."

"I got the impression he was top of their list," Harry said.

"Yeah, well, my guess is the witness couldn't ID 'im," Stooley said.

"Witness?" Harry asked.

"Yeah. Nobody's coughed up a name yet. But I've got feelers out."

"Howard Bethune, maybe?" Terry said.

"Naw. Cardona found Bethune up the coast a couple days ago and grilled him. Wrote him off."

"You didn't interview Bethune?" Harry asked.

"What'd be the pernt of driving all the way out to the nudist farm? Cardona's a hard-nosed prick but he knows how to copper. He says the guy's got zip, he's got zip."

"The nudist farm?" Harry asked.

"Yeah. Bunch o' goddamn nudists and beatniks squattin' on this hunk of prime real estate up near Morro Bay."

"Howard Bethune with nudists and beatniks?" Terry said. "Hard to imagine that match-up. Ballroom dancers would be

219

more like it."

Stooley stopped mid-chew. He stared at Terry for a beat, then grinned and swallowed. "I hope you're not sayin' Stooley gets his facts wrong, Red. That's not gonna happen in this lifetime. This Bethune bird ain't struttin' himself in no ballroom. He's—"

The crime reporter was distracted from finishing his sentence by a woman rushing toward their table. She was in her thirties, thin and wiry, and she walked in a masculine fast stride. Her short brown hair and round, tortoise-shell glasses weren't in style, but they seemed to work for her. She said, "The game's afoot, Sherlock."

"Worth my indigestion?" Stooley said, pushing back from the table.

"And then some."

"Where you goin'?" Colin shouted as the fat man followed the woman to the door. "You got pie comin'."

"Tell 'em to keep it warm for me," Stooley said, disappearing into the bar area with a speed and agility Harry found surprising in a supposedly inebriated fat man.

"What put th' bee in his britches," Colin said. "Never known him to cut a meal short before."

"Too bad," Harry said to Terry. "Another minute and he'd have narrowed down Bethune's location for us."

She seemed to ignore his statement. "Are you gonna eat your creamed spinach, Uncle?"

"Definitely not," the old man said.

She searched for and found an unused spoon on the table. Sampling the gooey greens, she asked, "How many 'beatnik' farms could there be near Morro Bay?"

Harry shrugged. "Maybe if we had a spare week or two, we could find out."

"Well, we'll just have to wait for Stooley to come back for his pie."

"That could take a week, too," Harry said.

"Don't be such a pessimist," she said, finishing her uncle's spinach. "He could be back before you know—see?"

Stooley had just entered the kitchen and was barreling toward them. Only slightly out of breath, he reclaimed his chair, staring at Harry with a hunger that he'd previously reserved for his meal. "You got a green Mustang convertible parked on Bellville Street?"

"Yeah. Why? Something happen to it?" Harry was in the midst of rising, but Stooley waved him down.

"Your car's okay," the crime reporter said. "It's just that somebody tossed a stiff onto your backseat."

33.

She was being dangerously foolish, Ida Connor knew, but the feel of Milton deep inside her was simply too extravagantly glorious to deny. She fooled herself into thinking she'd entered his office to discuss the next step in their plan to have Trower Buckley committed. But he'd known immediately what she was after, even if she hadn't.

There had been no hesitation on his part. He'd shut the door and moved toward her. He knew not to smile or say a word, knew to pull her roughly toward him, to take her in his arms and kiss her deeply. Just the way she'd wanted. It was his true genius.

She'd been vaguely aware of her notebook falling to the carpet, but had no memory of how they'd wound up on the couch. The feel of his body, hard and warm against hers came as even more of a surprise, since she did not recall them removing their clothes.

God, this was dangerous.

If . . . someone were to see them . . .

Then she felt Milton slide inside her, filling her, completing her and she thought of nothing else but the magical sensation coursing through her as she rose to meet his thrusts with a hunger more powerful than even mother love.

Later, lying beside him on the couch, her body drying under the central air conditioner's cool breath, she heard him say, "I feel like that guy in the story about the three spoonfuls of sugar."

"I don't think I've heard that one," she said.

"All his life, he's been putting two spoons of sugar in his coffee. One day he forgets and puts in an extra spoonful. And it's the best goddamned thing he's ever tasted. But instead of being happy, he's pissed off at how many great cups of coffee he's missed."

"You're saying I'm the best goddamned thing you've ever tasted?" she asked.

"Like honey from the hive."

"Ready for another sip?" she asked.

He shifted on the couch and she could see that he was.

The phone rang.

His hand rose along her inner thigh. He bent his head and caught her right nipple between his teeth.

The phone rang again.

The nipple was freed. "God*DAMMit!*" Armstead yelled, pulling away from her, rolling onto the carpet.

With a groan he rose and grabbed the noisy instrument. "WHAT?" he roared into the receiver.

Almost immediately, his temper cooled. "Right," he said, moving his hand near the dimmed desk lamp. He consulted his wristwatch and said to the caller, "Right, Buck. I . . . got a little sidetracked. I'm heading up now."

He placed the phone on its cradle and smiled at Ida. "Well, maybe not now now."

He moved to rejoin her, but for her the bloom was off the rose. She slid from the couch and began searching the carpet for her clothes. "What's Buck got cooking?" she asked.

"The fucking party." He seemed in no particular hurry. He lit one of his black cigarettes and sat down on the couch, naked, watching her dress with a wolfish smile on his face.

"No one mentioned a party meeting to me," she said.

"This is a boys-only get together, where we go over the guest list and make sure it's filled with fuckable ladies."

"Lovely," she said, adjusting her skirt.

"You'll definitely be at the top of my list."

"Bastard."

"Why don't we go together?" he asked.

"As a couple, you mean, for all the world to see?"

He nodded.

"Won't that crimp your style?"

He stood, smashed the cigarette in an ashtray and took her in his arms. "I set my own style," he said.

She gave him a peck on the cheek and slipped from his arms. "Let's see how we feel come party day," she said and left him standing there wearing only a bemused smile.

To use the elevator, she'd have to pass T.J.'s inspection at the front desk, so she opted for the stairs. In her private bathroom, she took a quick shower, redressed, applied new makeup and sat down at her desk.

She stared at the brown intercom for a beat, then clicked on the little switch at its rear. The special wiring she'd had installed did its thing and Kevin Dobbs' whiny voice rattled through the small speaker in mid-sentence. ". . . don't feel comfortable with that."

"Then leave early." This was Trower Buckley's voice. "It's my bloody party.

"And look who finally deemed us worthy of his presence."

"Sorry I'm late, Buck," Armstead replied. "Something came up."

"I'll bet. You look like a cat who's just eaten someone. Who was she?"

"You know I don't kiss and tell, Buck."

"Bullshit. You always kiss and tell."

"Not this time."

"That special, eh? Now I am curious. C'mon, give."

"What say we drop it?"

"Your call, old sport," Buckley said. "So let's get down to the business at hand."

Ida frowned. She was flattered by the obvious shift in Armstead's attitude toward her. But she wasn't looking for a romantic entanglement with the man, merely a nice, occasional roll in the hay.

She'd have to think of a way of turning him off without ruffling his plumage. Meanwhile . . .

She settled back and eavesdropped on the boys planning their little soiree.

34.

"I saw Lemming with a lovely blonde piece a few weeks ago," Buck was saying. "Anyone know who she is?"

"Lemming's wife Janice, probably," Kevin Dobbs said. "Bit of a nymph, I understand. Good stock, though. Plays tennis every day at the Jonathan. Father is on the board at—"

" 'Nymph' will suffice," Buckley said. "Take a note, Al. Let's make her an exception to the 'no-spouse' rule."

Of the five men in Buckley's office—Buckley, Dobbs, Armstead, ad director John Bingham and himself—the brainless chore of keeping the invitation list had fallen to Hewitt. A good thing it required little thought, because he was drunk. "I 'sume we invite Scotty, too?" he asked.

Buckley frowned. "That may be a problem. I can't stand the little creep."

"Send him to San Francisco on some senseless errand," Milton Armstead said.

"Perfect. Make a note of that, too, Al."

Earlier that evening, Hewitt had more or less made up his mind to pack quietly and leave before the presumably stolen semi-pornographic photos of Angel and himself found their way to Buckley's desk. The man had been more than generous to him and he didn't want to have to witness Buckley's reaction to his perceived betrayal. Also, he'd seen enough of the publisher's hair-trigger anger to understand some bodily injury could result.

But once back at the suite, where the emphasis was on Raymond the sick frog and not on any incriminating photos, Hewitt had decided to press his luck and stick around a little longer.

He had nowhere else to go.

Still, he'd tensed a bit when he'd heard Buckley yell from down the hall, "Come on in here, Al. On the double."

The editor-publisher was standing near the door to his office, scowling, with one hand hidden behind his back. "Angel's gone to Boston with Raymond," he said. "You and I are here all alone and so, the time has come."

The ex-archbishop tried to remain calm.

A grin broke on Buckley's face and his hand appeared offering a delicate glass filled with a clear fluid and one olive on a pick. "Martini time."

Awash with relief, Al Hewitt accepted the glass.

"Only alkies drink alone," Buckley said, lifting his own martini from the desktop.

They clinked glasses and Hewitt had his first sip of gin. It was surprisingly aromatic and surprisingly tasty. He had to stop himself from downing the whole thing immediately.

"Sit down, Al," Buckley said, taking a chair himself. "Some of the guys are dropping by at any minute to talk about the party. After that, we'll have to figure out something to amuse ourselves. Maybe get a couple broads and go check out Mort at the Crescendo."

Hewitt didn't know who Mort was, or what he, or anybody, did at the Crescendo, whatever that was, but the plan sounded fine to him. He replenished their glasses. These martinis were all right.

There were only a few hits left in the pitcher and he was pleased that Dobbs and Bingham both turned down Buckley's offer of a drink when they arrived. Clearly, neither was in a festive mood.

"I'm not sure why I'm here, Buck," Bingham said. "We're

not going to be inviting advertisers.'"

"Why the hell not?" Buckley asked.

"I was told there would be nudity."

"Damn well better be. It's what we're famous for."

"Of course," said Bingham, his face a bright red. "I just didn't think you'd want a bunch of squares showing up to . . . slow things down."

"Mmmm. I see your point," Buckley said. "But we've got to have advertisers, or it won't qualify as a business expense."

"I can probably come up with some, uh, swinging ad guys," Bingham said.

"Give their names to Al. He's the list-keeper."

Which is how Hewitt discovered he was not there merely to drain the martini pitcher.

Armstead arrived nearly half an hour after the others, looking both rumpled and oddly relaxed. It quickly became obvious that he was Buckley's master of revels, his first suggestion being the employment of Zorina, a legendary Hollywood madam whose courtesans had been transformed by delicate surgery to resemble the most desirable actresses of the era.

"Hookers?" Bingham said. "Buck, please. That's exactly the wrong im—"

The phone rang and Buckley held up a quieting hand before answering it. "This could be Angel."

He put a cheesy smile on his face and lifted the receiver. "Trower Buckley here," he said.

Immediately, the smile was replaced with a furrowed brow. "Police? Why . . . ?"

The room went quiet. Like the other three men, Hewitt was staring at Buckley.

"Good Lord! Well, I don't know . . . Just a minute." He held the phone to his chest, as if that might serve the same purpose as putting the caller on hold. "Did we have somebody named

Proneswagger working here?"

The word "Police" had dulled Hewitt's martini glow. Buckley's use of the past tense brought him to total sobriety. "Florence Proneswagger," he said. "A secretary in Photography."

"She was in our Photography Department," Buckley told his caller. Hewitt could hear a responding chirp from the other end. "Where have *I* been? Right here in this goddamned building for the last five hours. Are you suggesting I may have strangled this woman I never heard of?"

Strangled? Al Hewitt made a silent request that his God ignore Florence's failings and accept her into heaven. That done, he allowed himself to be puzzled by Buckley's statement. Hadn't Buck known Florence? Hewitt thought so, but couldn't remember what had given him that impression.

"Detective, there are over a hundred people working for *Ogle*. I don't know all of them personally," Buckley was saying. "Who? Harry Trauble?"

He looked at the others. "Harry Trauble one of ours?"

"One of mine, in Promotion," Armstead said. "He dead, too?"

Buckley shook his head. "Trauble works for us," he said into the phone. "Why do you want . . . Oh? Well, I'm gonna send you back to the duty watchman. He's being paid to keep track of who's in the building . . . Of course, detective. Always happy to cooperate with the police."

He replaced the receiver. "Can you believe it? A cop yells murder and our fucking watchman puts him through to me. Doesn't Ida explain to them that nobody gets put through to me?"

"Another murder?" Bingham said.

"Apparently so," Buckley said. "Passersby saw the body lying on the backseat of an open convertible owned by this Trauble."

"My God," Dobbs said, ashen. "Trauble could be hiding out in this building right now. Waiting to kill us all."

"For Christ's sake, Kevin," Armstead said, "I know we don't always hire the best prospects. You're living proof of that. But do you seriously think Trauble would be that dim a bulb—to throttle some bimbo and then leave her there in his own parked car with the top down?"

Buckley slammed a hand down on the desk. "We've wasted enough time on this. Let's get back on track. Milton, you were in the middle of telling us about Madame Zorina."

"Jesus, Buck," Bingham said. "The bodies are piling up and you're still on your party kick?"

"What's one thing got to do with the other?" Buckley asked. "Explain our party philosophy to him, Milton."

Armstead seemed uncharacteristically at a loss for words. "I . . . I like a good blowout as well as the next guy, Buck, but I'm with Johnny on this one. Along with one employee at the funny farm, another just released by the cops and now a dead secretary in the car of one of your junior execs. It's not party time."

"Et tu, Milton?" Buckley said. "What am I not seeing? Al, can you tell me what the problem is?"

Hewitt had only been listening with half an ear. His thoughts were on Florence. Back in his former life, he'd had to administer last rites to a victim of strangulation, a very sweet woman whose husband drank heavily and abused her and one dismally rainy evening killed her. There had been very little evidence left of her patrician profile and none at all of her playful blue eyes and generous smile. Just a grotesque mask with bulging, bloodshot eyeballs and distended tongue.

As unchristian-like as Florence had been, for her to die of strangulation . . . how ghastly. And what had the motive been? Did it have something to do with the missing photographs? He wondered where Carlos was. Alive or dead?

"Earth to Al," Buckley said. "Can you tell me why I shouldn't have a party?"

All eyes were on Hewitt. "It's about timing, Buck," he said. "Florence's death may have had nothing to do with the magazine, but she didn't work at the May Company. She worked here. That's what will make her passing newsworthy. It'll make your party newsworthy, too. And not in a positive way."

"I don't care," Buckley said in childlike petulance. "I'm having the party."

Armstead began to hum a familiar tune that took Hewitt a few seconds to identify as the *Twilight Zone* theme.

"You suggesting I've lost it, Milton?" Buckley almost hissed.

Armstead shrugged. "I don't know, Buck. There was a time it might have occurred to you to offer sympathy to the broad's family. Send flowers. Maybe even go to the fucking funeral. Instead, you want to throw a party."

"I'm not throwing the party because the broad died. I just don't see why her dying means I have to change my plans. I didn't even know her."

"Thinking of parties at a time like this," Bingham said, "it's not . . . normal."

Buckley's eyes began to blink rapidly. "Normal? Fuck normal. I hate normal. Normal is for squares. Normal is bore-ring."

Hewitt caught Armstead exchanging a brief glance with Bingham.

Buckley must have seen it, too. "Fuck all of you!" he shouted. "You don't understand the importance of . . . maintaining . . . an image. The party suggests we're beyond such mundane matters as sorrow or worry or fear. We're on this planet to enjoy ourselves. How did Christ put it, Al?"

"I'm not sure which quote you're thinking of, Buck."

"The one about pleasure being the be-all and the end-all."

"That doesn't sound much like Jesus," Hewitt said. "Possibly Epicurus. Or Ba'al."

"No matter," Buckley said. "It's the thought that counts. Tell me, Al, what is it out in that car? Is it a woman, someone we should have feeling for? Or is it just a pile of dead meat?"

"I suppose you could say that with the animas having departed—"

"The animas. That's like the essence, the soul, right? Yeah. So, here's the deal. You can go weeping and gnashing your teeth at some funeral for a soulless pile of rotting meat. Or you can come to my party and have one hell of a good time. Up to you. But I want to know your decision now."

Bingham and Dobbs both voted for the party.

"Milton?"

"Wouldn't miss it for the world," Armstead said.

35.

"Sit down, bucko," Stooley was saying to Harry. "The stiff's not goin' anywhere. And neither are the cops. You can spend a couple minutes with me first."

Terry was gesturing for him to sit, too. She was still working on getting Bethune's precise location from the reporter.

"But they're probably looking for me," Harry said.

"It won't help 'em much to find you," Stooley said. "Unless . . . you choked the lady."

"I've been here with you," Harry said.

"They haven't figured out the time of the murder yet," Stooley said. "Corpse looked pretty fresh."

"I was at my desk across the street since just after lunch," Harry said, hoping he didn't sound too defensive. "Then Terry inter—came by and we walked over here."

"You know the Proneswagger dame?"

"I . . . was talking to her earlier today," Terry said. She seemed quite affected by the murder. Harry thought she was on the verge of tears. He'd never seen her look so vulnerable.

"What about you, Trauble?" Stooley asked. "You know her?"

"I'd seen her around the office," Harry said. "She gave me a tour of the place when I was hired."

"Any idea why she wound up in your car?"

"Not a clue."

"Is that what she did over at the naked body shop, give tours?"

233

"Her main job was in the Photography Department," Terry said.

"Doing what, exactly?"

"I think she assisted the photographers," Harry said. "Helped them with the models."

"She knew her way around the photo lab, too," Terry said.

There seemed to be some commotion in the bar area. Voices raised in anger or protest. Then Detectives Cardona and Oskar were filling the doorway and heading toward their table.

"Got your five minutes, Stooley?" Oskar said.

Stooley shrugged. "A wasted hat," he said. "He didn't know the dame personally, don't know how she got in his car. Have fun, detectives."

The bar quieted down to just the "Push-Pull-Click-Cick" Schick razor ad on the TV as the cops led Harry toward the front.

Out on the street, Cardona said, "This is getting to be like our home turf."

They headed toward the parked Mustang where an assortment of uniformed police and technical people were milling about. Gawkers had begun to gather, too, and were being held in check by a couple of aggressive cops.

Another plain-clothes officer was talking with T.J., the night security guard. "You say she left the building twenty minutes ago?"

"That's about right," T.J. said, "I got the exact time in my log."

"Might as well get the basics done," Oskar said, distracting Harry from listening to the other interrogation. "You know the victim?"

Florence Proneswagger was still sprawled along the small rear seat of the Mustang, her extended, purple face a grotesque caricature of the one Harry remembered. A technician was kneeling on the car's front bucket, leaning over the back, using a small penlight for a rough examination of the corpse.

"I've seen her at work. I don't think we've said more than ten words to one another."

"We've been told by our crack lab team that the murder probably didn't take place in your car. Best guess, it happened in that alley and the killer saw your open car and took advantage of it."

"I'm lucky that way," Harry said.

"Teach you to keep your top up," Oskar said. "You strangle her, Mr. Trauble?"

"No."

"No offence, but I had to ask that. Sort of a thing we do."

"Kind of a waste of time, though. I mean, if I had killed her, would I have simply confessed to it? Just like that?"

"It happens," Oskar said.

"Any idea who she might have been meeting tonight?" Cordona asked.

Harry shook his head. "I don't know a thing about her."

"No hot and heavy office romance?" Oskar asked.

"Not that I know of."

"Never saw her at the Grasshopper with anybody?" Cardona asked.

It suddenly occurred to Harry that he had seen her in the Grasshopper a few months before. Soul-kissing with Maurice Grumbacher. "Not as I recall," he lied and wondered why.

"Thank you, Mr. Trauble," Cardona said. "I imagine, God help us, we'll be talking to you again, the death rate around here."

"At the risk of sounding like a selfish asshole," Harry said, "you have any idea when I'll be getting the Mustang back?"

"Couple days, probably," Cardona said. "We'll see it gets a nice detail job for you."

Harry couldn't tell if he was being facetious but decided he probably was. "One other thing? You did locate Howard Bethune, right?"

Cardona stared at him. "Why?"

"I just . . . would like to get in touch with him," Harry said.

"Sure you don't want to bump him off?" Oskar asked, winking at Cardona.

"Of course not. The guy's a friend of mine," Harry said.

"He's at this hippy commune near Moro Bay. Nirvana," Cardona said.

"I kinda liked that poetry reading gal," Oskar said. "She had a real nice set o' jugs."

"Yeah? Her and everybody there struck me as low tide on the beach," Cardona said.

He and his partner had no further use for Harry. They left him standing on the sidewalk, which was fine with him. Heading back to Herkie's he passed T.J. standing under the *Ogle* marquee. "This place is getting a little too spooky," the security guard said. "I figured the most I'd have to deal with was drunks and letches trying to get into the building. I didn't sign on for murders."

"None of us did," Harry told him.

36.

"Have the police sought access to your notes on our executives, Ivor?" Ida Connor asked the diminutive Dr. Magnus in her office the following morning. The doctor had dropped in to get her signature on an expense voucher.

"They've been rather insistent," he said, eyeing her hand that was holding the pen. "But as I explained to the rather disagreeable Detective Cardona, nothing in our sessions has made me cognizant of any employee of the company with homicidal tendencies.

"A touch of schizophrenia, paranoia. Depression, sublimation, an Oedipal complex here or there. These executives belong to the group we psychologists like to call 'fruit and nuts.' A mixed bag of neuroses not overwhelming enough to cause a rent in the social fabric."

"You seem to have missed the boat on Larry Beagle," she said.

"I had only one session with the man," the doctor said. "He exhibited the obvious symptoms of having undergone severe trauma in the past: the trembling hands, a tendency to become distracted. These are consistent with the findings of many studies made on returning members of the military who had undergone particularly stressful wartime conditions. Usually, these men go on to lead productive civilian lives."

"But not Mr. Beagle?"

The little man shook his head. "It was Mr. Beagle's misfortune to have had to deal with the stress of working under Mr. Armstead who, in his mind, became one with that wartime enemy."

"Mr. Armstead does have that effect on some people," Ida Connor said. "Was there any problem arranging for Mr. Beagle's release from prison?"

"No," the doctor replied. "I think the police were happy to get him off their hands. They're not really equipped to handle catatonia."

"Are they going to be able to do anything with him at Somerset?" she asked.

"Oh, my, yes. They're famous for their coddling of celebrity nut-jobs. The studios have been using them for years. Dr. Kandofer feels that given the proper therapy, Mr. Beagle will do just fine."

"Tell me, Ivor," Ida said, leaning forward, the pen just an inch or so above the expense voucher, "did your session with Mr. Buckley provide you with any insights I should know about?"

"Typical high-level executive. Alpha male. Aggressive. Perhaps a bit unrealistic in his demands of others. There are some grey areas . . ."

"Is he fit to head up this company?"

He hesitated before replying. Something in the way she'd asked the question made him wonder if she weren't hoping for a negative answer.

"I would say that, under ordinary circumstances, he would be considered what you would classify as norm—"

"What about empathy?" The pen moved back from the voucher.

"I don't understand."

"You do know what empathy means, doctor?"

"Of course. The ability to understand and sympathize with

the feelings of another. Are you suggesting that Mr. Buckley suffers from a lack of empathy?"

"One of our employees has been murdered. Likewise, Joseph Tobella, a man who worked for us, and his . . . roommate. Our assistant promotion manager has been considered a prime suspect in the Tobella deaths. And Mr. Beagle has just been confined to a rest home. In the face of all this, Mr. Buckley insists on having a party. What would you call that, doctor?"

"Definitely uncaring."

"Let's go whole hog and call it a lack of empathy. What would that indicate to you?"

"Any of a number of neuropsychiatric conditions. At the most pervasive end of the developmental disorder scale, you have narcissism, autism, antisocial behavior. In Mr. Buckley's case, I would think it more a case of improper social skills."

"Can you think of any ways these improper social skills could detract from the prosperity of *Ogle* magazine?"

Dr. Magnus smiled. "It's possible that they are responsible for its prosperity. A variation on the joke about the man who thought he was a chicken. His family didn't want him cured because they needed the eggs."

"Assume the chicken has stopped delivering and has in fact begun to poke holes in the eggs we have."

"Ah, now we're moving on to what we call the Gorilla Golfer Syndrome. The golfers at, let's say, St. Andrews, are a bit surprised to see a huge gorilla arrive, carrying his own clubs. He tees up, selects a fairway wood, approaches the ball and . . . whamo! . . . drives the ball four hundred yards straight as an arrow to the green where it plops down only a foot or two from the cup.

"It's an astonishing drive, clearly marking the gorilla as some kind of golfing wunderkind. The other golfers follow him down the fairway, eager to dote on his next moves. He studies the ball's position on the green, notes it's proximity to the cup, wets his thumb to gage the direction of the wind. Satisfied, he selects his club, approaches the ball and . . . whamo! . . . another four hundred yards."

Ida gave him a brief smile. "We are no longer in need of the four-hundred-yard drive," she said.

Dr. Magnus stared at her. "And you seek a way, preferably legal, to pry the golf club from your gorilla's clenched fingers?"

She nodded.

"I've had considerable courtroom experience as an expert witness in cases involving mental competence."

"So I've been led to believe," Ida said.

"I have to be honest with you. Thus far, I have heard of not one example of erratic behavior that a judge or jury might construe as being undeniably harmful to the future success of *Ogle.*"

She studied him. Was that slight twitch of the lip smirk or smile? "Have you a suggestion?" she asked.

"There is a so-called 'miracle drug' known by the letters LSD," Dr. Magnus said. "You've heard of it, I'm sure."

"There was a short piece in *Ogle,* prompted, I confess, by an article in Life. Therapists have used it in on alcoholics, drug addicts and criminals, with some success. Our piece covered its recreational use by members of your profession and the more adventurous members of the upper crust."

"Precisely. One of the reasons it came to mind was its use by one of Mr. Buckley's fellow publishers, Henry Luce, and his lovely wife."

He paused, noting her puzzled expression.

"If LSD helps to cure psychosis or deepen one's sense of self, then what would we gain . . . ?"

"Forgive me. I thought you were more cognizant of the effect of the drug on the psyche. Let me explain. First, it is colorless, odorless and nearly tasteless, especially when added to food or drink. Then, depending on its dosage, it produces a state some describe as schizophrenia while others consider it a rapturous euphoria. In either case, from what I've seen, during the period a person is under its spell, he or she often appears to be quite insane."

"Hold that thought, doctor," Ida said, reaching for the phone. "There are a few others I think should hear this."

"As long as you don't forget to sign my expense voucher," he said.

37.

"Couldn't we have waited for the weekend?" Harry asked as Terry steered her battered old Volkswagen along the Pacific Coast Highway heading north.

"Don't we deserve a day away from the office every now and then?" she asked.

"I was thinking the drive would be a little more comfortable in my Mustang."

"There's no guarantee the police will be finished with it by the weekend. And there's nothing wrong with the Zoombuggy."

"The windshield seems awfully close to my nose," Harry said.

"Then try looking through it at this wonderful view."

To their left, a bright sun was rising in a cloudless blue sky. Gulls floated and fell on invisible air currents. An unusually choppy ocean sent waves crashing along the coast, sending up a fine mist to sanctify as well as cool off the morning.

"Nice," he said without an ounce of genuine appreciation.

"You really can be a big baby sometimes," she said.

"I'm hungry. I'm tired. I didn't sleep well at all. I kept seeing Florence."

"Poor Florence," she said. "I don't understand why you didn't tell the detectives you saw her and Maurice Grumbacher kissing. He's connected to the other murders, too, which pretty well puts him at the top of my suspect list."

"Does Maurice really look like a serial murderer to you?"

242

"I've got only two words to say to that—Charles Stark-weather."

"Good point. Whoa, Seafood Shack," he said, pointing to a rundown-looking roadside diner with a giant grinning fish statue on its roof. "Turn in. I'm starved."

The stone fish, standing on its tail, was approximately the same size and shape as the *Ogle* frog but its colors had turned pastel from sun and salt air. It wore a chef's hat and apron that read "Come in and Shack Up." One of its fins was wrapped around a skillet. In the skillet was a fried fish.

"That is absolutely gross," Terry said. "It's like Colonel Sanders deep-fat frying a small child."

"You're not hungry?" he asked.

At ten-fifteen in the morning the Seafood Shack seemed to be in the short-order purgatory between breakfast and lunch. A perky little waitress said she could probably find some scrambled eggs and maybe fry some trout. She also informed them that she'd swum to work that morning.

Seemingly unimpressed, Terry settled on a cup of black coffee, eggs and a large wedge of the pumpkin pie even though the waitress warned her it had been "sittin' there since yesterday." Harry went for the eggs and trout.

There was only one other customer in the diner, a thin young man with long blond hair that nearly reached his boney shoulders. He was wearing a tie-dyed T-shirt, stained cut-offs and sandals cut from an old automobile tire. Smoking incessantly, he stared at the empty chair opposite him as if it were being used by some invisible raconteur who had him enthralled.

Harry and Terry had taken the table beside a window that looked out on the parking lot, a section of highway and, beyond, the ocean, sky and sun.

"What do you think we're going to get out of Bethune?" Harry asked.

"Even if we get nothing," she said, "we will have accomplished more than if we'd gone to the office. For example, on the way back, we might stop off for a swim at Trancas. Couldn't do that, going to the office."

"Trancas? The nude beach?" he asked.

"Did you bring your trunks? I seem to have forgotten mine."

"The nude beach," he said, thinking about it. He decided the idea appealed to him. The wonderful thing about sex, he had discovered thanks to Terry, was that it was like an addictive drug. The more you had of it, the more you wanted.

"There," she shouted suddenly, pointing out of the window.

The object of her attention was an undistinguished white van lingering on the other side of the highway. There was too much dust on the window for Harry to make out the driver.

"I saw that van when we left the apartment," Terry said. "And I'm sure it was behind us when we passed the Santa Monica incline."

The vehicle zoomed off.

"It's headed south," Harry said. "We're headed north."

"Don't you see? We turned in here before the driver had a chance to react. He kept going until he could turn around and the reason he was stopped out there was to make sure where we were."

Harry hadn't seen the van before. On one hand, he was worried she might be getting just a tad paranoid. On the other, with the body count continuing to rise, he was also worried she might not be paranoid at all.

"Maybe we should forget about seeing Bethune and just go back," he said.

"Not with food coming," she said. "Danger kinda makes me hungry." She smiled and he felt her bare foot suddenly wiggling on his lap. "And sexy."

"The thing that really bothers me," he said, "is that I'm starting to feel that way, too."

"Do you see the van?" she asked, as they took to the Coast Highway again.

"No. But your car windows are tiny and there's a lot of traffic back there." He pressed his stomach. "I wonder how long ago they caught that trout?"

"It's much too soon for you to be feeling sick. It'll be at least five or six hours before you start . . . oops, here's our turnoff."

The sign was small and surprisingly tasteful—a redwood plank with a painted red heart, an open golden eye in its center, the symbol of the facility called Nirvana. Under it, its rules and regulations were outlined in raised redwood lettering. "No Solicitors Allowed—No Cameras Allowed—No Clothes Allowed—Free Souls Welcome."

"See," Terry said, "we're welcome."

Harry was staring through the tiny back window, noting that no white van or any other vehicle seemed to be following their lead.

A winding, somewhat treacherous dirt road rose up into the mountain, twisting and turning, threatening at any second to tumble the Zoombuggy into one crevasse or another, eventually daring visitors to push through a wall of greenery to an open road that continued until the crest of a cliff prompted an abrupt left turn into more foliage and more turns.

Finally, they arrived at a parking area of sorts—a man-made plateau—where twenty or so vehicles, obviously purchased more for utilitarian purposes than cruising Sunset Boulevard, rested in vague order.

Terry found a nest for the Zoombuggy between an ancient Ford truck and a rusted out Nash station wagon whose hardtop had been removed by nonprofessional means.

Nirvana was another three-quarters of a mile or so up a path that had been dotted by hunks of rock to dissuade any drivers from trying to save themselves the climb, though single tire tracks suggested cyclists had made the trip. One of these had parked his chopper near the entrance—sleek and black and in considerably better condition than any of the four-wheelers down below. The heart and eye logo decorated its fuel tank cover.

An archway of intertwined vines—pink bougainvillea mixed with bright red bottlebrush—marked the entrance to the retreat. Harry might have missed the lens nestled among the vines had it not picked up just a nanosecond of sunlight as it panned to follow their progress. Evidently not all cameras were forbidden at Nirvana.

Trying to ignore the lens, he followed Terry through the floral portal. Past it was a large, very modern building on flat ground and beyond it, on plateaus in the still-rising mountainside, a collection of white cottages, all of a box-like pattern, shimmered in the morning sunlight, their casement and awning windows rolled out to full extension. It was like some unimaginative movie set designer's idea of a village of the future where robots dwelled.

No robots were visible. Just humans and a gathering of cows on a distant, tree-studded plateau and chickens hunting and pecking near twin barns that resembled two small airplane hangers.

Some of the humans were weeding and digging in patchwork gardens up past the last group of buildings, others were moving in and out of the barns and still others were making repairs on a massive generator in a wooded area to the right.

The non-workers, the off-shift, Harry assumed, were enjoying such leisurely pursuits as playing tennis on four courts to the left of the large building and romping in an Olympic-size pool to the left of the courts. There was a high chain-link fence surrounding the courts, presumably to keep the balls from flying off and a smaller one around the pool, probably to keep children, of which there were several, from falling in.

Those fences were the only man-made physical boundaries Harry could see.

The people of Nirvana—mainly young, active, healthy and tanned—were all naked.

Working for *Ogle*, Harry was not exactly a stranger to nudity. But since the magazine showed a definite preference for attractive feminine nudes, usually pampered and powdered, the sight of men, especially on the tennis courts, as well as hot and sweaty women on the thin or plus size, gave him a moment's pause.

"Honey," Terry said sweetly, "if we have any hope of getting into this joint, you're just going to have to hang loose a little."

He followed her to the main building and a door bearing the red heart and eye. A small redwood sign under the logo read: "The eye sees what the heart feels." Under it was a signature burnt into the wood, "Bert Needham."

Harry knew the name. He'd dug out an article titled "Nirvana's Mahatma" that *Ogle* had published in 1961, the year the retreat had officially opened. Its mahatma, Herbert L. Needham, had been an executive at the Howard Hughes Corporation for a number of years when he decided to quit for what he called "personal reasons."

Specifically, he wasn't that happy about working for a company that leased certain offshore islands from some millionaire named Bush, the better to allow the CIA access to raids on Cuba, this after some of Hughes' officers had been involved in a jackass scheme to assassinate Castro hatched by the CIA and several Mafia patriots.

It wasn't that Needham was in any way sympathetic to Fidel's cause, whatever the hell it was. He just didn't think that sending a murder squad to bump off a political opponent, no matter how pesky, was something the good guys should be doing. He also thought that Hughes, an avowed Mormon, had dropped the ball on the only thing about that religion that made any sense, considering the state of contemporary male–female relationships.

He was a particularly effective speaker—a talent that had landed him at the company to begin with. But since he was in no position to convey his beliefs to old Howard in any meaningful way, and, in truth, was a bit chary about doing or saying anything that might put himself in the CIA's crosshairs, he thought it the better part of valor to simply take a pass.

Every Tuesday, on his weekly drive along the Coast Highway to the Hughes Research Lab in Malibu, he'd noticed a "For Sale" sign beside a barely blazed trail that disappeared up into the spectacularly overgrown mountainside to his right. Finally, adrift from Hughes and Maheu and that whole crowd, he used his generous profit-sharing severance bundle to put a down payment on a seventeen-acre plot of mountain wilderness two thousand feet above the Pacific Coast Highway.

Since, as noted, he was a very convincing salesman, and since the product he was pitching—sexual liberation under the guise of a natural, healthy, totally free lifestyle—was far from a hard sell, particularly in Southern California, he quickly convinced a significant number of dissatisfied and independently wealthy men and women to share his happy, hedonistic dream. They became the core members of Nirvana.

Others followed their leads.

Harry assumed some of them had probably grown bored with all that sexual freedom and healthy food and returned to a more focused and conventional way of life, but judging by the looks of the place, Bert Needham's dream had definitely taken earthly root.

The reception area inside the main building was circular with white walls that curved up into a domed ceiling. The floor was patterned in alternating black-and-white tiles, polished to a high gloss. A recessed overhead light was focused down on the only furnishing to speak of—a huge glass tank filled with emerald water in which several beautiful and exotic fish glided in and out of some leafy growth.

One particularly odd brownish-green fish, magnified by the water to the size of a house cat, reminded Harry of a caricature of the actor Edward G. Robinson. It appeared to be studying him, then, its large lips opening wide, zoomed toward him. Harry took a backward step, just as a frosty female voice said, "Welcome to Nirvana."

The speaker was a short, wiry woman in slacks and a starched man's dress shirt who had entered from a door on the other side of the tank. Her hair was cut short in the pixie-like fashion popularized by the actress Jean Seberg. Her handsome face was deep-tanned, lightly wrinkled and void of any obvious cosmetic enhancement.

"I am Dorella. How may I help you?"

"We're here to see one of your guests," Terry said. "Howard Bethune."

Dorella studied them both and asked, "Is Howard expecting you?"

"No," Harry said. "We were sort of in the neighborhood."

"Frankly," Terry added, "we've heard so much about Nirvana, we were hoping Harry could show us around."

Dorella cocked her head to one side, pondering the request. Before she came to a decision, a man entered the room behind her. Harry recognized him from the photos in the *Ogle* article, Bert Needham, the mahatma of Nirvana, a strangely ordinary-looking guy except for his sun-bronzed skin. He was dressed in West Coast casual business attire—pale yellow silk pants, nubby brown jacket and white shirt open wide at the neck, the better to show off his tan. He combed his short brown hair forward, Caesar-like, to hide a receding hairline.

Raising one eyebrow, he said, "If these folks are prospects, Dorella, they get my vote." He flashed a set of pearl-white choppers at Terry. "Not that that counts for much around here. I'm Bert, by the way."

"I'm Terry and that's Harry." She extended a hand which Bert seized in both of his and raised to his lips.

"Welcome to Nirvana, Terry."

"Better get a move on, Bert," Dorella said. "They're here for Howie."

"Howie, eh?" Bert said. "That zane. You must know Lenina, too, of course. Now there's a handful. You'll be staying a while?"

"Maybe," Harry said, wondering who Lenina might be.

"Stick around. We're not gonna be gone all that long."

Dorella turned toward the open door. "Kiki?" It wasn't a shout, but it seemed to carry through the building.

A tall brunette, naked except for her eyeglasses and flip-flops, joined them from the rear. She had a lanky, athletic body, pale enough to suggest that she spent more time indoors than out. "Yes, Dorella?"

"These visitors are here to see Howie. Show them where they can put their clothes and then lead them out to the pavilion, please."

"Sure 'nuff," Kiki said.

"How do you like our new skins, K.?" Bert asked her, doing a parody of a model's turn.

"Very nice threads," Kiki said, "but you know what I always say, Bert, clothes just get in the way."

"Not when you're dealing with bankers," Dorella said. "Come on, Bert."

The mahatma lingered long enough to wink at Terry and

mouth the word, "stay."

"Bert digs you," Kiki told Terry, as she led them through a sort of study-common room to a door leading to the rest of the retreat. "Of course, he digs every bitchin' body he meets."

"I feel blessed," Terry said as they stepped into both sunshine and a blast of music—Nancy Sinatra telling the world what her boots were made for.

"Bert can't be beat in the sack," Kiki said. "It's like makin' love to a baby-oiled Louisville slugger on springs."

"Sounds irresistible," Terry said, smiling sweetly at Harry.

The music shifted, Nancy's boots giving way to the Beach Boys having "Fun Fun Fun."

"Okay," their guide said, "here's where you take it off, take it all off."

They were standing at the far edge of the main building near an open door to a room filled with bicycles and sports equipment. Just to the left of the door, a muscle-bound nude guy had twisted himself into a Yoga pretzel. "That's Jimmy Bob," Kiki said. "When he's not meditating, he hands out towels for the swimmers and tennis rackets and stuff like that. You can just put your clothes in there on top of the pool mats."

"Thanks," Harry said. "If you point out the—what did Dorella call it, the pavilion—we can probably find old Howie. You must have work to do."

"Dorella made me responsible for you two," Kiki said. "You are my work. So let's see what you're made of, mister."

Terry slipped out of her clothes without a second's thought, visibly disturbing Jimmy Bob's meditation and causing Kiki to exclaim, "Hot bod."

Harry took a little longer to strip down. "My shoes are okay, right?"

"Shoes are fine," Kiki said.

Harry's nudity was not commented on.

Just as well, he thought. Discomfort had a shriveling effect on him. As Kiki led them past her fellow Nirvanians, he tried to tell himself they were no less naked than he. But he felt pale and out of shape and, with all the Louisville slugger talk, a bit under-endowed. Then they approached a blonde, her voluptuous body coated in suntan oil, who winked at him and licked her lips and his concern shifted to a more outwardly thrusting form of embarrassment.

The Beatles sang and played "She Loves Me" as they climbed the sloping lawn to a leveled space with a crowded Jacuzzi and a tiled dance pavilion shaded by a canvas top. A quartet of little kids were wiggling on the tiles to the yeah-yeah-yeahs.

An altered Howard Bethune was at the rear of the pavilion, seated behind a console on which rested a reel-to-reel tape deck, two turntables and an assortment of vinyl records, stacked or scattered. Howard, his hair electrified into a frizzled white man's afro, nodded in time with the music. It was amazing how much relaxation changed his face, unlocking his pursed lips, erasing worry lines. He looked ten years younger. His eyes were closed and he seemed in such a beatifically dreamlike state that Harry felt bad about disturbing him, especially with dark questions.

He'd been Nirvana's Mister Deejay long enough to have become familiar with the machines. Without opening his eyes, he reached out and touched a button that shifted the source from one turntable to the next, making a professional segue into The Stone's version of Bobby Troup's "Route 66."

Kiki hunkered down beside his chair and whispered something in his ear that made him smile. "Anytime, darling," he said.

"Some friends are here to see you," Kiki said.

Bethune's eyes popped open and, for a moment, the tension returned.

"Hi, Howard," Terry said.

He looked from her to Harry, warily. "Who sent you?" he asked.

"Nobody sent us," Harry said. "We're here on our own. Just wondering how you were doing."

"It's okay, them being here?" Kiki asked, noting Howard's re-action.

He frowned and nodded. "It's okay, I guess," he said. "Thanks, Kiki."

The young woman backed away, uncertain.

"Thanks for your help," Terry said.

Kiki looked questioningly at Howard.

"It's fine, Kiki, but maybe you could take the kids down to the pool?" he said.

She did as he requested, herding the tiny dancers down the hill to the swimming area.

Bethune waited until they were out of earshot and said, "I'm trying to put all that *Ogle* crap behind me. I heard on the radio there'd been another murder. The woman who did the office tours."

"Right," Harry said. "I know you've probably been over all this stuff, but if there's anything you can tell us about those last few days you were at the magazine . . ."

"I don't know a goddamned thing," Howard said, his right hand automatically switching on the reel-to-reel. "My lifemate, Lenina, and I drove here the same night the sculptor was killed. At about the time the murders were being committed, we were here, getting assigned to a cabin. That's what I told the police and that's the way it happened.

"What makes any of this your business, anyway? You're what—a copywriter or something?"

"He's here because I asked him to come," Terry said. "And I'm here because the people who were murdered were my friends. And the police seem to be moving in circles."

"So you're gonna solve the murders yourself? Get serious. The cops know what they're doing."

"They still think the guy whose place you took, Nick Hobart, died accidentally," she said. "Is that what you think?"

Bethune opened his mouth and shut it again. He shook his head. "No. I believe he was murdered. I even found a threat he'd received."

"And the police blew it off?" Harry asked.

"They . . . never heard about it," Bethune said. "I was told I'd misinterpreted it, that it wasn't a threat at all."

"What did it say?" Terry asked.

"I . . . I've put all that ugly crap from my mind."

"Please. For the sake of my friends who were killed."

"It was something like, 'treacherous bastards are out to get you and there's something personal, too.' I think that's pretty close."

" 'Bastards' makes it more than one killer," Harry said. "But it doesn't sound as much like a threat than it does a warning. Somebody warning Hobart that others were out to get him."

"I don't know. I just know I was told to forget all about it."

"Who told you that?" Harry asked.

"Kevin Dobbs. I trusted him enough to give him the note. He said he'd take care of it. He did that all right. Next thing I knew every executive in the company was telling me to forget about it, that it meant nothing. But I knew they were bullshitting. They were only concerned with one thing—the public sale of *Ogle* stock. They were having enough trouble getting Buckley to go along with that plan and a murder investigation would have put it off indefinitely."

Harry had heard nothing about the company going public. "When the sculptor and his buddy were murdered, why didn't you tell the police any of this?" he asked.

"I didn't see a connection between those murders and Hobart. Even the papers were calling it a coincidence. Anyway I just . . . I've got a great life now. I'm living with a beautiful, passionate woman whom I love very much. Everything is open and happy and limitless. I'm doing things I never thought possible, experiencing sensations I'd never imagined. Hell, I've even started to like rock 'n' roll. I don't want to get dragged back to that terrible, secretive, primitive old existence."

"Let's say the murders are tied to the public offering of *Ogle*," Harry said. "There must be millions involved. Could Hobart have been goosing the circulation figures to make the company look better?"

Bethune shook his head and his wiry afro seemed to vibrate. "No. That was the first thing I thought about. I checked his totals and they were right on the money. His forecasts may even have been on the conservative side. The company is doing well. Circulation is strong. Anyway, none of the principals suggested I juggle any figures. And they would have."

"When you mention the principals," Terry said, "you're talking about Milton and the ad guy . . ."

"Bingham," Harry said. "And the editor, Dobbs, Ida and, of course, Buckley himself."

"The note mentioned 'bastards,' " Terry said. "Maybe they're all in on it."

"Look, I don't wanna be rude, but that's my past life," Bethune said. "Too much negativity. Too much ugliness. I'd like you to go now."

"We didn't mean to disturb you," Harry said. "We're just . . . you said that the threat Hobart got mentioned 'something personal.' Any idea what that could have been?"

Bethune stared at him for a beat. "I think Hobart had a thing going with one of the *Ogle* girls," he said.

"Somebody who worked in the office?" Harry asked, looking at Terry.

"No," Bethune said. "An Eyeful. A centerfold."

"What makes you think that?" Terry asked.

"Look, I never even met the man," Bethune said. "But I . . . well, hell. The job was stressful. I'd relax when I could and it was usually on the couch in my office. One of the last times I used it, the cushion under my head made this rustling noise. Very distracting. I unzipped the cover and found a file folder that I assume Hobart had stuck in there. One of the things in the file was a centerfold. I thought that was a little, well, odd. Even for that place."

"Anything else in the folder?" Harry asked.

Bethune hesitated, but answered the question. "It was even weirder than the Eyeful, a copy of Trower Buckley's birth certificate."

"What was he doing with that?" Harry asked.

"I've no fucking idea and, frankly, I couldn't care less."

"Buckley's family history is a matter of record," Terry said. "Was there anything unusual about the birth certificate?"

"Here's my take on *Ogle*," Bethune said. "There always was something damn creepy about that whole joint—the unprofessional behavior, the secretaries who knew more about your department than you did, because they were sleeping with Armstead or Buckley or both, the air of secrecy, the sadistic behavior of some of my fellow executives. The pettiness. As my life partner, Lenina, noted just the other night, for a magazine that claims to be in the forefront of sexual freedom, it's the least free place she'd ever heard of.

"So, to answer your question, I don't really know what was unusual about Buckley's birth certificate, because I didn't spend a lot of time studying it. I was too damn afraid somebody would walk in and catch me with it in my hand. I put it and the centerfold back in the pillow and, from that moment on, used another pillow for my headrest."

"Did you recognize the Eyeful?" Terry asked. "Or notice the month?"

"Please. No, I barely glanced at it. As I recall she was in a supine position, maybe pretending to read a book."

"They're all pretending to read books," Harry said.

"Look, you two seem like nice kids," Bethune said. "And you've got something going, right? Forget about murders and *Ogle* and all the horrible things that go on down below. Nirvana is at one-hundred-percent capacity right now, but Bert has opened up an area above the cattle pens for campers. Join up. Set up a tent. You'll get full use of the facilities and I'll see what I can do about getting you the first cottage that opens up."

"Thanks," Terry said. "Maybe we'll take you up on that one of these days. Right now, I'd like to think we can be of more use in the real world."

"Okay," Bethune said. "It's your fune . . ."

The report of a rifle echoed through the canyon. Bethune was spun back against the turntable, clicking off the reel-to-reel and filling the area with the voice of Mary Wells far into the chorus of "My Guy."

Something whizzed past Harry's cheek, followed by another echoing crack. He dived toward Terry and tumbled with her onto the floor of the pavilion. Two bullets smashed into the chair where she had been sitting.

Harry and Terry lay flat on the tiled pavilion floor, waiting for the next shots. But they didn't come.

From below came shouts and someone yelling, "By the main house."

Harry inched forward to the edge of the pavilion plateau. A large man, fully dressed in khaki pants and shirt, was running toward the rear doorway of the main building with a rifle in his right hand. A blue baseball cap low on his forehead and sunglasses effectively masked his features.

"How the hell does this work?" Terry was asking behind Harry.

She was hunkering beside Howard's table, a microphone in her hand. She flipped a button at its base and Mary Wells' bouncy song was replaced by Terry's voice, sounding a bit higher pitched than usual, as she said, "Howard Bethune has been shot. Someone please call for help."

Below them, most of the Nirvanians were still hugging the ground. The muscular Jimmy Bob and another man were running toward the main building.

The shooter was gone.

Harry got to his feet.

Terry stood beside Bethune, pressing a forefinger to his neck. "He's alive," she said. "The pulse is strong."

A beautiful young woman was bouncing up the hill on a run. With a cry of "Oh, my God, Howard," she rushed toward Bethune.

He groaned.

"Oh, my precious," she said, helping him back onto his chair.

Blood was matting his afro and pouring down his forehead.

"Damn, it hurts," he said.

The woman parted his wiry hair and studied the wound. "It doesn't look so bad, baby."

"But it hurts."

She cradled his head against her breasts. "Don't worry, precious. The bad man's gone and Lenina's here."

"We'd better go make sure somebody called for an ambulance and the police," Harry said to Terry. He wanted to distance himself from the couple. He was almost sick with guilt, knowing they'd brought the violence with them to Nirvana.

38.

"Is today a frigging holiday?" Armstead asked, looking at the small assembly in the conference room. In attendance were Ida Connor, Roger Weeks, Al Hewitt and Kevin Dobbs' editorial assistant, a frail young man with a sour milk odor to him, six-and-a-half feet tall, with long oily hair, rumpled white Brooks Brothers button-down shirt and khaki pants, whose name no one bothered to remember.

"What are we celebrating, Father Feeney," Armstead asked, "St. Fucking Swithins?"

"We're a trifle late on that, I believe," Hewitt said.

"Well, where the hell is everybody?"

"K-K-Kevin is at a s-s-speaking engagement," Dobbs' assistant barely managed to reply.

"Maurice called in sick," Ida said. "I'm not sure where John Bingham is." She noted the other empty chair. "Or Harry Trauble."

"Harry's at . . . Harry's sick, too," Weeks said.

"Well, Weeks," Armstead said, "you seem to be the sole survivor of what was once a proud and noble promotion department. Please be attentive."

"Milton, since we barely have a quorum," Ida said, "perhaps we should table this meeting 'til tomorrow. You and I should discuss a suggestion of Dr. Magnus'."

Armstead turned to Hewitt. "Okay if we close this bore-ass down, padre?"

Hewitt rewarded the "padre" with a meager smile. "I've just a few things to pass along. Buck asked me to tell you that, whatever else you may have heard to the contrary, the party is very much a go project."

"Yes, yes," Armstead said impatiently. "Death will not dismay our continuous search for sex and booze."

"But what is new, as of a half hour ago, is that Buck wants it to be held tomorrow night."

Armstead's eyebrows rose. "He's expecting us to whip up a full-blown *Ogle* bash, broads, celebrities, food, drinks, entertainment and more broads in about," looking at his watch, "thirty hours, not including sleep. We can't even get the invitations printed by then. What's the rush?"

"There has been a convergence of events," Al Hewitt said. "First, the operation on Raymond the frog went well, I know you will be happy to hear, and Angel will be returning with the cunning little amphibian on Saturday. In other words, she will not be here for the party, allowing Buck the opportunity to make new friends.

"Second, the party venue, ex-Governor Moody's home, has suddenly become available, since Mrs. Moody and their daughter will be driving to her sister's in Santa Barbara. And, finally, Buck has an announcement he wants to make to the executives and department heads ASAP, and thinks the party might be the perfect place to do it."

Armstead turned to Ida with a questioning look. She turned hers to Hewitt. "Care to give us a little preview of the announcement, Al?"

"I really don't know anything about it."

"Why don't I ask Buck?" Armstead said, reaching for the phone.

"He's not in the penthouse," Hewitt said. "He headed out a while ago."

"Going where?" Armstead asked.

"His lawyer, I think." Hewitt stood and adjusted his coat and cuffs. "I'd best let you folks get busy with the party plans," he said. He turned to Ida, "And your chat about Dr. Magnus."

"I-I-I'll be g-g-going, too," the editorial assistant said. "The b-b-blue lines for the n-n-next issue j-j-just came in."

"Good. Good," Armstead said. "It's been getting close enough in this room to gag a rodent."

Ida watched the ex-archbishop exit, wondering just how much he knew about their plans for the takeover.

Armstead turned to Weeks. "Alright, you smarmy little ferret, now's your chance to show me your stuff. Get the Marx Brothers in publicity to start corralling the A-list guys and D-cup starlets. Use as many of the secretaries as you can find to order up the catering and the booze. Get the security guy—what's his name?"

"T.J.," Weeks said.

"Yeah. Tell him to order up a gang of leg breakers and—"

"I will arrange for security," Ida said, "as well as staff—butlers, maids, etcetera."

"Bravissimo. Weeks, get whoever's left in photography to line up the Eyefuls."

"Talk to my assistant, Darlene, about it, Roger," Ida said.

"Okay, Weeks. At it, chop chop."

When the copywriter had left the room, Armstead said, "Now, what's this about the head-shrinker?"

Ida was just beginning to summarize her earlier conversation with Dr. Magnus when she saw that she'd lost Armstead's attention. He was staring at the door, where Darlene stood anxiously, her ice-queen demeanor a bit melted by concern.

"What is it, my dear?" Ida asked.

"On the radio," she said. "Someone tried to m-m-murder Mr. Bethune at that retreat place, Nirvana. He's in critical . . ."

the young woman began to weep.

Ida was on her feet, offering her assistant a shoulder to cry on. "There there, dear."

"I still have feelings for him, Ida . . . even though he . . ."

"I know, Darlene." From the corner of her eye, she saw Armstead making his way toward the door. "Men can be such bastards, but we still can't do without them."

"My curiosity is piqued enough that I'm going to double-check why Kevin and the huckster missed our meeting," Armstead said. "Find out how they've been spending the morning."

"Buck, too," Ida said, without thinking.

"Buck, too," Armstead said, his shark's grin in place. "Now wouldn't that be something?"

39.

"They kill Flor-jence," Carlos was saying to Al Hewitt. "I am next."

Hewitt had gone to the photo studio to see how the photographer was faring and found the man in a state of near-petrifaction.

"Why do you think she was killed?"

"Why?" Carlos looked at him as if he were on a mental level somewhere between an idiot and a doorknob. "Because of the focking photographs."

"You think she stole them?"

"No, man. What's with you? Because she knew about them."

"But everybody knows about them—at least every guy in the photographs. Why do you think her knowledge of them would cause her death?"

"I dunno. What you think, smart guy?"

"I'm beginning to think her death had nothing to do with the photographs," Hewitt said. "You've been taking pictures of executives with Angel for how long?"

"Four yeaz, maybe."

"And nobody got hurt and nobody tried to steal the pictures. Was I the most recent addition to the club?"

"No. The shrink, Magnus, we got last week."

"Any way he could know where you keep the photos?" Hewitt asked.

"No way. On'y me and Flor-jence knew where they was.

Whoever took 'em went right to the spot, busted the lock and vamoosed with the photos, the contacts and the negatives."

"Is it possible Florence helped the thief, who then killed her?" Hewitt asked.

"You mus' be nuts. Flor-jence has been scared shitless about the theft, same as me."

"And all the photos were taken?"

"Every las' focking one."

"Then the thief had everything he wanted," Hewitt said. "Why kill Florence?"

Carlos frowned, thinking about it. He seemed to relax a little. "You right. It doan make no sense."

"Unless she'd been doing a little blackmailing," Hewitt said.

"Flor-jence wasn't no blackmailer. She was a nice lady who wanted to get married and have kids and like that. Only she wound up falling for assholes like Grumbacher."

"Was she pressuring Grumbacher in any way?" Hewitt asked.

Carlos shook his head vehemently. "She wasn't like that. Anyway, the Grumbacher thing was pretty much over. Why all the questions about Flor-jence, anyway? You nervous about somethin'?"

"I'm very nervous about the photos and why they were stolen. I guess I just wanted to convince myself that Florence's murder was a coincidence and not a result of the theft."

"You convinced?"

"Yes," Hewitt said. He scanned the studio. "You know this place, Carlos. Was there anything different about it this morning?"

"What you mean?"

"I mean the police are saying that Florence was strangled in an alley and dumped into a nearby car. But suppose she was killed in this building? In this studio?"

A fearful look returned to Carlos' eyes as he searched the

room. "There wasn't nothin' out of place this morning I can remember. Except the darkroom door was open. Florence usually closes it when she's finished."

"Florence developed film?"

"A year ago, she ask me to show her how. Since then, she make extra money makin' prints for her friends."

"Show me," Hewitt said.

Carlos took him into a small room painted a flat black. It smelled of chemicals. Several clotheslines had been strung from wall to wall on which a few photos, mainly of naked ladies, were held in place by wooden clothespins.

Carlos flipped a switch and the room took on a red glow. "She also left a tub full of developer."

"But no photo prints?" Hewitt asked.

Carlos looked around the area, lifted packs of stock, sifted through galley sheets. "Doan look like," he said. "Wait. Here somethin'."

He picked up a folded sheet from the floor. A name was scrawled on it in red marking pencil. "For Terry O."

"Know who this Terry O. is?" Hewitt asked.

"Got a Terry who sits at the front desk down on three," Carlos said. "Great body. Mr. Buckley hisself ask her to be an Eyeful and she tell him no, which ain't so smart. Maybe this Terry O. is her."

40.

"You like those moody black-and-white crime movies, Trouble?" Detective Steve Cardona asked. "The ones where the heroes—I guess they call 'em anti-heroes—get hopelessly over their head in something they got no control over?"

"I guess they're okay," Harry said. Cardona was driving him south along the Coast Highway. Up ahead of them, Terry was driving Detective Oskar in the Zoombuggy. That was the way the two cops had wanted it. The sky was a cloudless pastel blue. The choppy Pacific was more reflective of Harry's anxious mood.

"Usually there's a sexy dame involved," Cardona said. "My favorite is Yvonne De Carlo. Now there is one beautiful piece of poisoned pastry. And she really let Burt Lancaster have it in that . . . hell, I can't think of the name . . . Know the one I mean? Dan Duryea is the bad guy pulling the strings, but she screws him over, too."

"Maybe I saw it on TV," Harry said.

"Anyway, all's I'm saying is broads can lead you into all kinds of shit. Is that what happened?"

Harry blinked. "Huh?"

"Your gal up there is definitely in the De Carlo ballpark. My guess is you found out about her and Tobella and kinda lost it. That it?"

"Whoa," Harry said. "I thought you were gonna be asking

me about the shooting back there. What's all this about To-bella?"

"We found some nudie shots of your girlfriend at Tobella's," Cardona said. "If it'd been my woman, I might've done the same thing."

"What the hell are you talking about?" Harry asked, anger trying to mask the sinking feeling in his stomach.

"I'm talking about an average, law-abiding guy finding out his gal was having hot three-way sex with some arty-farty types, and flipping his lid."

"Tobella and his partner were gay, weren't they?"

"I don't know how those things work," Cardona said. "But from what I've observed about your lady up there, she could give eyesight to the blind. And the photos . . ."

"They're having sex in the photos?" Harry asked.

"Like you don't know," Cardona said. "No. They're not having sex in the photos. It's just her, looking damn fine."

"The pictures were for a statue," Harry said. "The one in his studio."

"You were in his studio?"

"N-no. But Terry told me about the statue."

"But not about the photos?"

"You really think I killed Tobella?"

"All I know, brother, is that the murdered sculptor has naked pictures of your gal, a strangled dame winds up in the backseat of your car and now a guy gets shot with you in attendance. Even if I believed in coincidence that'd be pushing it.

"So you and Miss O'Mara are gonna be our guests for a while."

Harry felt as though the car seat was dissolving beneath him. "Y-you're saying we're under arrest? For murder?"

Cardona scowled. "This isn't an arrest, kid," he said. "I'm not an idiot. Even that brain-dead trooper back there at the nudist camp could tell there was no way you coulda done the shooting. And there are enough people who saw you in Herkie's at the time the Proneswagger woman was being choked. Tobella and his pal, Orlando, now, that's a different ball game.

"What we'll call this is protective custody."

"How long you gonna keep 'protecting' us?"

"That depends on how long you and Miss O'Mara want to keep pulling our chains. You know damn well you weren't at the nudist farm just to say hi to your old pal Bethune. He was yapping to the state trooper that you two were questioning him about the late Nick Hobart. You got any reason to think Hobart's death wasn't an accident?"

Harry wondered how Terry was answering that question. He decided to try and finesse it. "Howard Bethune thinks Hobart was murdered," he said.

"Yeah-yeah, I heard his theory on that one. We'll be checking out the couch in his old office for Hobart's so-called 'secret papers' and trying to find somebody who saw the written threats Bethune says he got. It woulda been nice if he'd mentioned them when we had our little talk a couple days ago. Then, he didn't know nothing about nothing.

"Kinda like you and Miss O'Mara."

Their destination was Parker Center, the headquarters for the LAPD, which, with its crowded public areas, cracked walls and agonizingly slow elevators had the appearance of a building twice as old as its ten years.

Cardona maneuvered Harry up to Robbery-Homicide, through the bullpen and into an interrogation room–a small space with pale green walls, a large mirror, obviously one-way, and a black and grey tile floor, brightened by a single light recessed behind a protective grill in approximately the center of the off-white ceiling. Its furnishings consisted of a metal table and three metal chairs.

"Get you anything? Cigarette? Coke?" Cardona asked.

"Where's Terry?"

"Good question. Lemme check." The detective left the room.

The lighting was harsh. Harry shut his eyes and slumped back in his chair.

This was the worst thing that had ever happened to him.

How far was Cardona going to take it? Did the detective know he'd been at Tobella's the night of the murders? Was he being arrested? His picture in the papers? His parents seeing it? Jesus.

Where was Terry and what was she telling them?

What the hell were you supposed to do when you got arrested? Get a lawyer. He didn't have a lawyer. Did they really have to give him one phone call, or was that some movie bullshit? He'd ask for the call and see.

But whom to call?

His thought process took an off-road hike. Images softened, melded, broke apart.

He awoke to someone shaking his shoulder.

The man was in his fifties, fit, wearing an immaculate three-piece charcoal-grey suit, white shirt with a Dean Martin extra-high collar, midnight blue silk tie. His dark hair was streaked with grey. His flat, handsome face was tennis court–tan, marked by very blue eyes and a half smile. "My name is Miles Corrigan, Mr. Trauble," he said. "I'm your lawyer."

"Oh?" Harry was still a little fuzzy from sleep. "How'd I get a lawyer?"

"Ida Connor called me. I've been getting quite a lot of business from *Ogle* these days."

He took the chair across the table from Harry. "Detective Cardona says he hasn't questioned you yet. Correct?"

"We talked on the drive here. But I guess there hasn't been, you know, an official kind of thing."

"What did you tell him?"

"That we saw—"

"The 'we' being you and Terry O'Mara?"

"Right. That we saw a white van following us on our way to Nirvana. Couldn't really see the driver, but it had to be the guy who shot Howard Bethune.

"Cardona started off talking about that, then, out of the blue, he started asking questions that made me think I was guilty of something, so I shut up. What are they accusing me of?"

"You're being held as a protected witness. Unofficially, I gather, you are a suspect in the murder of Joseph Tobella and Orlando Royale. Any idea why?"

"Cardona says they found pictures of Terry . . . she's here, too. I'm okay. You should see how she's—"

"They're not holding Miss O'Mara," the lawyer said. "She's the one who got Ida to call me on your behalf. You were saying they had pictures of her?"

"Nudes. Taken by Tobella for his sculpture work. They think I was jealous enough to . . . kill him."

"But we know better, right?" He smiled. "If they had anything at all by way of evidence, fingerprints, hair, a button from your shirt, you'd be an official suspect. Unless they're being uncharacteristically coy. Is there anything you can think of that could put you at the crime scene?"

"N-no. I never even met Tobella. Saw him once when he was at *Ogle* but that's about it."

"Nothing you said to anybody or mumbled in a dream they can use? No other connections or motives other than the absurd jealousy theory?"

"No."

"All right, then. The only reason you're here is that they have a witness who saw somebody go into Tobella's house on the night of the murder. They want you to take part in a lineup. That worry you?"

"No," Harry lied.

"Good. Then let's get that done and I'll have you out of here in time for Johnny Carson's monologue."

41.

Trower Buckley seemed distracted at dinner. He toyed with the chicken that the cook-housekeeper Henrietta had fried just the way he liked it. He pecked at the potatoes she had mashed with loving care and selected maybe three green peas to nibble on. He barely touched the apple pie a la mode.

From time to time, his sole dinner companion, Al Hewitt, tossed out a potential subject of discussion—the attack on Howard Bethune, the futile police examination of a white couch that, Bethune's claim to the contrary, contained no secret folder of the late Nick Hobart's, the air of unrest in the office building, the weather and, finally, the upcoming party.

Buckley had had nothing to say about Bethune, except that his statement regarding the birth certificate in the couch cushion indicated "the poor fellow has to be delusional. No wonder somebody shot him." As for the party, "It's in God's hands now," he said. "God's and Milton's."

Hewitt winced at that partnership. "What's bothering you, Buck?" he asked. "Was it something that happened at the lawyer's this morning?"

Buckley shook his head bemusedly. "No. That went as expected. I guess I miss the lady."

"You mean Angel?"

"Who else?"

"Any chance she can fly in tomorrow for the party?"

Buckley frowned at him. "I said I missed her. I didn't say I wanted her to inhibit my party fun. A Saturday arrival will be just fine. But I think I will give her a call, see how she's faring."

He slid his chair back and stood. "You will excuse me, Al?"

"Of course."

As soon as Buckley stepped from the dining room, Henrietta was out of the kitchen glaring at Hewitt who'd just started on the pie. "You a slow eater," she said. "I got me a life, you know."

"Why don't I just take this pie and my coffee into the living room?" he said. "Let you finish up in here, so you can get home."

Henrietta merely nodded and began clearing the table.

The living room was vacant. Hewitt placed his pie and coffee on the table in front of the couch, sat and stared at the darkened TV screen. Wearying of that, he got up and turned on the machine.

A courtroom drama was in progress.

The gruff defense attorney, Perry Mason, was grilling the wild-eyed leader of a religious sect who had witnessed an argument between the victim, his supposedly devoted follower, and the attorney's client, a beautiful but perplexed woman who had been trying in vain to get her younger sister to leave the sect. Mason was prying loose the hidden fact that the follower had been leading a takeover of the sect.

The plot's combination of religion and betrayal of leadership were enough to catch Hewitt's fancy and he was deep into the episode when Buckley wandered into the room, complaining about the telephone.

"It's my goddamned company and my goddamned WATS line, and they're making me wait."

"I'm sorry," Hewitt said, half an eye still on the TV courtroom. "What's the problem?"

"Evidently the WATS line is being used by someone in the building. For a personal call, I have no doubt."

"Can't you just make a regular long distance call to Angel?"

"I have. Three of them. The hotel says her room line is busy. She's talking to that mother of hers, I bet. Ghastly woman."

Hewitt gave up on the TV.

"Even at station-to-station rates," Buckley said, pouring himself a tot of brandy, "these calls are killing me."

Hewitt figured the man was a millionaire several times over. He didn't blink at sending a frog on a first-class flight to Boston. But he was balking at making a few long distance calls.

"Besides, it's three hours later there. It's eleven-thirty," Buckley said. "God dammit, I want that WATS now. What do you say, Al? Will you do this for me?"

"Do what, exactly?"

"Search the building and find out who's using the WATS line and tell them to hang the hell up."

Hewitt stood. It was a simple enough request, he supposed.

"Begin with Milton," Buckley said. "He seems to use his office as a late-night salon."

T.J. the security guard was just starting in on a pizza that nearly covered the desktop when Hewitt stepped from the elevator. "Oh, hi, Al," he said. "Heading for your nightly?"

"Actually, I was wondering if Milton Armstead was still in his office?"

"He left about an hour ago."

"Anybody else on the first floor?"

T.J.'s forehead wrinkled in thought. "A light was on when I made my last pass. One of the copywriters. I didn't look in to see who. Don't like to disturb people when they're working. You looking for somebody specific?"

"Somebody's got the WATS line tied up and Mr. Buckley wants to use it."

"That's a big no-no." T.J. put down the pizza slice and started to rise. "Lemme help you look."

Hewitt waved him down. "No. Eat your pizza while it's warm. I can handle it."

"There are some guys up in Editorial playing poker."

"I'll look in on them next," Hewitt said and opened the door to the first floor.

"Good luck," T.J. said. "Just don't open any windows or exit doors to the street. Those alarms go off, all hell . . . all heck breaks loose around here."

"Thanks for the warning," Hewitt said as he left the lobby.

He scanned the dimly lit first floor area. Only one of the closed doors was outlined by light.

It was the office shared by the two copywriters—Trauble and Weeks.

Heading for the closed door, he was reminded of the rather unpleasant sensation he used to experience when proctoring the Sunday School Bible tests at his former church in Buzz. One got an ugly pleasure from being able to frighten and judge.

He heard a low murmur coming from the room.

A foot from the door, he recognized the speaker as Roger Weeks, even though Weeks was forcing his voice into an unnatural, lower register. "Oh, baby, I hope it was as good for you as it was for me," he was saying.

Hewitt didn't quite get the drift of what he was hearing until Weeks' description of his orgasm exploded into graphic detail. The ex-archbishop decided the whole scene was much too sordid for him.

He was backing away when he heard a word that froze him in his tracks. The word was, "Angel."

"You and me, Angel," Weeks was saying. "Our bodies intertwined forever."

It had to be another Angel. No way would the Angel he knew risk a premium relationship for a fling with a balding, unattractive little slug like Weeks.

"Roger's hungry for his honeybun," the slug was saying. "Hurry back from Boston, baby."

Hewitt's heart sank.

He understood Buckley well enough to realize that he could not tell him about Angel and Weeks. The bearer of bad tidings would receive no reward, instead would probably be banished from the happy *Ogle* kingdom.

What was the silly woman thinking? he wondered. Ah, of course. She was probably using Weeks to make Buck jealous. Which meant that she'd make sure Buck found out.

Well, it wasn't his business, really. He would just step back and try to forget—

What did Weeks just say about photos?

"I finished the note that's gonna go with the photos, baby. Wanna hear it?"

Evidently she did.

"It's like this: 'Dear Bla-Bla, thought you might like a copy of this for your personal file. We've another copy ready to be mailed to' . . . and here we put either Buckley's or the guy's wife's name or both . . . 'unless we receive a mere' . . . and we stick them for $2,000 to $4,000, whatever we think the guy can scrape together . . . 'in cash. In return, we will send you the only other print and the negative.'

"We'll instruct them to send the loot to a P.O. Box at the marina I'll rent under a fake name."

Weeks was silent for a bit, apparently listening to a comment from Angel. Then, "I don't think they'll risk it. But even if they do, you know your Rog isn't dumb enough to retrieve the cash myself. I'll con somebody else to do it. Harry, maybe. He's simp enough to do me a favor and he lives out near the marina. Or I'll just pick up a stewbum from the Venice Boardwalk and promise him a pint to go get my 'mail.' If the cops grab him, c'est la vie. Back to square one.

"But nobody's going to go to the cops if we don't squeeze 'em too hard." He chuckled. "Forty-seven photos. I figure we've gotta clear at least one hundred grand. Added to what we get for the artwork and manuscripts and the three *Ogle* No. 1's I've snagged, we'll be living like royalty in old Me-hi-co."

Al Hewitt had heard more than enough.

He quietly made his exit.

"Find 'im, Al?" T.J. asked around a pizza slice.

"Nope. But the line's probably free by now, anyway."

When he arrived at the penthouse he heard the drone of Buckley's voice deep within the main suite and supposed Angel was satisfying her second caller of the evening. Or third. Or fourth. Why presume she had only two men on the string? In the real world, anything was possible.

He entered Henrietta's spotless kitchen and located a tin of coffee and an old-fashioned porcelain drip-brew pot. During his pre-teen years, after his mother had left for parts unknown, his father would sit beside the stove in his pajamas and robe for an hour each night, ladling boiling water into just such a brew pot, one spoonful at a time.

The resulting coffee would be thick and black and delicious, but that was not the point, his father explained. The point was that, by focusing on a single, simple task, one was able to clear one's mind of all the detritus it collected during a normal day.

His father had such wisdom. And integrity. Moral fiber, he called it. He wished the good man were still alive and he could phone him for advice. No, that wouldn't be good. He wouldn't have wanted his father to see the way his moral fiber was fraying.

He pulled a chair close to the stove and began to ladle the boiling water onto the dark brown grounds.

"Now that smells like the real McCoffee," Buckley said, sailing into the kitchen, naked under his loosely wrapped, red-and-black silk robe. "Come fly with me," he half sang, half mumbled as he opened the refrigerator and withdrew a carton of milk. "No caffeine for yours truly. I don't see how you can drink that stuff and sleep."

"It's for the morning," Hewitt lied.

Buckley half filled a tumbler and took a long gulp. "The gal loves me," he said, with a foolish grin on his face and milk on his moustache.

"Of course she does," Hewitt lied again.

"Of course she does," Buckley repeated. He polished off the milk, deposited the glass on the counter and headed out. "We've got to get you a lady," were his last words of the night.

42.

Terry was waiting in the Zoombuggy in a "No Parking, No Loitering" zone in front of Parker Center when Harry emerged a free man, at least temporarily. "Oh, God, was it awful?" she asked as he slid into the VW.

"Close enough." He looked at her, wondering how she could be so bright-eyed and cheery and beautiful at a little before 1 a.m.

"It'd be appropriate, as well as nice, if you had a big kiss for the girlfriend," she said.

"I smell bad and taste bad and thanks to the cot in the cell where they finally stuck me there are some very tiny crawling things that keep biting me." To emphasize that point, he began scratching his side.

"What're human odors and a few little lice when you're in love," she said, moving toward him with eyes closed and lips parted.

He barely pecked at those lips. "Really, honey, I feel like something *Wagon Train* left on the prairie. And I would dearly love to get the hell away from this garden spot."

"A good hot bath," she said, putting the Zoombuggy in gear.

"Maybe a drink first?"

"Definitely," she said. "Herkie's?"

"No-no. Home and stiff drink and shower."

She waited until she was headed toward the freeway to ask, "What went on in there, anyway?"

279

"Well, Cardona's got this theory that you mentioned a long time ago: I killed your pal Tobella and his boyfriend because he or they were sleeping with you."

"Ummm."

"Were they?"

"Not . . . exactly."

"Both of them?"

"Of course not. Neither one, really. They were gay as geese. But there was a night Joe and I got a little high and he decided to see if he could change his luck. It turned out he couldn't."

"He must have been really queer," Harry said.

She smiled. "That may be the nicest compliment you've ever paid me. So . . . why would Cardona think Joe and I did the deed?"

"They found nude photos of you at Tobella's. Didn't they mention them to you?"

"Well, yeah," she said. "Then they reminded me that I'd told them I barely knew Joe. And I said, well, I posed for him once, which to me is barely knowing somebody. That seemed to satisfy them so they let me go. They said they were keeping you for a while; wouldn't tell me why. And I went directly to Ida and she got you a lawyer."

"Thanks, honey. If he hadn't shown up, I'd still be collecting body bugs and listening to my cellmates describe in intimate detail the things they wanted to do to Julie Andrews."

"Mary Poppins?"

"Heck yeah. I was about to chime in when—" He stopped talking to jam his foot helplessly against the floorboard as the Zoombuggy nearly zoomed into the rear of a bus. "Anyway, as Stooley mentioned, Cardona and Oskar have a witness and they wanted him to take a look at me. They were going to hold me for a lineup in the morning, but the lawyer, Corrigan, insisted they do it then and there or let me go."

"Were you worried?"

"What do you think? Somebody could have seen me go into Tobella's that night."

"But if a witness saw you, they'd have seen me, too. So Cardona would've been looking for a couple. And they'd never have let me go."

She aimed the Zoombuggy up onto the Harbor Freeway. They were almost to the 10, before she said, "I'm guessing the witness gave you a pass."

"Nothing conclusive," Harry said. "He was on Staysail, so whoever he saw definitely wasn't me. But, according to the lawyer, Corrigan, the witness said the suspect was about my height. He's not really sure about facial features, because he was too far away and it was dark. But he thought the guy was thicker through the chest and had an entirely different build."

"What was this witness doing on the street at that time of night, anyway?"

"Walking his pet spider monkey."

"You're joking, right?"

"It's Venice, California," he said.

"He say anything else?"

"Well, that's the thing," Harry said. "The guy ran out of Tobella's and got into a van."

Apparently ignoring the fact that they were on the Santa Monica Freeway, heading west at approximately seventy miles per hour, she turned to stare at him. "Didn't Cardona connect that to the white van that followed us to Nirvana?"

"This one was a grey van. And could you keep your eyes on the road, please? I don't want to die with jail lice on my body."

She blithely changed lanes, barely avoiding the left bumper of a new Lincoln. "White, grey. Close enough for nighttime, right?" she asked.

"Not for Cardona," Harry said.

"If you're the killer, who was the man everybody saw shoot Howard?"

"Somebody I hired."

"What a meathead," she said.

"Anyway, the witness—why don't I call him Tarzan?—Tarzan says another guy left Tobella's a minute later. Understand, this is all second-hand, from Corrigan, who was quizzing Tarzan while they were getting ready for the lineup."

"I assume the second guy didn't look like you, either," she said.

"Too thin. Tarzan said he was tall and looked like Satan in a beautifully tailored suit and he drove off in a black Mercedes, license plate not noted. Who else could it have been but . . ."

"Milton," she said.

She was quiet for a mile or so, long enough for Harry to dare hope she was finished with the subject of murder for the night. He'd certainly had his fill. But alas . . .

She slapped the steering wheel and said in angry frustration, "We just don't know enough."

"We don't know anything," Harry said.

"We know Milton was there, but we don't know why. We know he arrived before Tarzan happened by. Let's say he finds the door open and goes in. Then what?"

"He bumps into the killer on his way out?"

"No," she said. "If Milton had seen the killer, he'd be dead now, too."

"Unless he is the killer," Harry said.

"Oh, Harry." Her voice took on a tone of disappointment. "We know for a fact that the man in the van—definitely not Milton—shot Howard. And he was at Joe's when he was killed. Therefore, the man in the van is the killer, not Milton."

"That's faulty logic," Harry said. "To begin, we don't know for a fact that Howard's shooter was driving the white van we saw. We don't really know that that van was the same one Tarzan saw on Staysail Street. And we don't know that Milton and he weren't working together. Like I said, we know nothing."

"You can be really infuriating," she said, spinning the wheel so suddenly to the right he was thrown against the door as the Zoombuggy took the Lincoln Boulevard off-ramp on two wheels. "You just wait until I get you in bed tonight," she said. "I'll show you what we know."

43.

At 12:30 a.m., fully alert thanks to the extra-strong brew, Al Hewitt took the inside stairwell down to the first floor. He assumed Weeks would have departed for home long ago. His main concern was bumping into T.J. It was why he decided to wait until the half-hour. T.J. had explained to him once that he made his rounds every hour on the hour, and the security guard struck him as being one of the most literal-minded inhabitants on the planet.

Still, he was very cautious upon entering the first floor.

The night lights provided enough illumination to guide him past the empty desks. He could even see that someone had placed a similar sheet of white paper on each desktop.

Once inside the totally dark office shared by Weeks and Trauble, he closed the door and clicked on the flashlight he'd brought.

The cleaning crew had given the room only a minimal sprucing, probably because they'd had to work around Weeks. The wastebaskets were empty. The floor had been swept if not mopped. The twin desktops of simulated wood that faced one another were dust free. Each held an electric typewriter, a phone, a stapler, a tape dispenser, a staple remover, a letter opener, an *Ogle* mug containing pens and pencils and a bi-level IN/OUT basket.

And a white sheet similar to the ones on the desks in the outer office.

An ant farm, preserved between two sheets of glass, had been taped to the far edge of the desk closest to the door, the one with Weeks' nameplate on it. That desktop also supported a black onyx tray on which rested an assortment of gewgaws, an unused ashtray from the Hotel Las Hamadas in Acapulco, cuff links, a tie clasp, a drinking glass and a coffee cup, each emblazoned with the *Ogle* frog.

Ignoring the white sheets of paper, Hewitt began to test Weeks' seven desk drawers. Only one was locked—the bottom right.

He picked up Weeks' letter opener and slid it between that drawer and its guide. He paused, straining to hear any sound that would indicate the near presence of T.J.

Satisfied that there were no scuffs or steps, he forced the letter opener against the desk lock.

The lock wouldn't give.

He tried prying up and had better success. The metal drawer buckled slightly.

He pried harder and the drawer popped free.

Eagerly, he shined his flashlight on the fruits of his labor. A stack of mimeographed sheets blocked his view of the rest of the drawer. He placed them on the desk and played the light over the drawer's remaining contents. Nothing but a checkbook, a five-dollar bill and scattered Mexican coins and paper money.

Hewitt flipped through the checkbook. Weeks deposited his biweekly salary checks of $438.50 and kept a total of just under $1,000 in the account. Nothing unusual there.

He looked at the top mimeoed sheet. "Party Party Party. Tonight!" it announced. He turned over the white paper on Weeks' desktop. It was from the same batch. He continued reading. "Trower Buckley is happy to invite every member of the *Ogle* staff to a party at the fabulous estate of former governor George Moody."

A map to the ex-governor's home was included, along with the advice to get there early and "bring your swimsuits . . . or not."

At the bottom of the page was a forged signature of Buckley's that in no way resembled the genuine article.

Hewitt almost had to admire Weeks' gall. Not only was the man cuckolding Buckley and attempting to blackmail the magazine's executives, he was now undermining Buckley's plans for a gala with a five-females to one-male ratio. With all the magazine's male employees—from the delivery guys to the typesetters—party party partying, instead of exercising his droit du seigneur, Buckley would probably have to wait in line.

As amusing as that prospect was, Hewitt was still stuck with the problem of locating the incriminating photos. They were probably at Weeks' home. It wouldn't be that difficult to find the address, but Hewitt hadn't much heart for housebreaking.

He sighed and flashed the light around for a last look at the office. There was a cabinet running the length of the wall behind Trouble's chair.

He circled the desks and began with the panel on the far right. Behind it were office supplies—white typing paper, pens and pencils.

The next panel led to legal pads and boxes of transparent tape and staples. Panel three housed books—a Webster's dictionary, a thesaurus, *Bartlett's Quotations, The Elements of Style*, several slang dictionaries.

Then things got a bit less organized. The final three panels were hiding papers and folders, old magazines—*Life, Time,* et al., as well as *Ogle* and its competitors—all jammed together.

Hewitt dug into the mess, spilling it onto the tile floor—clipped pages, mainly of advertisements, torn and cut up magazines, interoffice memo envelopes, unopened junk mail, centerfolds, even an empty beer can. It was as if Weeks and/or

Trauble had scooped everything off the floor and jammed it into that space.

He was about to examine the trash more closely when he heard rubber soles squeaking toward the door. He flicked off the flashlight and ducked into the kneehole of Trauble's desk.

The squeaks paused just outside the closed door.

Then they continued, moving away now.

Hewitt slumped, sitting down on the tile while he waited for his heart to stop pounding. Looking heavenward, he got only as far as the underside of Trauble's desk, less than three inches away, where even in the dim light he saw a key held in place by masking tape. Of course the sly Weeks would hide it there, keeping himself one step removed from its possible discovery.

Hewitt picked it free. The flashlight showed up the number "298" and under it the words "Union Passenger Station."

Fueled by caffeine, anxiety and adrenaline, the ex-archbishop decided he had to go to the station before the workday began to make sure the photos and negatives were there. He could replace the trash back into the cabinets, but there was no way he could adequately disguise the damage he'd done to Weeks' desk drawer.

The copywriter would immediately assume someone was on to his blackmail plans. He might send the photos to Buckley out of spite.

Hewitt returned to the fifth floor via the inside stairwell where he refined his plan of action. He had only a vague idea where Union Station was located. At that hour of the morning, the choice of a guide to the city was rather limited.

"Taking a train trip?" T.J. asked. "You'll miss the party." He held up the now familiar mimeographed invitation.

"I'm not taking a trip. There's something I have to pick up at the station." He pointed at the invitation. "When did those get delivered?"

T.J. shrugged. "Beats me. Somebody passed 'em out after my eight o'clock round and when I got back from the nine o'clock, this was on the desk here."

"Well, anyway, I need directions to the station."

"Right. You know Beverly Boulevard, Al? Just take it all the way east 'til you hit . . . no, wait a minute. Beverly turns into 1st Street somewhere downtown around Olivera or Chinatown and then you take that . . . or maybe 2nd Street until . . ."

Confusion twisted his face into a simian scowl. "Oh, heck," he said. "I know how to get there, but I can't put it into words." He looked at the large plain-faced watch on his wrist and brightened. "Herm should be showing up at two to take over here. That's just twelve and a half minutes from now. You don't mind waiting, I'll drive you."

The idea of sharing a long car ride with T.J. wasn't very high on Hewitt's wish list, but he had precious little confidence in his ability to navigate L.A.'s urban sprawl on his own. Especially in an unfamiliar vehicle such as the bright red rental convertible Buckley had put at his disposal. Especially at night in a city where—if one believed the news—pockets of racial unrest were ready to ignite.

"I wouldn't want to . . . ," he began halfheartedly. "I mean, you're probably weary after. . . ."

"No. Not at all," T.J. said. "I'm a night person. I'd be happy to have something to do."

"That's very kind of you," Hewitt said, sitting down on the same Naugahyde and chrome chair next to the ersatz mulberry bush that he had used on his arrival at *Ogle*.

This time, the wait was slightly shorter.

Herm Philbrick, whose seven-hour security shift was sched-uled to begin at 2 a.m., didn't show up until nearly 2:15. The dog-shift guard struck Hewitt as something of a mystery gender-wise, pudgy, with a salt-and-pepper crew cut, his or her round, jowly face featured rather long lashes over bright sapphire eyes, the lips of a pouting Cupid and soft, smooth skin that showed not a hint of a beard.

The hand Herm offered when T.J. introduced them was small and soft but had a surprisingly strong grip.

"Sorry I'm late, buddy," Herm said to T.J. with a forced gruffness that did little to mask his or her soprano voice. "Friggin' alarm didn't go off."

He or she gave T.J. a manly arm punch. "I'll make it up to ya. Okay, amigo?"

"Huh? Oh, sure," T.J. said, jamming his pizza box into the wastebasket. He removed his gunbelt and handed it to Herm. "There's a big *Ogle* party tonight at some guy's house." He pointed out the mimeoed sheet. "Everybody's invited. If you go, don't forget me here. Maybe I can catch the tail end."

"You got it, my man."

Walking away from the building, Hewitt asked T.J., "Is Herm's name Herman or Hermione?"

"What do you mean?"

"I couldn't really tell if Herm was a feminine man or a masculine woman," Hewitt said.

"Gee. I don't know." T.J. was leading him down an alley to the rear of the building. "I guess I just assumed he's a guy."

"Where are we going?" Hewitt asked.

"The garage."

There was a larger alley behind the building, wide enough for vehicles to use. T.J. pulled out a ring of keys and poked one of them into a lock holding a hinged metal garage door to a hook recessed into the concrete floor.

With minimal urging from T.J., the freed door slid up on rollers into a position parallel to the ceiling of a brightly lit small garage.

"I never knew this existed," Hewitt said.

"Not many people do. That's the boss's wagon." T.J. pointed to a maroon Bentley. "Most times he uses the limo, so I get to take it for a drive just to keep the battery charged.

"The 190SLs," he said, indicating two sleek sports convertibles—one white with a black top, the other black with a white top, "are kinda like company cars. When the Eyefuls get invited to an event, sometimes they drive up in them. A while back, they let a writer from New York drive the black one for a weekend visit and he got stoned and ran it into the side of the Chateau Marmont. $7,000 damage."

"That seems a little out of place," Hewitt said, pointing to a boxy white van.

"It's for hauling magazines and stuff, mainly when the Eyefuls make an appearance at a convention or the like," T.J. said. "Doesn't get much use, except when Bingham or his ad guys need it."

"Who parks in the empty spaces?"

"The top execs," T.J. said. "Milton Armstead and . . . the others. Bingham. Dobbs.

"That little beauty is mine." It was a black Hillman-Minx cabriolet with a red top. "Just bought it a month ago. Only two years old and had hardly any miles on it. A sweet deal."

"Nice car," Hewitt said. "Rank has its privileges, eh?"

"What do you mean?"

"I mean Herm probably parks on the street."

"Oh." T.J. grinned. "I'm sort of the garage guy. I get a few extra bucks to make sure the vehicles are clean and polished and gassed up. Doesn't take more'n an hour or so every few days and I save nearly that much time not having to hunt for a place on the street. This time of night, Herm has his pick of places."

T.J. used another key from his ring to unlock the door to the Hillman-Minx. He got into the vehicle to roll down the windows, then stepped out again. "Okay if we push the top back."

"Why not?" Hewitt said.

"It'll go faster if you give me a hand. We can make it just half-convertible or do it the whole way."

"Your call."

"Great. All the way."

Together, they managed to unhook the frame of the cabriolet's top and push back the heavy but flexible canvas. "The last car I had was this really old Buick that used to die on me all the time," T.J. said. "Happened on the Ventura Freeway once. Man, was that scary. I do my best not to use the freeways any more after that. But sometimes you can't avoid 'em."

The Hillman-Minx seemed toy-like to Hewitt, but it was clean and surprisingly comfortable. And it had that calming new-car perfume.

He had never thought much about automobiles. They were strictly transport. But this odd little vehicle was pretty charming and it ran smoothly. And he liked driving with the top down, the feel of the warm wind on his face and the view it provided of the city's neon glow as it drifted upward to lose itself in the inky, star-filled sky.

Union Station with its 135-foot-high clock and observation tower was something of a surprise. He'd assumed the architecture would be of the Spanish Mission variety. But he wasn't prepared for the perfection with which that had been blended with a Thirties deco style, or the beauty or oddness of the place at night, so lonely, with pastel colored lights casting shadows across its clean surfaces and slim, towering palm trees guarding the entrance while hula-ing in the breeze.

T.J. had stopped the Minx close to the entrance. "Want me to come in with you?" he asked. "I could park over—"

"Stay where you are. I'll just be a minute."

T.J. said that was fine with him.

The station was far from deserted. Long wooden benches were serving as makeshift beds for weary travelers caught between trains, many of them wearing military uniforms. Of those awake and alert none seemed to be appreciating the carved wooden beams high overhead or the polished marble floor under their feet.

Hewitt was so fascinated by the beauty of that shadowy beamed ceiling that he had to force himself to attend to the job at hand.

A weary clerk stifled a yawn long enough to point out the storage lockers at an area near the tracks. Number 298 was at the far end of the second tier.

Hewitt put his hand in his pants pocket and found coins but no key. With a hint of unease, he tried the other pocket. Unease turned to panic. He ran his hands over his clothes . . . and felt the outline of the key on his right side. It was in the tiny pocket within his coat pocket—the one called, appropriately, the "key" pocket.

Hand shaking, he inserted it into the lock and opened the door.

A thick manila envelope rested inside the locker.

He withdrew it and backed away, forgetting to close the locker door.

He undid the envelope's metal fastener and pushed back the flap. He paused to make sure no one was paying him any mind, then pulled the stack of photographs partially out of the envelope.

He saw enough of the top photo to convince himself that this was Weeks' stash. Now, if the negatives were there, too . . . yes, long strips encased in protective plastic sleeves.

He shoved photos and negatives back into the envelope and returned to the Hillman-Minx. T.J. had kept the motor running and was leaning back, looking at the night sky and listening to some smoky-voiced songstress on the radio. He clicked off the music when Hewitt got into the car.

"What's in the envelope?"

"Some personal items."

"You mean like letters and stuff?" T.J. asked without too much interest.

"Exactly."

"I get letters every now and then," T.J. said and aimed the car in a westerly direction. "Uh, Al, I don't suppose you'd want to grab a burger?"

Hewitt was anxious to get back to the penthouse where he would have all the time he needed to destroy the photos before Buckley returned from dreamland. "It's a little late," he said.

"Yeah. I guess it is. I'll drop you off and then go to a drive-in by myself." There was only a touch of wistfulness in T.J.'s voice, but the young man exhibited such a lack of affect in general that it struck Hewitt as a cry for companionship.

"I'm not very hungry," he said, "but I suppose I could have a glass of milk while you ate."

T.J.'s drive-in of choice was Tiny Naylor's, a sleek and flashy diner on Sunset and La Brea that looked like it had been designed with The Jetsons in mind. He'd barely nestled the Minx into one of several empty slots under the broad canopy roof when a waitress approached. Her white paper cap was slightly askew and the canopy's sparkling lights accentuated her weariness.

T.J. ordered a vanilla milk shake with his cheeseburger and

Hewitt surprised himself by saying, "Make that two."

Watching her depart, T.J. said, "I heard the girls used to be on roller skates. But that was before I ever came here."

"You're not from L.A.?" Hewitt asked. His thoughts were on the package in his lap, but he made a game effort to seem interested in the young man's mainly one-sided conversation.

"I am. I mean, I was born here. But when I was a little kid we lived in the Valley, Sherman Oaks, and I didn't even know about this place. And when I was older, I was going to boarding school in Santa Barbara and then to college at San Luis Obispo."

"A college man, eh?"

"Not exactly. It wasn't working for me so I quit and came back here last year. But I haven't given up on getting a degree. In Law, maybe."

"Your folks from here?" Hewitt asked.

The question seemed to dampen T.J.'s spirits. "They are," he said. "I see 'em all the time. I just wish . . ."

Hewitt stared at him expectantly.

"I guess I wish we were more of a family."

"Your parents don't get along?" Hewitt knew something about that situation.

"They get along okay. They just don't live together." He brightened suddenly. "But it looks like that might change."

Hewitt knew something about that sort of dream, too. "I hope so," he said, as the waitress returned with a loaded tray that she hooked to T.J.'s door.

T.J. thanked her politely. He opened the Minx's glove compartment and, using great care, placed Hewitt's shake and plate with burger and fries on its flat surface. Satisfied that he'd completed his duties as host, he took a huge, happy bite of his own late-night snack.

As Hewitt reached out for his burger, his hand froze. A very sinister-looking little pistol rested in the glove compartment.

T.J. must have noticed his reaction. "I bought that yesterday," he said. "And his brother, too." He patted a bulge in his uniform pants pocket. "It's too darn dangerous around *Ogle* these days. Florence getting killed was the last straw. Anybody that tries to break this boy's neck is gonna get a big surprise."

He grinned and took another bite of his burger. "Eat up, Al. Burger's don't come any better than this."

But Hewitt's appetite had gone south.

44.

"What the goddamned hell?" Trower Buckley bellowed as he entered the kitchen of the penthouse at 9:30 the next morning. He slammed a copy of the mimeographed invitation onto the table beside Al Hewitt's dry toast.

Hewitt stifled a yawn and looked up from his cup-of-coffee breakfast. He'd returned to the penthouse approximately six hours earlier which was when he'd discovered that there was one more negative than there were photographs in the collection. He thought he knew which one it would be. The romantic Roger Weeks had kept evidence of his own welcome-to-*Ogle* engagement with Angel.

It had taken Hewitt until nearly 4:30 a.m. to locate that extra negative and another fifteen or twenty minutes to slavishly scissor everything else into pieces small enough to be flushed down the toilet.

Now, after less than five hours' sleep, with Buckley's voice still ringing in his ears, he leaned forward to look at the invitation that he had come to know quite well. "What's all this?" he asked.

"These were placed on every bloody desk in the whole bloody building," Buckley said in a clipped, pseudo–British accent that he used in moments of high annoyance. "Dammit, Milton knew the kind of party I wanted. He must've lost his sex-besotted mind."

"What makes you think he's responsible? Anybody working

here could have done this."

"Good point," Buckley said. "Well, it's going to be up to Milton to undo it, pronto. I'm not going to have my party ruined by the presence of riffraff. My God, even the bloody messenger boys—"

He was interrupted by a bronze beauty named Orma, one of three super-efficient secretaries who kept his office and his life in order. "You might want to check this out," she said, handing him a thick envelope.

From it he withdrew several handwritten pages.

He began to read aloud: " 'We the undersigned want to thank you from the bottom of our hearts for the privilege of working for such a fine and noble man as yourself who would be so appreciative of his devoted staff to invite one and all to his grand party.' "

His scowl softened as he read and Hewitt thought he observed a little mist in the publisher's eyes as he continued:

" 'You are indeed a rare employer and we will work long and hard to show our appreciation for this kindness.'

"Damn it, Al, there must be nearly a hundred signatures on this thing."

He turned to the secretary, "You'd better get Dobbs to inform the ex-governor that instead of a select little gathering of sixty or so, there will be nearly three times that. He should also expect most of them to be yahoos with no regard for his station or possessions. Notify Milton, too, that the food and drink order should be tripled."

As she went to do his bidding, Buckley sat down at the table across from Hewitt and sighed. "Did I do the right thing, Al?"

"Without a doubt. You chose love and devotion over mutiny."

"Dammit, I suppose I do want to be loved," Buckley said.

When Harry and Terry arrived at work that morning at a little after nine, the reception area was jammed with people talking about the party. No one questioned the lateness of the invitations or the fact that this was the first time in the magazine's history that the staff had been invited to anything but the lame company Christmas outing at the Santa Monica Pier. It was party time and very little work would get done that day.

Weeks did not seem to be sharing the high spirits of the rest of the staff. He sat at his desk, morosely staring out of their solitary window.

"Morning, Roger," Harry said, expecting no reply and getting none.

Circling Weeks' desk, he saw that the floor was littered with trash. "What happened here?" he said, stepping over the magazines and papers.

"Why ask me?" Weeks said angrily.

Harry pulled his chair to the mess, sat and began shoving the trash back into the far cabinet. "Isn't this crap yours?" he asked.

"Fuck you, Trauble," Weeks said. He rose and left the room.

Harry was used to Weeks' moods, both high and low, but this seemed to be verging on a serious depression. Something had really brought the man down. Probably the mystery girlfriend, if she even existed.

He grabbed another handful of tear sheets and magazines and exposed a familiar centerfold. It was the one he and Weeks had discussed a while back. The pretty brunette nude with horn-rimmed glasses. He realized she was reading Kinsey's *Sexual Behavior in the Human Female*.

Good prop, he thought.

He was about to send the bookish brunette into the cabinet with the rest of the junk when he recalled what Bethune had said about the centerfold the late Nick Hobart had stashed in the white couch. That Eyeful had been reading a book, too.

The white couch had been in their office when this centerfold had first turned up. Had it fallen from its hiding place when the couch was carried in?

He looked at the remaining pile of trash, wondering if the Buckley birth certificate might be hidden in it.

"So you finally decided to drop in, huh, Trouble?" It was the aggravating voice of Maurice Grumbacher, coming from the doorway, followed by the unmistakable wave of toxic musk. "In my office, right fucking now."

"Gee, Maurice, nice to have you back," Harry said.

Grumbacher was already heading away. "Now," he shouted.

Harry slipped the centerfold into a drawer and stood. He paused briefly to move some of the trash around with the toe of his shoe, but didn't see anything resembling a birth certificate or a document of any kind.

He strolled unhurriedly across the floor to find that Grumbacher's door was closed.

"In here." The voice came from Larry Beagle's office.

Grumbacher had taken over the larger space and, Harry presumed, the title of Promotion Manager. He was sitting behind Beagle's desk. Beagle's military knickknacks and framed family photos had been replaced by an ugly brass paperweight, a china statue of a horse rearing up, front legs extended, a radio in a brown plastic case and an empty IN/OUT basket.

"Close the fucking door."

Harry did that. He started to sit down on the couch, but was ordered to take a chair closer to the desk.

Grumbacher sat back and put his feet on the desktop, almost knocking over the china horse. "So, Trouble, what was it like?"

"What was what like?"

"Killing the queers."

"Are you nuts?" Harry was on his feet.

"Hey, take it easy. C'mon, sit. I'm not judging you. If anybody needed killing . . ."

"Maurice, what the hell are you talking about? I didn't kill anybody."

"Okay. Sure-sure." Grumbacher swung his feet off of the desk and slid his chair closer, assuming a more businesslike position. "Sit. Fill me in on what's been shaking around here. I've got a parley with Milton in 60 and want to be up to speed."

Harry sat down again. "Well, there's the party tonight, which I guess you heard about at the meeting yesterday."

"I, ah, didn't make it in for the meeting," Grumbacher said. "Anything new on the Image Campaign?"

"I think it's Weeks you should be talking to," Harry said. "He's the one in the loop."

"Really? I never thought of him as loopster potential. You're the guy who impresses me, Trauble." He leaned in closer, lowering his voice. "C'mon. Just between us old dogs, you sliced up those fruiters, right?"

Harry finally understood what was happening. He smiled and said, "Maurice, you're the one who threatened to kill those guys. If anybody killed 'em, it was you."

"Now wait a minute . . ."

"Right in front of this building, you told Tobella you were going to get him."

"I . . . I've been cleared. The witness . . ."

"The witness cleared me, too," Harry said. "But the difference is, you threatened those guys. I bet the detectives could find a bunch of people who heard you."

Grumbacher grabbed the radio and was trying to pull its cord free when the door opened and Cardona and Oskar came in. Oskar yanked the radio from Grumbacher's grasp and placed it on the desk. He gave the cord a tug and a tiny microphone at its end popped out of the rear of the case.

Cardona stared at Grumbacher and said, "Well?"

"Well what?"

"You threatened to kill Tobella?"

"Now wait a minute," Grumbacher whined. "You said this was to get a confession from Trauble."

"I'll take what I'm offered," Cardona said. "Did you threaten to kill Tobella?"

"I was . . . annoyed, upset. They were climbing all over the marquee. No permission. And they smart-mouthed me. You get a little riled at that, but you don't kill anybody for smart-mouth."

"It's happened," Cardona said.

"He was having an affair with Florence Proneswagger," Harry said.

"Better and better," Cardona said. "Let's go three for three. If you weren't at work yesterday morning, Grumbacher, where were you?"

"I . . . spent the morning at home."

"Playing hooky from the office?" Cardona asked. "Missing a big meeting? Why would you do that?"

"I, ah . . . thanks to that swill they serve in lockup, I had a bad case of Montezuma's Revenge."

That prompted a chuckle from Oskar. Cardona didn't seem too amused. "Your wife will back you up on that?"

"My wife left me," Grumbacher said.

"Probably worried she'd be next," Harry said.

"Shut up, Trauble," Cardona said.

Oskar was still having fun with it. "You didn't happen to hang on to any evidence of that diarrhea?"

His partner shot him a flinty glance, then turned to Grumbacher, unclipping the cuffs from his belt. "You know the routine."

"Awww. Not again."

"Trauble, you mind telling me why you lied that evening up at your girlfriend's when you said you didn't hear Grumbacher threaten the sculptor?"

"I didn't exactly lie," Harry said. "I just sort of shaded—"

"What about the night of the Proneswagger killing, when you told me you didn't know anything about her personal life?"

"Well, that might have been a lie. I just couldn't see Maurice killing anybody."

"And now?" Oskar asked.

"I don't know."

"Neither do we," Cardona said. "But we're gonna find out. And you're joining us downtown."

"Me?" Harry asked. "Why?"

Cardona grinned. "To give us an official statement."

"Swell," Harry said.

All first-floor conversation ceased when they emerged from the office. People stood rigid as statues as the four of them, Grumbacher in handcuffs, marched from the building.

"Any chance your lab guys might be finished with my car?" Harry asked.

"They were," Cardona said. "But now that there's a connection between Proneswagger and Grumbacher, we're gonna have to give the prints on it another long look."

"Swell," Harry said again.

When they released him, Terry was waiting for him in the Zoombuggy, parked within view of the entrance of Parker Center. "We've got to stop meeting here like this," she said as he got into the car. "Did they give you your old cell back?"

"No cell. Just a cheesy-looking office and a stenographer. Maurice, on the other hand, is enjoying the full services of the lockup."

"You think he did it?"

"I don't have a clue. Except that there wasn't any musk odor at Tobella's. I wouldn't have thought him smart enough to go muskless when he's in murder mode. But maybe I've underestimated him."

Terry felt it was hardly the place to give him the present she'd wrapped earlier that day. But he looked so depressed, she reached into the car's tiny well and withdrew the brightly colored gift.

"What's this?" he asked, brightening in spite of himself.

"Today's our anniversary," she said. "We met one month ago."

"Just a month?" he asked, tearing at the paper. "It seems like . . . yesterday."

It was a framed photograph of them standing on the street near the *Ogle* Building on that fateful morning a month before.

"This is from the marquee shots," he said.

"Right. I asked poor Florence to blow up the photo and crop it. She was such a sweet woman. If that louse Maurice Grumbacher strangled her, I hope he swings for it."

"They don't hang people any more in this country, honey. But I share your sentiments. And I love the photo. I wish I had something for you."

"I'm expecting something," she purred with mock sexuality, "at my place after the party."

"The party?" He grimaced. "Don't tell me you want to go?"

"I have to," she said. "Receptionists don't get an option. They want girls at these things. But you don't have to . . . unless you want to save me from the lustful clutches of all the guys who'll be there. Including, I understand, Mr. Gary Lockwood."

"Who's that?"

"A very handsome actor. He was in Elvis' last movie."

"Gee, then I guess I have no choice," Harry said.

45.

At five o'clock, the employees of *Ogle* magazine put away the tools of their trade and vacated the building with all the speed of ravening wolves scenting meat on the hoof.

Lew Mitteer and Cholly Grandiose were the first of the revelers to arrive at the Moody compound high in the Pacific Palisades. They traveled in separate cars and set the style by parking in the middle of the ex-governor's manicured lawn. Then they bustled to the entrance to the sprawling hacienda-like main building, where they took a welcoming committee stance.

On their heels came the Editorial Department staff, leaping out of a Volks autobus and an ancient Nash Rambler. They rushed past the reception committee's outstretched hands and locust-like, buzzed through the cavernous home until they found the groaning tables laden with ham, beef, roast pork, Southern fried chicken and at least a dozen varieties of cheese. Ignoring the liveried help, they clawed at the food, stuffing it into their mouths as fast as their ink-stained fists would move. Then they yelled for drink.

At the entrance, Lew and Cholly continued trying to personally shake each and every hand, but the eager crowds were having none of their professional courtesy. The only hands that allowed themselves to be shaken belonged to the members of the Phil Remus Quartet, the musicians the publicists hired for the event.

By eight-fifteen, when Harry and Terry arrived, the party was in full swing. The food table had been leveled and re-loaded thrice, and was again showing bare spots. The drinks were flowing freely from bottle to glass to carpet. Phil Remus and his men were squeezed against the south wall of the great dining hall by the mob of frenzied, grasping, inarticulate, freeloading employees who drank, danced, sweated, shouted, spat, belched and wheezed and who, for this one night of nights, agreed that Trower Buckley was one hell of guy.

"I don't see Buck or any of the executives," Harry said to Lew Mitteer.

"An *Ogle* party has two phases," Lew explained, shouting above the noise of the crowd. "Phase One is for the amateurs. Phase Two is for the pros. That'll start around ten when everybody gets here."

"Swell," Harry said.

He found Terry teaching a strawberry blonde bartender how to mix an old-fashioned. "Can we go now?" he asked.

" 'Fraid not," she said.

She sampled the bartender's concoction, rolled it around her mouth and said, "Not bad, especially in a paper cup. Let's have another for my boyfriend."

Harry surveyed the gluttonous and grimly determined fun-seekers. He'd never been one for parties, was much more comfortable in one-on-one situations. Terry handed him a cocktail in a cup and said, "Gotta circulate. See you later."

"Wait," he said. Too late.

He watched her moving through the crowd. A gawky, acned teen "accidentally" fondled her butt. Two mail room bozos double-teamed her, momentarily sandwiching her between them, pressing against her fore and aft while rocking to the Phil Remus Quartet's rendition of "You've Lost That Lovin' Feeling." Extricating herself from their bodily embrace, she took only one step before Angus Flood, the ancient, diminutive, legally blind keeper of the *Ogle* galleys, ran into her, his face pressed hard against her breasts. He apologized profusely, but when she'd passed, he grinned and moved on to his next tall, full-breasted target.

After that, Harry stopped watching.

"Hi, Harry." *Ogle*'s art director Scotty Lemming was standing beside him. "Some party, huh? I was supposed to go to Frisco on business, but I didn't want to miss this."

Next to him was a stunningly beautiful woman with platinum hair whom Scotty introduced as his "better half, Janice."

With feline grace, the woman took Harry's hand in both of hers, brushing his palm with her long fingernails. "So handsome. Like a young William Holden." She followed that remarkable compliment with a lioness growl.

Blushing, Harry tried to concoct a suave reply. Scotty saved him from that struggle by angrily yanking his wife toward the dance floor. Looking over her husband's shoulder Janice Lemming blew Harry a kiss.

"William Holden, my ass." Roger Weeks was standing beside him. "The best she could do for me was Van Heflin."

"He's a good actor," Harry said.

"He's losing his hair and he's got this big brow. Trouble, you didn't find a key . . . no, of course it wasn't you."

"What're you talking about? What key?"

"Never mind."

"What?" Harry asked.

"It's too painful to talk about," Weeks said. "Are you getting drunk tonight? I'm getting drunk tonight."

Weeks dragged Harry back to the bar, where he got the overworked strawberry blonde to fill a cup with scotch, no water. "Let's go find a good seat for the show," he said.

"What show?"

"You weren't at the meeting on Thursday," Weeks said. "Buckley's gonna make some kind of major announcement to the senior executives. I don't want to miss it."

"It's hours before Buckley's supposed to arrive," Harry said. "Anyway, we're not senior execs."

"That's why we've got to get there early. Before the Pemberton Guards take their posts to keep people like us out."

He headed off through French doors leading to the pool area.

Harry searched the crowd. Terry was on the dance floor twisting around the clock with Wilbur "Snake Willie" Terhue, the skinny head of Accounting, garbed in one of his money-green, all-weather wool suits. Terhue grinned like he was counting cash; Terry seemed to be having the time of her life.

With a sigh, Harry followed after Weeks.

It was 9:24 p.m. when Buckley, Al Hewitt and Cholly Grandiose made their way to the Spanish-style guest house just beyond the tennis courts at the far end of the ex-governor's estate. By then, the two copywriters had been holed up for over an hour in a small, dark, accoustic-tiled film projection booth in the guest house.

Early on at the party Weeks had discovered the location of the meeting from an oddly naïve Pemberton Security Guard who'd fallen under the spell of his Pockets of Information questioning technique. The copywriter had proceeded to give the building a thorough vetting, deciding that the projection room made the ideal observation spot, offering a clear view of the big, comfortable living room, with its paintings of early Californios and Indians and the Pacific coastlines decorating its rough plaster walls, its bloodred tiled floors covered with subtly patterned Mexican rugs and its soft leather sofa and chairs draped with earth-colored serapes, the sight of which made

Harry's skin itch.

"This place is bigger and nicer than my folks' home on Lake Hamilton," he had said.

"I heard JFK used to boff starlets in the bedroom upstairs," Weeks had replied, and they'd run up to take a look and been disappointed to find sleeping quarters as clean and impersonal as a hotel room.

The two copywriters were keeping silent now, intent on overhearing the conversation in the living room.

"What the hell are these guards doing out there by the tennis courts?" Buckley asked the publicist. "They demanded to see my identification."

"They're just a little . . . overeager," Cholly said. "Wanna make sure the meeting is totally private."

"Private? Who the hell wants privacy? I want everybody to hear what I have to say. Why the hell do you think we invited the media? Because we like 'em?"

"I understood . . . ah, Milton said—"

"This is my party, not Milton's. Drag the yellow journalists in here and send those guards packing."

"We might need the guards later," Cholly said, "to toss out the drunks."

"Fine. Tell 'em to take a walk until then."

Harry tried to get Weeks' attention, to give him the finger for putting him through seventy minutes of unnecessary boredom, but Roger kept staring through the projectionist's window.

"What's this announcement all about, Buck?" Hewitt was asking.

"If I told you, Al, it wouldn't be a surprise. Ah, here come some familiar faces."

John Bingham and Kevin Dobbs stepped into the room. The Advertising V.P. was complaining about disrespectful treatment at the hands of the Pembertons. Dobbs was complaining about the damage done to the ex-governor's house and property. "That lawn will have to be completely re-sodded. And the main house looks like a cesspool. Have any of you seen the governor? I looked all over for him, to offer my apologies."

"I'm sure he's around somewhere," Buckley said. "When the Eyefuls strut in, he'll be front and center. Let's get this show on the road. You didn't happen to see Ida or Milton?"

"They were getting drinks," Bingham said. "How long has that been going on, by the way?"

"How long has what been going on?" Buckley asked.

"Ida and Milton. They're, you know, involved."

Buckley blinked in surprise, then smiled. "Politics and *Ogle* make strange bedfellows. Al, let's go round up the happy couple and offer 'em our heartiest congratulations."

As soon as Buckley and Hewitt had left the room, Dobbs said, "I've never seen him more alert or on point. This is not going to work."

"Relax, for Christ's sake," Bingham said. "If it works, great. If not, no harm."

"I'm concerned about this so-called romance of Milton and Ida," Dobbs said. "With Buckley out of the picture, their shares add up to more than yours and mine."

"We're all supposed to be on the same page about the company's future," Bingham said. "If they've got some other cute idea, if they try to screw us, we just put Buck back into the picture. Go to him and fall on our knees and confess."

"I suppose you're right," Dobbs said. "I hope to hell it doesn't come to that."

Harry understood that something fishy was going on, but he couldn't imagine how the other shareholders hoped to take Buckley, who owned a majority of the voting stock, out of the picture. He looked over at Weeks who remained mesmerized by the living room tableaux.

"Where's the Buckster?" Milton Armstead asked as he and Ida Connor breezed into the living room.

"Out there looking for you two," Dobbs said. "You must've just missed him."

Ida noticed a smudge of lipstick on Armstead's mouth, yanked his display handkerchief free, wiped it off and stuck the kerchief back into his pocket.

"That creepy shrink ready?" Bingham asked.

Ida nodded. "Ready and eager."

"Anybody have a clue about Buck's mysterious announcement?" Bingham asked.

"Maybe it'll be loony enough we won't need the doctor's drug," Armstead said.

"He visited the lawyers," Dobbs said. "Maybe he's gonna do what we want—go public and expand the company."

"We'll know in a minute," Ida said. "Here he comes, with about fifty or sixty of his closest friends."

The noisy crowd filled the guest house with laughter and talk and the occasional break of glass. Harry saw Terry enter with some curly-haired stud in a loud Hawaiian shirt. He didn't recognize the guy. Maybe the actor, whatever his name was. He said something to her, smirked and kissed her bare shoulder. Annoyed, she took a step away from him. He seemed to be delighted by this rebuff.

Harry felt like a creep, spying on her.

The publicists, Grandiose and Mitteer, yelled for attention and, when the noise level dipped just a few decibels, made an impromptu introduction.

"Ladeeze and gen'l'men," Cholly Grandiose said, "here's the man who's made tonight possible . . ."

"The sex sultan of Southern California . . ." Lew Mitteer added.

"The Wazir of woo who turned a frog into a franchise . . ."

"Trower J. Buckley, who has an important announcement to make."

"Thank you, Lew, Cholly," Buckley said, standing before the room's huge, cold fireplace. "And thank you, employees of *Ogle* and our great and good friends in the media and in the business world for taking time out of your busy schedules to join our little celebration.

"What are we celebrating, you ask? Well, it's the beginning of a new era for *Ogle*. When I and a few other brave souls began the magazine nine years ago, I knew we were on to something. But I never dreamed it would become the fabulous success . . ."

Harry yawned. Weeks was leaning back in his chair, making the bullshit sign by extending his index and little finger and wagging them from side to side. They'd both had to watch an indoctrination film featuring Buckley using those same words to provide new employees a historical background of the magazine and the company.

Judging by the rapidly glassing eyes of the assemblage, they'd heard the pitch before, too. The curly-haired stud didn't seem to know anybody was talking. He just kept moving in on Terry and she kept moving away. Finally, she flicked a finger against the man's nose and he yelled, "Ow," momentarily distracting the speaker.

Buckley looked over at the curly-haired stud, who was holding his nose and seemed to be crying. Shrugging, he continued his speech. "Blablabla . . . need to celebrate sexual freedom . . . blablabla . . . my pet frog, Raymond . . . blablabla, blablabla . . . circulation rise from a mere one hundred thousand copies to just under a million, and then . . . blablabla . . ."

The curly-haired stud was squinting at his refection in a windowpane, trying to judge the damage to his schnoz, but Harry had lost sight of Terry. He was scanning the room for her when something Buckley was saying caught his attention. ". . .

in all those years, I never met an employee I thought could take over for me when I . . . retired. But now I have met that man. Bright, honest, hardworking and completely dedicated, that's my new best friend and, as of tonight, *Ogle*'s new publisher, Al Hewitt."

Hewitt seemed to be as stunned as everyone else.

"Come on over here, Al," Buckley said, smiling broadly as Hewitt reluctantly worked his way though the crowd.

"Dig Milton," Weeks whispered to Harry.

Armstead was glaring at both the men now standing in front of the hearth. Ida Connor wasn't any happier. Dobbs and Bingham seemed merely shocked.

"Not that I'm going off into the wilderness to raise wildflowers," Buckley said. "I'll still be around as president of *Ogle,* Inc. But the magazine is gonna be Al's baby. And, as befitting his new status, here you go, Al." He reached into his pocket and handed Hewitt a shiny key. "This key, like the one I and the other four major executives carry, opens every lock at the *Ogle* Building."

Moving as if in a trance, Hewitt accepted the offered key.

"That's not all. We're getting rid of that red convertible that you never seem to want to use and get you a car more in keeping with your position, a brand new 190SL in the color of your choice.

"And, Al . . . to show just how much faith I have in you, old man, I have made arrangements for you to be the second-largest stockholder in the company.

"You may all now applaud."

Everyone did, except the two copywriters in the dark room and the other four shareholders.

"This is big," Weeks said. "Milton and Ida each have an eighth interest. The only free shares are the ones bought back from Nick Hobart's estate. That's about one-sixteenth interest. The extra shares are gonna have to come from Buckley's personal stock."

"So?" Harry asked.

"So it means he's not just giving up the magazine, he's also giving up his 52% control of the stock."

Harry got it. He stared through the portal at the two highest-ranking executives. Buckley had Hewitt trapped in a bear hug.

"Our boss is one trusting son of a bitch," Weeks said.

Even in the warm night, with Buckley's body heat radiating against him, Al Hewitt was feeling a chill. He didn't know the first thing about being a publisher. Oh, he'd run off a weekly mimeographed newsletter for the church, but that was hardly in the same league as being responsible for a monthly magazine worth millions.

"Don't worry, Al," Buckley whispered in his ear. "I'll be showing you the ropes."

"It's an incredible responsibility," Hewitt said.

"You can handle it. I sensed it the first minute I laid eyes on you. You'll pick it up as quickly as I did. We're brothers."

Hewitt was so moved by the man's faith in him that he began to believe he could do it. How difficult was it going to be, really? The magazine had an editor, an art director, a full staff. They'd been working together successfully for years.

He felt Buckley moving to his side, keeping one arm around his shoulders, heard him address the crowd. "Now, let's go have some fun."

As the crowd rolled out of the guest house, dragging their feet across the ex-governor's clay tennis courts, Cholly Grandiose yelled to the media folk that both Buckley and Hewitt would be available for interviews the following week.

The four other stockholders watched them go.

Satisfied that they were alone, Armstead said, "That was freaking amazing. What the hell is Buck thinking?"

"Sounds like he's in love," Bingham said.

"The question is: where does this leave us?" Dobbs asked.

"I don't see that it changes anything," Ida said. "It's just one more example of his diminished capacity. Turning over his magazine to a man with no experience as a publisher, with no experience in the world outside of a very limited religious community in a very small town."

Armstead cocked his head and smiled. "This could be a very good thing," he said. "Buck's position in the company is now vulnerable. All we have to do is get a naïve fool to vote with us."

"The naïve fool and Buck are thick as thieves," Ida said. "And we both may be underestimating Hewitt. Let's just proceed with the plan."

"The plan is sloppy," Armstead said. "Drugs are undependable and, from a public relations point of view, an ugly courtroom battle over Buck's sanity won't help the company's image. Tonight Buck admitted it was time for a change. He picked his successor. All we have to do now is to get that successor to climb on board our bus."

"I like that," Bingham said. "Hell, with Buck relaxing his grip on the magazine, maybe we ought to sound him out before doing anything drastic."

"God, yes," Dobbs said. "It's bad enough having to deal with murdered employees and police. We shouldn't go looking for trouble."

"You'd better call off your shrink, Ida," Armstead said.

"You're idiots if you think Buck has changed," she said, moving away from Armstead. "This dog and pony show tonight means nothing. He's still in control and still has to be dealt with."

"We can outvote him now," Bingham said.

"Get your head out of your ass, John," she said. "You've known Buck long enough to realize he'll never give up his 52%. This was all bullshit, some harebrained scheme that nobody but he can hope to understand."

"Honey, you may be right," Armstead said, "but the three of us think otherwise. So call off the shrink."

She glared at him, and then at the others. "All right," she said. "But you'll regret this. And, Milton, if you ever call me 'honey' again, you'd better hope there isn't a weapon within my reach."

She stormed off.

The three men waited a bit in uneasy silence, then made their exit.

46.

"Well, that was interesting, in an 'Executive Suite' sort of way," Weeks said as he and Harry wandered from the guest house.

"Good to know the company has such a stable leadership," Harry said.

"It's the same in any big business," Weeks said. "You reach a point where bullshit ideals like morality or aesthetics or friendship get pushed aside by good old-fashioned black ink profit."

"They were going to slip Buckley some kind of drug to make him look loony," Harry said. "That's pretty low."

"Low? Some corporate heads would call it kindness," Weeks said. He turned to look at the guest house. "Did you see a phone back there?"

"On a table next to the sofa," Harry said.

"Swingin'," Weeks said and left him.

The lights were turned low in the main room and Harry could only make out vague shadows on the dance floor. After a few minutes of being jostled by writhing or rocking couples, he gave up trying to find Terry and withdrew to the bar.

The curly-haired stud who'd been hitting on Terry in the guest house had switched his attention to the strawberry-blonde bartender who looked like a trapped animal.

"Could I have a Coke?" Harry asked her.

"Gladly," she said.

The stud's curly head rolled on his neck like a puppet's.

"Who the hell are you?" he asked, slurring.

"You first," Harry said.

"Adam Troy," the stud said. "I'm in th' nex' issue o' *Ogle*. Fashion stuff. Brioni."

"You're a male model?"

"Ahma actor. Some *77's*, *Hawaiian Eyes*. Wha about you?"

"My name is Buckley," Harry said, taking his soft drink from the bartender. "My dad owns *Ogle*."

"No shi'?"

"No shi'," Harry said. "And, my dad and I, we'd like you to leave."

The bartender mouthed the words "Thank you."

"Huh?"

"Leave. It means to go. Away. And not come back."

"Yeah, well fuck you, Buckley."

"If you're not out of here in two minutes, we redo the fashion spread and cut you out. Or maybe we'll touch up the photos, put a little lipstick on you, eyeliner."

The stud seemed to sober immediately. "You c-can't . . ."

"You've got a minute left," Harry said, looking at his watch.

"Fuck you, Buckley," Adam Troy repeated and staggered out of the party and out of Harry's life.

"You deserve a medal," the bartender said. "The guy is seriously warped. He said he wanted to give me a tongue bath, like that sounds so appealing, you know. Mr. Buckley really your dad?"

"Don't you see the family resemblance?"

"No."

Harry smiled. "My dad's in the motel business," he said.

"It'd be neat to have a dad as rich as Mr. Buckley," she said.

"I guess," he said, though he was thinking how un-neat it would be, having people your dad trusted trying to screw him over.

"Thanks for the drink," he said and went into the dancing area.

He headed for Lew Mitteer who was in a far corner, applying wet napkins to the forehead of a business reporter for *The Toluca Lake Tattler* who had either eaten or drunk to excess.

"Lew, any idea where Mr. Buckley is?" Harry asked.

The distracted publicity man said, "Upstairs . . ."

A few seconds later, Lew yelled, "But you can't go up there."

By then, Harry was at the top of the stairs, facing a series of closed doors.

A cry of pain penetrated the nearest door and Harry opened it on a brightly lit room where Trower Buckley sat in a chair while an effete young man applied makeup to his face.

Buckley emitted another cry and Harry realized that a woman with familiar platinum hair was kneeling on the floor between his legs engaged in frenzied fellatio.

Harry was unnoticed by those in the room. Buckley's eyes were closed. The makeup artiste was concentrating on his work, as was the kneeling woman. Suddenly the door was pulled closed by a person that Harry initially thought was a male security guard. Studying the figure now, he wasn't at all sure of its gender. It looked soft and may have had breasts under the uniform. The face was round and cherubic. The shove that it gave Harry was anything but feminine.

"Downstairs, buddy," the guard said in a voice that sounded like a parody of a tough guy. "Nuthin' for you up here."

Harry was too puzzled by the guard's ambiguous sexuality to obey immediately.

The guard patted his/her gun holster and said, "Do like I say, kid. Head on down."

Harry shrugged and obeyed.

The guard escorted him down the stairs. "Upstairs is out of bounds, kid. Don't piss me off."

There was no reason for him to go upstairs again, anyway, Harry thought as he watched the chubby guard returning to duty outside Buckley's door. One look at Buckley dispassionately being serviced by Scotty Lemming's hot-to-trot wife was all he cared to take. It made him wonder if warning the man about his disloyal executives was worth the bother. Maybe, as his dad kept insisting, *Ogle* really was the magazine equivalent of a brothel.

He passed the doorway to what was apparently a study or den. It was empty save for one man sitting on a chair.

Harry blinked, caught his breath and entered the room. "Hi, Larry," he said.

Larry Beagle, looking more peaceful than Harry had ever seen him, smiled and said, "Harry, my boy, what do you think of this so-called piece of art?"

His reference was a painting that occupied ten square feet of wall space, a blown-up comic strip version of the famous Iwo Jima flag-raising scene. A dialogue balloon coming from the mouth of one of the Marines read, "Ira Hamilton Hayes, I bet you wish you'd never left the reservation, you redskin bastard." In the background were the words "Zonk" and "Blit, Blit, Blit" in orange.

"Pop art," Harry said.

"So little respect for the military," Beagle muttered. "In a ex-governor's house, yet."

"Vietnam is giving war a bad name," Harry said.

Beagle stared at him and frowned.

"You're okay now?" Harry asked.

"So they tell me. Look." He held up his right hand. "Steady as she goes. Of course, I'm medicated, but not so much that it impairs my thinking process. It was nice of Buck to send me an invitation. I understand we have a new publisher."

"Looks that way. You . . . coming back to work soon?"

"One of these days," Beagle said. "When I'm ready. Miss me, Harry?"

"Very much."

"That's good," Beagle said, getting to his feet. "It's good to be missed. I'd better be going now. The bed check at Somerset is at midnight."

"You snuck out to come here?"

"I prefer to say I took my leave. See you around, Harry."

What a weird frigging night, Harry thought.

Terry was on the dance floor, perspiring and definitely tipsy. Her partner was the brunette receptionist from the first floor. Harry thought her name was Astral or maybe Esther. Weeks was also dancing, being pushed and pulled by a giant dark creature with a bored expression.

Harry suddenly needed fresh air. He stepped through French doors onto a large patio at the end of which was a rectangular pool, its waters glistening black in moonlight.

He wandered to the pool's edge where the bronze frog designed by Scotty Lemming had been placed. Its wide, big-lipped mouth seemed to be sneering at him and, thanks to a reflection of the moonlight on the water, one heavy-lidded froggy eye winked obscenely. Harry shrugged and started to walk back to the party.

"Quite a crowd in there, isn't it, young man?" In the darkness, he could barely see a plump shadow seated at a wrought-iron table at the far end of the flagstones.

He recognized the familiar figure. "Governor Moody?"

"Guilty as charged," the man said with false humor. "And who might you be?"

"Harry Trauble."

"Well, Harry Trauble, maybe you could tell me when the *Ogle* Eyefuls are supposed to arrive."

"I really couldn't say, sir, but I did notice they were putting makeup on Mr. Buckley, so I guess they're getting ready for the pictures. They'll be dragging some lights down here for shots around the pool."

"Let there be light," the old man sighed. There was a full bottle of whiskey on the table beside him. He picked it up and offered it.

To be polite, Harry took a tiny swig.

"Will they really take a dip in my pool, bare-ass naked?"

Harry, his throat burning from the booze, croaked, "Sure. They're used to it."

"Amazing. They look so clean cut and all-American. Like the girl next door."

"Do you read the magazine a lot?" Harry asked.

"Read? In forty-one years of political life, young man, I've been accused of many things. But reading *Ogle?* That's carrying it a bit far. I look at *Ogle,* to be sure. But read it? I don't think so."

"The girls," Harry said haltingly, "the girls . . . in real life they don't look exactly like the pictures. I mean, they touch them up a little. There's a way they have of getting rid of blemishes that—"

"Please," the ex-governor interrupted, raising his hand. "Let an old man have something to hold sacred. But I do hope they show up soon. I've an early flight to D.C. in the morning."

"Business or pleasure?"

"Definitely the former. I'm going to try and talk to Bill Fulbright like a Dutch uncle."

"Senator Fulbright seems to be pretty outspoken about the war," Harry said.

"Outspoken?" ex-Governor Moody chuckled bitterly. "I suppose you could say that. And unless he shuts up, Lyndon'll hang our whole committee out to dry."

"What committee?" Harry asked.

"Foreign Relations," ex-governor Moody said and took another swig of whiskey.

"Do you agree with Senator Fulbright about the war?" Harry asked.

The ex-governor stared at him and then smiled, "Not for publication, Mr. Trauble."

"I'm not a reporter. I just write copy, nothing very serious."

"What bliss that must be," the ex-governor said. "Actually, I don't care if you do print it. There's not much Lyndon or anybody else can do to me now. Otherwise, I certainly would not have agreed to this orgy in my home.

"To answer your question, I suppose a man would have to be an idiot to say he was in favor of a war that can't be won. An idiot or an unscrupulous thug who hoped to profit from the conflict."

"But you don't want Senator Fulbright to voice his opposition," Harry said.

"Peace in the valley. Politics, in a nutshell." The ex-governor leaned back in his chair, sighed and added, "Have you ever considered what it's like to be in your early seventies?"

Harry shook his head.

"Well, if you had been a baseball pitcher who lived only for the game, and one day you woke up to find your arm gone, you'd have some idea. You'll see someday. Until then, forget politics and get all the fucking done you can, Mr. Trauble."

The old man passed him the bottle. This mouthful went down easier. From inside the house came the sound of glasses breaking and laughter. The old man perked up. "The Eyefuls, do you think?"

"I'll go see," Harry said. Getting out of his chair, he noticed a female silhouette framed in the doorway to the main house. At that distance, he could just make out a nicely rounded figure clothed in a dress with a plunging neckline that stopped just short of the knees.

"I think they're here, sir," he told the ex-governor.

The old man squinted at the girl in the doorway. He adjusted his glasses, and groaned. "Guess again, Mr. Trouble," he said. "That's my daughter."

"Oh, I'm sorry," Harry said.

"Not as much as I. Because if Georgina is here so is her mother."

The old man grabbed his bottle with both hands. "Never marry a woman twenty-five years your junior," he said. "Screw her, but don't marry her."

Daughter and mother, both tall, willowy and blonde, and seeming more like sisters, descended upon them. The ex-governor struggled to his feet to greet the missus.

"George you senile son of a bitch," she screeched. "They've destroyed our home."

"Now, Helena. Buck has promised to put the place back in apple-pie order."

"He'll do more than that. He'll also be paying me for the mental anguish and humiliation I've suffered, having to hear it from the goddamn TV news, in a room filled with my relatives and their friends, that my husband has opened up our private home to the scum of the universe."

"You don't look so scummy," the daughter said to Harry. "I'm Georgina."

"Harry."

She tilted her head in the direction of her mother, "She'll be at him all night. Let's go take advantage of that shitty music."

Harry let her pull him into the party, which had grown wetter, noisier and uglier. Bright lights blinked on and off as the event was captured for future generations by Carlos and his team of crack photographers including a pair of Austrian twins named Hans and Franz.

He hoped Terry would see him dancing with Georgina, but she had disappeared again.

"You wouldn't have any rugs on you?" Georgina asked, plastering her body against his.

"Rugs?"

"My code word for drugs."

"Oh. No. Sorry."

"Then let's see what you do have," she said and moved her hand down his back, squeezing his right buttock. He pushed forward in surprise. "Nice Pavlovian response," she said.

"Look, I—"

She quieted him with a finger to his lips. "Harry, I have just spent nearly five hours in the car with my neurotic mother, separated by another three hours listening to my salt waterlogged cousins talk about the bitchin' nightlife in Santa Barbara. So less talk, more action, okay?"

With that she pulled his head down and kissed him, her tongue entering his mouth like a particularly warm-blooded snake. She tasted of cigarettes and spearmint gum.

"Not bad at all," she said, pulling away slightly. "Why don't you and I get a bottle of something and head up to my room?"

He didn't respond because he was staring at Terry who was standing at the edge of the dance area, regarding him with a look of profound disappointment.

She turned and walked away.

Harry freed himself from Georgina's arms and left her surprised and annoyed on the dance floor. He heard her yelling at him. He assumed she wasn't complimenting his dancing.

Coming from a culture in which neither sobriety nor constancy was prized, Terry was not exactly surprised by the sight of her intended sucking the face of a well-endowed bimbo temptress.

But she'd expected more from Harry. And she knew damn well that if their relationship were to blossom into a long and fruitful marriage, an object lesson was called for right at the jump.

She waited until he saw her and his face took on that stricken look. Then she turned and began to walk away, moving at an oblique angle to keep him in her peripheral vision as he ditched the bimbo and started after her.

She walked through the dimly lit hacienda, certain he was following. She was trying to decide just how much she was going to put him through before forgiving him.

She heard him call her name just as she pushed past the heavy oaken front door. She would lead him to the Zoombuggy. There, she would do an ice queen, haughtier-than-thou number on him, letting the ice melt gradually into her acceptance of his apology. That would lead to a passionate kiss that would then lead to their departing the bullshit excuse for a party.

She paused by the vehicle and turned.

The hacienda's front door remained closed.

He'd seen her leave, she was certain. It would only be a few seconds before he'd be following.

The heavy door stayed in place.

It had just been a minute. She'd give him a little more time. She couldn't have misjudged the situation. He loved her. He'd had too much to drink. He kissed a pretty girl and pushed her aside when she, Terry, had arrived.

He would not have gone back to that bimbo in the de la Renta dress.

Unless . . . had she overplayed her hand?

The heavy door didn't move.

There was no way she could go back to the party. Not if her romance with Harry had any hope for survival. The next move had to be his.

And the front door creaked open.

She tried on a pose of complete indifference. That melted away when Al Hewitt, not Harry, left the hacienda.

She crossed the lawn to meet him. "Excuse me," she said. "Do you know Harry Trauble?"

"Yes."

"I thought he was on his way out here."

"Actually, I just saw him heading upstairs," Hewitt said. "Probably to talk to Buck."

"Oh."

"Were you waiting for him to give you a ride?" Hewitt asked. "I'm supposed to have a cab coming. If the driver can find this place."

"I have a car," she said. And, realizing she had no other choice now but to use it, she added, "I'd be happy to give you a ride."

"And Harry?" he asked.

"He'll have to find his way home all by himself."

47.

Harry had started after Terry, but he'd been momentarily blinded by the blink of the photographers' strobe lights. Then he'd stumbled over a couple huddled on the floor.

He called out to her just as the front door was closing behind her. His intention to run after her was sidetracked by the sight of someone creeping up the main stairs with a glass of clear liquid in one hand.

"Dr. Magnus?" he called out.

The strange egg-shaped cranium turned to observe him. The doctor looked a bit nervous. "Sorry," he said, probably not placing Harry, "I can't speak now. Very busy."

He continued up the stairs.

Harry raced after him, taking the stairs two at a time. "Doctor. The deal's off."

"I beg your pardon." The hand holding the glass seemed a bit shaky.

"The deal's off," Harry said. "They voted against using the drugs."

"Who are you?"

"Harry Trouble. We talked about my family in Hot Springs."

"But you're not . . . what do you know about drugs?"

"I know the plan was for you to give Mr. Buckley some kind of drug. But that plan was voted down a little while ago. Ida Connor was supposed to tell you."

"I don't know what you're talking about," Dr. Magnus said

and continued up the stairs.

Harry slapped the glass from his hand. It hit the carpeted stair, sloshing most of its contents. With a yelp, Magnus made a grab but it eluded him by inches. He reached down just a bit more than the laws of gravity allowed and as the glass rolled downstairs, he tumbled after it.

Sitting on the tile main floor, holding the empty glass, his pince nez now dangling from the ribbon pinned to his lapel, he glared up at Harry. "You imbecile. Do you know how much money you've just cost me?"

With that, he threw the glass at Harry, a wide toss that cleared the stairwell and shattered on the tile beyond. Then the little therapist leapt upon Harry and began pounding him on the head and face with his tiny fists.

It had probably been ten years since Harry had hit anyone, and that had been his brother Vaughan who, God knows, needed a punch every now and then. But it wasn't something one forgot how to do. He clipped Magnus on the cheek. The therapist responded by trying to choke him.

"You men, stop that immediately."

Harry looked up to see Trower Buckley, immaculate in a summer tux, face artificially tanned, puffs of Kleenex separating the makeup from his glow-white shirt collar. "Violence solves nothing," he told them as he gingerly stepped past their struggling bodies. "Go get drunk or get laid for heaven's sake. Do something useful."

Harry and the therapist watched as Buckley marched toward the pool, the photographers swarming around him like hummingbirds to sugar water.

"You haven't heard the last of this," Dr. Magnus said, getting to his feet.

Harry was about to reply when he remembered Terry.

He rushed from the hacienda in time to see the Zoombuggy

exiting the estate. Al Hewitt was in the passenger seat.

Damn. Not only had he lost a girlfriend. He'd lost his ride home.

Back at the party, the action had moved to the pool area which a series of bright lights had turned into center stage. Carlos had managed to find seven or eight Eyefuls, now typically starkers. He was draping them around Buckley who was standing in the pool, fully dressed in his summer tux with the water lapping at his cummerbund.

Harry found Weeks on the now-empty bandstand, microphone in hand, whispering the lyrics to "Who Wrote the Book of Love."

"You drunk?" Harry asked him.

Weeks paused mid "who-bidoo" to say, "No. Not even close."

"Ready to leave?" Harry asked him.

"I guess," Weeks said. "I can't make my phone call here. Some bastard limited the lines to local calls only."

"Gimme a lift?" Harry asked.

"All the way out to the ocean?"

"It's on your way back," Harry said.

Weeks shook his head. "No, it isn't. I've got to go to the office. Make my call."

To the office. Hewitt lived in the *Ogle* Building. He and Terry would probably wind up there. Eventually.

"A lift to the office will be fine," Harry said.

There was a huge splash by the pool. Buckley said something they couldn't quite hear and everyone laughed uproariously.

"Some party," Weeks said.

"One for the books," Harry said.

48.

On the trip from the ex-governor's compound to the *Ogle* Building, Terry did the thing she usually did when meeting someone she thought might be worthy of her friendship. She asked Al Hewitt to tell her a little about himself.

"Before we get into that," he said, "I wonder if you could tell me what sort of photography work Florence Proneswagger did for you."

The question was so surprising it made her blink. "What makes you think—?"

"There was a slip of paper with your name on it on the floor of the darkroom," he said.

"Oh. You didn't give it to the police by any chance?"

"No. Should I have?"

"No. It's nothing, really. She developed a picture of my boyfriend and me."

"That's certainly innocent enough. I suppose Harry Trauble is that boyfriend?"

"I hope he still is," she said, and began to go on and on about Harry, that they lived in the same building and fate had brought them together and even though he behaved like a jerk sometimes, she had no doubt but that they'd marry and have at least three children.

"Harry Trauble was the first person at *Ogle* to show me any kindness," Hewitt told her. "I think you made a wise choice."

Her plan had been to drop him off and then go immediately

to her apartment to await Harry's apology, either by phone or, better yet, in person. But it was barely eleven and she didn't feel the new publisher should be celebrating up in the penthouse all alone.

She suggested they have a drink across the street. "You and Herkie will get along like old pals," she said.

It was a typical Friday night in the bar. Laughter and tears and drunks everywhere you looked, while Scat the bouncer slowly cruised through the crowd, pausing from time to time to waggle a warning forefinger at a boozer who had ventured beyond the edges of propriety as he saw it.

A poker game was in progress in the kitchen, which Willem had shut down for the night. Herkie was with Colin and Stooley and a couple of other inebriates at a different table, one devoted more to drink and conversation than to cards.

The restaurateur correctly read Terry's eye message and greeted Hewitt with the warmth of a cherished friend. She filled him and the others in on the newcomer, ending with the comment that "Al was made publisher of *Ogle* at a party tonight."

Of those at the table, only Stooley seemed impressed by the news. "You mean Buck's really gonna let somebody else make a decision over at the frog pond?"

"That remains to be seen," Hewitt said, waiting for Terry to be seated before sitting down himself.

"So that's the reason for the party, huh?" Stooley said.

"One of them, I guess."

The columnist studied him intently. "Okay," he said. "You get made frog prince to the frog king at a big blast at that blowhard Moody's compound. Nothin' but food and booze and broads wherever you look. What the hell are you doing sitting here with us disreputable characters?"

"I never much cared for big blasts," Hewitt said.

"Me neither, brother," Herkie said. "That's why I'm back

here with these bums, instead of out there with the paying customers."

"Did you know the broad who got her neck snapped?" asked Stooley, ever the reporter.

Hewitt nodded.

"Snapped?" Herkie said. "I thought the cops said she'd been strangled."

"Coroner changed that to a broken neck about an hour too late for tomorrow's morning edition," Stooley said.

"Guess it don't matter too much to the lady," Herkie said. "Dead is dead." Then, realizing that the table had grown decidedly gloomy, he added, "You play pool, Al?"

"A little, back when I was at the seminary," Hewitt said. "But I haven't had a stick in my hand in years."

"Yeah, like I never heard that con before," Herkie said, rising from his seat. "Let's see what you got. Want some of this action, Terry, my love?"

"You boys have fun," she said. "I'm heading for home."

She didn't want to miss Harry's call, so she drove with a heavy foot along the nearly empty freeway. The drop in temperature at Overland and the briny smell of the ocean had been two of the strong selling points in her move to Bay City, but she ignored them in favor of thinking about how she should respond to Harry's pleas for forgiveness.

Judging by the lights in the seventeen-story apartment building, less than half of her neighbors were asleep. Approaching the parking entrance, she couldn't stop herself from glancing at Harry's windows even though she knew they'd be dark. He'd still be at the party.

But maybe he was dialing her number at that very moment.

She dashed from the Zoombuggy to the elevator and from it to her apartment door, fumbling the key into the lock.

She stepped into a room where everything looked wrong.

It wasn't just the lights from the hall and the moon playing tricks with shadows. The carpet had been ripped, books thrown from shelves. She spied a gutted sofa cushion resting beside an overturned flowerbox.

Her heart thumping, she took a backward step toward the open door.

The square of hall light disappeared and the door clicked shut just as she bumped into a hard human body.

The intruder must have been hidden beside the door when she entered the apartment.

He acted before she could shake loose of her panic, locking her neck in the crook of one arm.

Her fingers pried at the arm. When that didn't work, she dug her nails into the exposed flesh of his wrist. "Stop that," he ordered, bringing up his other hand and displaying her own bread knife, its serrated edges just inches from her face.

He'd meant to frighten her even more. But the knife had the opposite effect. Her panic disappeared, replaced by an instinct for survival. A scarred face was better than death. She kicked back at him, but he sidestepped and thrust a leg between hers. He pressed against her, pushing her forward, off balance. The specter of rape flitted through her consciousness. But she could tell from his body this was not about sex.

What, then? she wondered.

He tightened the pressure on her throat. "Where's the negative?" he said. It was the voice of someone experiencing a pleasant high, soft, without anger, without any emotion. Almost blissful. And she recognized it.

"Can't . . . talk," she said. It was a pretense and it got the result she wanted. He removed his arm, but kept hold of the collar of her blouse.

"Why are you doing this, T.J.?" she asked.

The *Ogle* night watchman touched the knife blade to a spot just below her right jawline, demonstrating how effortlessly he could slice her throat from ear to ear. "You better tell me where the negative is," he said.

"What negative?"

"One of the pictures the two homos took at *Ogle*," he said.

"Joe and Orlando?"

"Uh huh. They were evil, did things to each other."

"You killed them?"

"I didn't want to," T.J. said. "The one, the sculptor guy, answered the door and invited me in. He wasn't wearing any clothes and he was high on pot. He said he'd give me the negative if I gave him money. I told him I didn't have any money and he said a lot of mean things and made me mad. So, I grabbed this gizmo off a table, a kind of wire with handles and well, you know."

"And Orlando?" she asked, trying to get into a better balanced position. She took a step to the left, away from the knife.

"I didn't even know he was there," T.J. said. "I was looking for the negative in this creepy room upstairs with all the candles and statues and the smell of pot smoke when suddenly this guy sits up in bed and starts giggling. I figured I couldn't leave him to tell I'd been there, so I looked around and saw this metal rod. And that was that. He stopped giggling."

His hand had relaxed on the collar of her blouse and she was almost in a position to make a break for another room. The bathroom, where there was a lock on the door. "Why'd you put Joe in bed with Orlando?" she asked.

"I figured maybe the police would think they killed each other," he said. "Then they wouldn't be looking for anybody else."

She must have tensed to run, because he increased his grip on her collar and pulled her backward, bringing the knife to her neck again. "Enough talk," he said.

Trying to keep the fear from her voice, she said, "I don't have any negative."

"Florence said you did. She said you told her the homos were friends of yours and they gave you the negatives because there were pictures of you on the roll."

"Oh, God. Poor Florence," she said, realizing for the first time her part in her friend's murder.

"I liked her, too," he said, suddenly releasing her collar and taking a step back. But he kept the knife at her throat. "Florence was nice. She saw this negative on the sheet you gave her and she printed it out and she asked me about it. She wasn't asking for money or anything. But she'd seen the photo and . . . I had to do something."

Stay on track, Terry ordered herself. She'd started sinking into despair and guilt for Florence's death. She wasn't paying enough attention to what he was saying.

But she did get the drift of it.

"Did I ask you for any money?" she said.

"No. But that might be because you don't know what's in the picture. Do you?"

She wasn't sure which answer would serve her better. Might as well tell the truth. "No idea."

"Florence said you didn't. It's why I waited until tonight to come here. I thought you would be at the party and I'd have time to find the negative. And that would be that."

"Are you going to kill me?"

He hesitated before saying, "Not if you prove you're a good person by giving me the negative."

He was a lousy liar. Definitely no Irishman. The negatives that Florence had returned were in the bedroom, resting in a night table drawer. "All of that stuff is at the office," she said, knowing she would have to get out of the apartment if she had any hope of survival.

"Not in your desk," he said. "I checked."

"My desk doesn't have a lock, so I asked someone to keep them for me."

"Who?"

"I don't want them to get in trouble."

"Tell me who," he said and moved closer, the knife indenting her flesh.

"If you kill me now, you'll never find your precious negative," she said. "Whatever you're trying to hide will still be out there. My murder and all the others will be for nothing."

"That's enough, now," he said. But he stepped full away from her, removing the knife from her throat. "Turn around and face me. I don't want you running off and locking yourself in some room."

He looked much larger than usual, and downright spooky out of uniform in baggy denim pants, white button-down shirt and work boots that added an inch or two to his height. Glaring at her and clutching the knife, he asked, "If you didn't think the negative was special, why did you lock it up?"

Shit! She would not let herself get outplayed by an idiot. "It was personal junk. You know how they are about us keeping personal junk at the office."

He thought that over. "Why'd you keep it at the office?"

"Florence asked me to. She said she might want to pull a print from it."

"I bet you gave it to the guy you leave the office with sometimes. Harry."

"Bad guess," she said and said a little prayer that some good had come from her being descended from a long line of lying reprobates.

"I bet it's in his desk."

"Then kill me now and gamble on finding the negative."

She closed her eyes and leaned her head back, exposing her neck. "Our Father who art in heaven," she prayed, "hallowed be Thy name . . ."

He slapped her so hard she staggered. She would have fallen to the carpet if he hadn't grabbed the V of her blouse. Her head was ringing and her cheek was on fire. "I'm taking you with me, trusting you," he said. "That was just to let you know I don't like being wrong about people."

49.

Al Hewitt and Herkie were in the middle of a game of straight pool. It was a close game, with Herkie's 127 barely edging Hewitt's 119.

"The man sez he played 'a little,' " Herkie complained as Hewitt closed the gap by putting the 14 ball away in a corner pocket. "And him a former man of the cloth."

"It was 'a little'—every day for four years," Hewitt said, lining up a bank shot on the 7 ball. "We had a Ping-Pong table and a pool table at the seminary. I preferred the non-bouncing balls."

Worrying about the hubris implicit in that comment, he missed the bank and stepped back to observe the chuckling Herkie as he began to run the table.

"There's Terry girl," Colin said, staring out of the window. "Looks like she picked up a new beau."

Hewitt strolled to the window in time to see the couple entering the building.

He was puzzled by two things. What was T.J. doing out of uniform with his arm around Terry?

And . . .

Terry had seen Colin at the window of Herkie's, but T.J.'s arm was encircling her waist, the knife pressed to her stomach, and there was no way of sending a distress signal, even if her uncle had been sober enough to pick up on it.

It had been the same on the trip in from the Ocean. T.J. had given her no room to wiggle. He'd insisted they take the Zoom-buggy with her driving. As they exited the garage, she saw his white van parked beside the building. Why hadn't she spotted it before?

He stopped her from taking the freeway, so they traveled East via Olympic Boulevard. A lengthy drive was in her favor, but traffic was minimal. Her hopes rose when an LAPD prowl car came up beside them at a red light. But then she felt T.J.'s knife piercing the skin of her right side, and she'd watched the damned cops drive away oblivious to her situation.

Now she and her captor were in a contained space again, not quite as hopeless as her apartment, but hopeless enough. "Okay," T.J. said, "take me to the negative."

"In there," she indicated the first floor with her head.

"So I was right about the boyfriend?" he said, opening the door and marching her into the darkened office space.

"Was I right, Terry?"

"Yes. His office." She'd worked out a plan on the drive. When she'd sat at Roger Weeks' desk earlier in the week, she'd noticed he had a lock on one of the drawers. She would tell T.J. that the damned negative was in that drawer. Then, assuming he didn't cut her throat on the spot, maybe in the course of trying to jimmy the lock he'd give her the chance to hit him with something solid from Roger's or Harry's desk, though, in truth, she could not remember seeing anything remotely resembling a weapon.

Could she lift an electric typewriter? Was a phone heavy enough to knock a psychopath unconscious? Was this the worst plan in the world?

These thoughts and questions danced in her head as T.J. pushed her across the shadowy floor and into the darkened office.

Immediately, he slammed the door and turned on the light.

Her eyes desperately searched the desktops and counters. She saw nothing helpful. Hitting T.J. with an IN/OUT basket would only make him angry. To get her hands on either of the phones, she would have to reach past the big man and she didn't think he'd just stand there and let her do it.

"Okay, where is it?" she heard him say.

Why not just tell him the truth? Why prolong the agony? she thought. To live another minute, you dumb cow.

"It's locked in that draw . . ." she began, pointing to Weeks' desk.

She was surprised to see that the lock on the drawer had been bent and twisted into uselessness.

T.J. yanked the drawer open. It was bare, except for a few Mexican coins. He turned to her, with a sad look on his usually placid face. "You lied to me, Terry."

"No, I didn't. I swear. It was in there." She was improvising as quickly as she could speak. "You can see that somebody broke the lock to get to it."

He looked back at the drawer, puzzled now. "Who knew it was there? Who'd you tell?"

"Nobody."

"You had to tell the person whose desk this is. Roger Weeks, right?"

Even at so desperate a time, she didn't want to put Weeks on this goon's hit list. "Sure. But he has a key; he wouldn't have had to break his own lock."

"Weeks must've told somebody. Or . . ." He seemed to drift off. "Maybe he wasn't checking the WATS line. Maybe he was making fun of me the whole time we were . . ."

T.J. seemed stricken. He leaned forward on the desk, mumbling something about not being able to trust anybody. "I have no friends," he said and his eyes filled with tears. His fists, including the one holding the knife, were pressed against the desktop. This was her last chance.

It wasn't much of one.

She'd barely touched the doorknob, when she felt him grab her hair and yank her backwards against him.

She saw the knife blade catch the light as it moved toward her throat.

"Jesus, Trauble," Roger Weeks said as he guided his ancient but not classic MGA down the La Cienega exit from the 101. "I'm going as fast as I can."

"Okay. I'm just sort of anxious to talk to Terry."

"You don't even know she's at the building."

"Then I'll try to phone her at home. The problem is, I don't know what to say to her. I behaved like a real asshole."

"Tell her that's what being a guy is all about, behaving like an asshole at times," Weeks said. "Or that you're a big hero who saved our fearless leader from an acid trip. Or you can do what I've been doing to my honey: lie like a friggin' rug."

"What've you got to lie about?" Harry asked.

"Amigo, you got no idea how screwed up my life has suddenly become. And don't bother to ask for details." He braked, downshifted, roared around a city bus and raced forward until stopped by one of the frequent traffic lights on La Cienega.

"How about Buck making Al Hewitt his numero duo?" Harry asked. "The look on Milton's face was priceless."

"He'll just take out his frustration on us," Weeks said.

As soon as the MGA turned the corner Harry spied the Zoombuggy parked in front of the *Ogle* Building. "Great. She's here. Let me off."

"Hold on. There's a parking space just across the street."

"No. Let me off now."

Weeks braked and Harry stepped out of the MGA without

bothering to open the door. "Take it easy, Harry. I know in your naïve little heart of hearts you think she and Hewitt are up in his apartment having coffee and talking about you. But don't be too bummed if you bust in on quite a different scene. Hewitt is now Buck, Junior, don't forget."

Harry watched the MGA scoot away. Weeks was right about what was in his heart, but he had to be wrong about what was in Terry's.

He ran to the door, wondering how he was going to open it, since the security guard seemed to be away from the reception desk.

The front door was unlocked.

He rushed through it and went to the elevator. His plan was to go directly to the penthouse. He'd just pressed the UP button when the screaming started.

50.

Terry had no idea where Al Hewitt had come from.

Her eyes had been on the knife. Its descent had stopped when Hewitt had said, very calmly, "Hey there, T.J."

He was standing in the doorway, looking bizarrely confident for a slim man without a weapon trying to face down a psycho wielding a bread knife.

"You made me think you were my friend," the psycho said to him. "You were laughing at me the whole time."

"Never."

"You saying it wasn't you jimmied that drawer?" T.J. said.

"It was me."

"Then where's the negative?"

Terry thought Hewitt looked momentarily confused, losing some of his poise. "Negative? I destroyed the negatives."

"No more lies," T.J. said.

Terry screamed as she felt herself being tossed aside. Her left hip banged against the desk. Her left leg buckled and she fell, her head hitting the desk with a terrific *whack*.

Looking up from the tile floor through blurred vision she saw T.J. almost on top of the helpless Hewitt. "Don't," she croaked.

There was a loud pop.

T.J. seemed to tiptoe backward in slow motion.

He regained most of his equilibrium and started toward Al again. He was keening now, a horrible sound reflecting both rage and pain.

Another loud pop.

As she felt herself fading away she thought she heard Harry's voice.

Following a scream he knew had come from Terry's lips, Harry burst through the door to the first floor.

A gun was pointed directly at his face. "Whoa," he said, braking hard. "Take it easy."

"Damn fool, rushing in like that," Herkie said, swinging the weapon away from him. "Goddamn fool."

The restaurateur's eyes were wide and shiny. He looked a little insane.

Past him, two men were lying on the floor. Only one was moving, trying to get his legs under him. Al Hewitt. The front of his white shirt was ripped and bloody.

"I told you not to get too close to the prick," Herkie was yelling angrily as he headed for Hewitt. "Just draw him out where I could get a clear shot."

"He was . . . too fast," Hewitt said, wincing in pain but on his feet now.

"How bad is it?" Herkie asked, shoving his gun into a pocket and staring at Hewitt's bleeding chest.

"Much better than he," Hewitt said, indicating the man lying bunched on the tile floor, turning it a dark red.

Harry was stunned to see that it was the night watchman, T.J. He looked like a Samurai who had fallen on his sword, except that it was a bread knife he'd stuck in his own stomach.

"What the hell happened?" Harry asked.

"Long story short," Herkie said, "the dead freak had Terry. You better see how she is. I ain't got the stones."

Harry saw her legs stretched out in his office. He raced in and dropped to his knees beside her seemingly lifeless body. There was a bloody gash on the side of her head, a red smudge the size of a quarter on her blouse just below her right breast. "Jesus Christ, no," he whispered, making it a prayer.

She stirred.

"Thank you," he said, eyes raised in reverence.

He took her hand in his.

Her breathing seemed normal.

Her pulse felt strong and constant. He bent to kiss her cheek. She squeezed his hand and smiled and whispered something.

"What?" he asked, leaning closer.

"You were wonderful, Al," she said.

"Damn," Harry said.

"How's my gal?" Herkie asked from the doorway.

"A little banged up, but okay, I think," Harry said. "How's the wonderful Al?"

Herkie sat down on Terry's other side and studied the gash on her forehead. "That was some crazy sonofabitch. I put a pill in his chest and he still managed to give Al one third of a Zorro. But Al'll live to finish our goddamn game of pool."

"Damn it, Trauble," Weeks said at the door. "I left you less than a minute ago. How the hell did you do so much damage?"

51.

By the time the police arrived, the emergency medics had Hewitt's and Terry's wounds cleansed and taped and Stooley had sobered enough to make it across the street from the bar and grill to take down information for his paper.

"So the dead man, T.J. Muledeer, told you he'd murdered Florence Proneswagger?" he asked Terry, rechecking his facts. Terry nodded. She was seated next to Harry on a sofa in the conference room. Al, Herkie and Weeks were on leather-and-chrome chairs. Stooley was resting his large rump on the edge of the conference table.

"He told you he was looking for a negative of a photograph that Proneswagger had told him was in your possession."

"That's what he said. But I don't have any negative."

"Any idea why the late Proneswagger would have told him you did?"

"No idea," Terry said, wondering why Weeks had been giving her the evil eye ever since the subject of the negative had come up.

Stooley flipped a page of his notepad and went on. "You convinced Muledeer that the negative—the one you don't know anything about—was at the office, hoping that some opportunity for escape might arise or that someone might save you from the killer. That someone arrived in the form of Alphonse Hewitt, the newly appointed Publisher of *Ogle* magazine, who became suspicious when he espied Muledeer and Miz O'Mara entering the office building.

"This correct, Al?"

Hewitt nodded. "Something you said made me suspicious."

"What was that?" Stooley said, suddenly very interested.

"You mentioned that the coroner had just announced that Florence's neck had been broken," Hewitt said. "But T.J. had called it a break last night. So I was wondering about that and when I saw him with Terry, I—"

"You asked well-known restaurateur Henry Herkimer for a weapon," Stooley said, impatiently. "He told you that, as the owner of a tavern, he owned a legally registered .38, but could not, under law, allow anyone else to use it.

"He accompanied you to the *Ogle* Building where you both discovered the, ah, soon-to-be-deceased in the act of attempting to murder Miss O'Mara with a butcher knife."

"A bread knife," Terry said.

Stooley gave her a bleak smile. "Bread knife, no drama. Butcher knife, drama. On sighting Mr. Hewitt, Mr. Muledeer tossed Miss O'Mara aside and went for him with the butcher knife. He gave Mr. Hewitt a nasty slice across the chest and Mr. Herkimer had no choice but to plug Mr. Muledeer twice before he desisted.

"At that, Mr. Muledeer may have lived, but he had the bad luck to fall onto his weapon."

"It's a beautiful story that brings tears to my eyes," Detective Steve Cardona said as he entered the conference room. He'd obviously been standing just outside the door for a while. "Don't bother getting up."

He scanned the room. "I believe I know everybody. You were the shooter, Herkie?"

Herkie frowned. "I shot a man who was trying to kill my friend, Al."

"Looks like he came damn close. What about you, Trauble?

Just happen to be wandering by the office?"

"Just happened to need a lift because you're still holding my car," Harry said. "Mr. Weeks offered to drive me as far as the office where he wanted to make a phone call."

"That right, Weeks?"

"Yep," Weeks said. "A phone call I never made, by the way. Where's your partner, Oskar?"

"Busy with a little dustup in Watts. I'll let him know you asked. It'll boost his self-confidence."

"Can we go now?" Weeks asked.

"Stooley, maybe," Cardona said. "In fact, I insist."

The reporter launched himself from the desk and exited with a two-fingered salute to Cardona.

The detective waited until the reporter had passed through the door to the reception area then parked his butt on the same section of table that had previously held Stooley's. "Miss O'Mara, I'd kinda like to know the specifics of why Muledeer went Jack the Ripper on you."

"As Mr. Stooley just mentioned, he thought Florence Proneswagger had given me a photo negative."

"Did she?"

"No."

"You just frowned, Mr. Trauble," Cardona said. "You know something about this negative?"

"Nope. I'm frowning because I'm so happy to see you again."

"The feeling is mutual, Trauble. Does anybody here know anything about the negative?"

The question was greeted by a resounding silence.

"Okay. Let us move on to the subject of Mr. Muledeer," Cardona said. "While we wait for Miss O'Connor to arrive to give us a gander at his employment application, is there anything anybody can tell me about this bird?"

After a brief silence, Hewitt cleared his throat and said, "He was born in this city, grew up in the San Fernando Valley, a place called Sherman . . . Sherman . . ."

"Sherman Oaks," Cardona said. "You were a friend of his?"

Hewitt replied that he barely knew the man, but that on Thursday night he'd needed to run an errand and Muledeer had offered to drive him.

"What kind of errand?"

"I had to pick up a package. Mail, personal items I'd left behind when I moved here from Wyoming."

"I don't suppose any of those personal items was a photo negative?"

Hewitt tried to recall the morally acceptable excuses for telling a lie. He felt quite confident that the destruction of the blackmail photos had been a moral act. Surely keeping the photos a secret was just as moral. Unless, as he feared, T.J. had been killing people to recover one of those photos.

"Sorry, no," he said.

"So you and Joe Murderer were driving around Thursday night? What time was that?"

"Around two a.m."

Cardona's eyebrows went up. "A little late for errands."

"I was awake," Hewitt said. "I've a touch of insomnia."

"Guilty about something?"

"Nothing illegal," Hewitt said.

"What's open that late?"

Hewitt had been wondering what to do about Weeks, how to "convince" him to turn in his resignation quietly and without fuss. Buck's amazing promotion had provided the solution. Hewitt was now the second most powerful executive in the company and he knew that Weeks respected power.

Looking straight at the little weasel, he answered Cardona's question. "Union Station. That's where I picked up the package."

Weeks glared at him, then slumped in his chair.

"What else did Muledeer tell you?"

"He went to boarding school in Santa Barbara—didn't mention which one. He started out in college at UC San Luis Obispo, but quit and came back here to work."

"Know where he kipped?" Cardona asked.

"I don't understand."

"Where'd he live?"

"I don't know. Maybe with one of his parents. They were separated, but he believed they were about to reunite. Of course, children always hold out that hope."

"What kind of car did he drive?"

"A Hillman-Minx cabriolet. He was very proud of it."

"You identify it?" Cardona asked.

"Of course," Hewitt said. "He keeps it in a garage off the alley. Oh, yes, there's a gun in the glove compartment."

"Show me," Cardona said, shoving away from the table.

"Okay I go close up the shop?" Herkie asked. "It won't take me long."

"Yeah. The rest of you hang in here. It's gonna be a long night. Rough for all of us non-insomniacs."

52.

"He didn't say anything that would make this easier?" Harry asked, squinting through a magnifying glass at the tiny two-inch images on the contact sheets from Joe Tobella's negatives.

"Sure he did," Terry said from her living room, which she was trying to put back into some kind of order. "He told me the exact negative he wanted and I'm holding back that information to torment you."

Cardona had finally released them at approximately three in the morning. It was now past five and night was waning as their tempers waxed.

Harry was sitting on the bed, leaning into the light from the end table lamp. "Nothing but struts, bolts, bricks," he said. "I can't stand it anymore. I need sleep."

"Let's see. I got beaten up and almost had my throat cut. And you've lost your beauty sleep. Poor baby."

He had no reply to that. He placed the sheets and the negatives and the magnifier on an end table and turned out the light.

Terry entered the room and stood beside the bed. The only things she wore were two bandages, a large one on her forehead, a much smaller one below her right breast.

A huge dark bruise was forming on her hip.

She got into the bed and lay on her side, facing him. There were tears in her eyes.

"Head still hurt?" he asked. "I'll get you another pill."

351

"My head's fine," she said.

"Then what?"

"I don't like what's happening to us," she said.

"We've had a long, ugly night. Things always look better in daylight. Or maybe not."

"Why are you so angry?" she asked.

"Why are you?"

She frowned and then winced, touching the bandage on her forehead. "I guess I'm angry because you chose some party bimbo over me."

"That's ridiculous. You can dance and flirt with every male in the house and that's just great. But I take one step out on the dance floor with our host's daughter—"

"And stick your tongue down her throat."

"It wasn't my tongue doing the sticking. She caught me off guard."

"Oh? She caught you?"

"Yeah," he said. "Is that impossible, that she wanted to kiss me?"

"Of course not. But you might have at least tried to explain that to me."

"I would have if you hadn't run off like that."

"I didn't . . . Yes, I did. And you didn't try to catch me."

"I did try. But something came up."

He told her about overhearing the conversation in the governor's guest house.

"They were actually going to drug Buckley to make him look crazy? I always thought he was crazy enough without drugs."

"Anyway, they decided not to do it. And as I was running to catch you, I saw that ferrety shrink, Magnus, heading upstairs to where Buckley was with a drink in his hand. Nobody had told him the plan was off and he didn't believe me. I had to rough him up a little."

"Harry . . . ?"

"I did. I knocked the glass out of his hands and tackled him. And by the time I got out to where you'd parked the Zoom-buggy, you were driving off with Al Hewitt. Mr. Wonderful."

"What does that mean?" she asked.

" 'You were wonderful, Al.' I'm down on the floor with you, worried sick, and you wake up to tell me how wonderful Al is."

"He saved my life, Harry."

"I know it, dammit," he said. "He saved you and I didn't. And that's why I'm so angry."

She smiled and moved against him, her arm circling him and pulling him closer. "You make my life worth saving," she said.

53.

"You want some coffee, Al?" The question came from Marty, Trower Buckley's chauffeur, who'd just parked the company limo in the Loading Only section of LAX's Terminal Four. With his white moustache and Van Dyke–beard he resembled a goat with sunglasses. He held up a large thermos.

"I'm fine, Marty," Hewitt said, stifling a yawn. He was a little woozy from the pain pill that was keeping the sting of his chest wound to a minimum. He hadn't slept. He'd been on his way to bed at about 3:30 a.m. when Buckley called from the ex-governor's house to suggest he pick up Angel and Raymond the rejuvenated frog at 8 a.m.

"Tell Angel I'll see her for cocktails at six," Buckley had said.

"Okay, but you should know that both the police and the media are going to want to talk to you."

"Why?" Buckley asked.

"Your night security guard, a man named Muledeer, tried to murder one of your receptionists a couple of hours ago. It looks like he's the one who killed Florence Proneswagger and the sculptor and his assistant."

"Good Lord. Whatever was on his mind?"

"We may never know for sure," Hewitt said. "He's dead and his motive may have died with him."

"The police stopped him?"

"No. Your neighbor, the bar-owner from across the street, Mr. Herkimer, shot him."

"This is incredible. Where were you when this was going on?"

Hewitt hesitated. He didn't want to get into all that over the telephone. "I was with Mr. Herkimer."

"Are you all right?"

The wound seemed to twitch. The emergency tech had said it was up to him if he wanted stitches but didn't think they would be necessary. "I'm okay," he told Buckley.

"Excellent. Then we can safely say that all's well that ends well. And you'll make the run to the airport?"

"Sure."

There was a moment of silence, then Buckley said to someone on his end, "Now, you naughty minx, I'm all yours."

Hewitt heard a click followed by the annoying buzz of a disconnected line.

So, there he was, at the airport at precisely 8 a.m., sleepless, mildly sedated but not quite pain-free, waiting for Angel and the fractured frog.

"Looks like the flight's in," Marty said. "I'd better go get her before she starts squawking."

He opened his door a crack, emptied his coffee cup onto the tarmac and screwed the cup back into place on top of the thermos. He was about to step from the limo when Hewitt said, "Your cap."

"Right. Thanks, Al," Marty said, putting on his chauffeur's cap. "The lady don't go much for casual."

Hewitt leaned his head back against the soft leather seat and wished he could simply give in to sleep. But he had one more important task before he rested. Still, he could probably close his eyes for a second . . .

The sharp pitch of Angel's voice brought him back to awareness. She was complaining to Marty that he'd taken too long in gathering the seven pieces of luggage she'd needed for her four-day trip.

"And how long do I have to stand here before you open the goddamned door for me?"

Sweating under his chauffeur's cap, Marty parked the luggage carrier and opened the rear door with an exaggerated bow that Angel failed to notice.

She glared at Hewitt and climbed into the limo. She was carrying Raymond in a small straw Easter basket lined with a tiny white pillow. She settled into the leather seat, her already short skirt rising almost to her panty line. She placed the basket on the limo's carpeted floor and said, "Where the hell is Buck?"

"There was a party last night."

"I know fucking well there was. I read about it in the papers. The party. The shooting of some nut case at the magazine. Buck being unavailable for comment. Why do I have to find out about this shit from the papers? Buck couldn't stop screwing bimbos long enough to give me a call?"

"Things have been a little hectic," Hewitt said. He watched Marty get behind the wheel and start up the limo. He'd planned to have his chat with her on the drive back to Hollywood but now he decided to wait until they were in the penthouse. He wanted their discussion to be as private as possible and, considering her mood and tone of voice, there was no way Marty wouldn't get an earful.

"Where is he?" she demanded.

"Still at the governor's home," he said. "Probably trying to avoid the media."

"Or avoid me?"

"You folks want some music back there?" Marty asked.

"Couldn't hurt," Hewitt said.

Immediately the limo was filled with a bouncy Henry Mancini orchestration.

"How's Raymond?" he asked.

"On the mend," she said, lifting the Easter basket to her lap.

"What happened to the veterinarian who was traveling with you?"

"That slimy bastard was all over me on the flight to Beantown. I finally had to break his fucking thumb. Last I saw of him, they had him sedated and were carting him off the plane at Logan Airport."

She gave the sleeping frog a wan smile. "How's my little boy?" she whispered.

As they glided south, Hewitt looked out of the side window at wetlands that seemed to reach all the way to the Pacific.

She continued her one-sided conversation with the unconscious tiny critter, evidently having nothing more to say to Hewitt.

That suited him to a "t."

Back at the penthouse, once Marty had departed after dumping Angel's luggage in the master bedroom, Hewitt thought the time had come for more conversation.

Wearing only a sheer silk bra and panties, Angel was plucking tubes and jars of makeup from a small bag that was open on the king-sized bed. She looked up at him, a bit surprised, and asked, "Something?"

"Yes," he said, suddenly conscious of the vulnerability of his thumbs. "You should leave your things in those bags and pack up whatever else you want to take with you when you go."

"What the fuck are you talking about?"

"As I told your boyfriend, Roger Weeks, about seven hours ago, it's time you two lovebirds flew the coop."

"Roger who?"

He sighed. "Weeks," he said. "The guy who's been phoning you in Boston. Remember? You helped him steal Carlos' photos of you and various members of the *Ogle* staff for purposes of blackmail."

"You're nuts. When I tell Buck—"

She was stopped by a small 6 × 8 photo of herself and Roger Weeks that Hewitt had removed from his coat pocket. It was a particularly vivid snapshot of her and the copywriter totally lost in coital embrace.

"W-where did you get that?" she asked.

"Carlos developed it for me from the stolen proof sheets that Weeks was keeping in a locker at Union Station."

She seemed mesmerized by the photo.

"Weeks didn't phone to tell you the trouble you were in?"

"No," she whispered. "Is he . . . ?"

"In jail? No. *Ogle* has enough bad publicity as it is. But he's no longer working here. He packed up and left early this morning with a security guard named Herm making sure he didn't steal anything that wasn't bolted down."

"Shit. The little putz is all mouth and no balls."

"Well, you would know," Hewitt said. "You might want to think more positively about him, since you'll need someplace to sleep tonight."

"Sez you. I'm thinking maybe I'll be sleeping right here."

"It would be a mistake to overestimate your hold on Buck," he said. "How do you suppose he'll react after seeing this? You with a *copywriter,* no less?" He gave her one final look at the photo before sliding it back into his coat pocket.

When she didn't reply, he said, "Leave now and grab whatever you can carry. Or stay and have Buck toss you out without even a mink coat on your back. I don't imagine he'll mind if you take Raymond."

"Some fucking man of God, you are," she said as she began gathering her things.

He left her to her packing, satisfied that he was doing God's work, albeit in an unorthodox fashion. The final task would be to figure out some way to explain Angel's departure to Buck without exposing him to the ego-deflating truth.

He stopped off in the kitchen, drew a glass of water and took another pain pill. He needed as much rest as possible before Buck returned. He went to his room, removed his shoes and shirt. He used the bathroom mirror to check the bandage on his chest. It seemed to be clean. The bleeding had stopped.

On the cusp of exhaustion, he readied for bed. He decided his best bet for keeping his wound from reopening would be for him to sleep in an almost-sitting position. He was piling up pillows for that purpose when his phone rang.

"Al," Trower Buckley whispered into his ear, "how did it go with Angel?"

"Go?"

"Was the flight on schedule?"

"Yes," Hewitt said, wondering how to start laying the groundwork for her disappearance.

"Was she upset that I wasn't there?"

Hewitt wished his mental processes were sharper. "She, ah, seemed, ah, annoyed."

"Hmmm. Well, Al, I have another little task for you, one I wouldn't trust to another soul."

Hewitt yawned and closed his eyes.

"Bottom line, Al, I have made a . . . commitment to Georgina Moody."

"What kind of commitment?" Hewitt asked.

"The woman is incredible. Beautiful, intelligent, absolutely the most sensual, the most exquisite . . . We're engaged, Al. This time it's all the way."

In spite of both drugs and weariness, Hewitt was suddenly wide awake. "It's a little sudden, no?"

"There's no fool like a man who doesn't follow his heart,"

Buckley said.

There was also no fool like a middle-aged celebrity being fawned over by a clever young woman, Hewitt thought. "Congratulations, Buck," he said.

"That leaves us with the problem of Angel," Buckley said. "I want you to . . . get rid of her, I suppose. You have to handle this for me, Al. I'm absolutely worthless when it comes to severing emotional ties."

Hewitt had to remind himself that only a few days ago, Buckley was professing love for the woman he was now so eager to dismiss by proxy. The publisher was definitely not someone to depend on for lasting friendship. Or employment. But for the present the fickle Mr. B. considered him a wonder boy. Which, he supposed, he was.

"I'll take care of everything," he said, knowing that he had already accomplished that task.

Buckley ended the conversation with words of gratitude that relaxed Hewitt more than the pain pill.

He was drifting into sleep, when there was a knock at his door.

He assumed it was Angel with one last attempt to salvage her situation. He hoped it wouldn't be a seduction. His rejection of her sexually would only infuriate her more.

Being careful of his wound, he eased out of bed and opened the door.

Harry Trauble was standing there clutching a document in his hand.

"Did Angel send you?" Hewitt asked.

"Angel? No," Trauble said, as though the question had thrown him for a loop. "I just saw her dragging a bunch of luggage to the elevator."

"Good," Hewitt said, relaxing. "Then, you're here because . . . ?"

"Because I know why T.J. killed those people," Harry said. "And I know who's been behind the whole thing. And I need your advice about what to do next."

54.

Two hours earlier, Harry had been watching Terry dig into a huge chicken liver omelette that he'd transported from a brunch palace called The Good Egg on nearby Main Street. He'd placed it on a tray for her breakfast in bed. He wasn't much for fowl organ meat himself, but it was what she'd ordered and he was delighted to see her packing the food away and sluicing it with orange juice, apparently without a care in the world.

Her nightmare-prompted screams had awakened him not long after their lovemaking. He'd taken her in his arms and held her protectively until she'd lapsed back into a more peaceful dreamlike state. When she awoke again, she'd been concerned that the plaster on her forehead and her various cuts and abrasions had made her look like "the bride of Frankenstein."

"Wrong color hair," he'd said and kissed her.

"You still love me?"

"Of course."

"Then will you get me an omelette?"

Hence his trip to The Good Egg.

"Why don't we go to a movie today?" she asked, emptying a tiny tub of raspberry jelly onto a buttered toast triangle. "Something stupidly romantic and charming."

"I'll check the paper," he said. "But it'll have to be a little later. I've got to drive in to the office."

"Why?" She shivered at just the mention of the place.

"I should have thought of it while we were there last night," he said.

She frowned. "What are you talking about?"

"My manuscript," he said. "The only copy. With cops and everybody else going in and out of our office, I'm anxious to make sure the darn thing is still there and bring it home. Then, we'll hit the movie."

Reluctantly, she let him go, promising to stay at the apartment and rest up if he swore to be ultra-careful with her beloved Zoombuggy. "Promise me you won't skip second gear when you shift," she'd demanded.

The first thing he noticed when entering their office was that Weeks' desk had been stripped of everything but some white powder the LAPD lab technicians had left behind and the IBM typewriter. Gone were his office mate's personal gewgaws. The desk drawers were bare. Even the ant farm, which they'd purchased together, was missing.

Harry reached for the phone.

Weeks answered on the third ring, his mood dipping after hearing Trauble's voice. "Oh, it's you."

"I'm down at the office," Harry said. "It looks like you moved out."

"Yeah. I'm outta there," Weeks said.

"Why?"

"Because, aside from guys getting shot in the office, it's a shitheel place to work," Weeks said. "Look, Harry, you're a nice guy and all, but I'm waiting for a call and I don't really have anything to say to you. Okay?"

"Sure," Harry said. "Have a good life. And enjoy the ant farm."

He replaced the receiver, feeling a little stung. Not that he and Weeks had been best friends or anything, but still . . .

The office was a mess. Weeks or the police had thrown the contents of the cabinets back on the floor. He stepped over the tear sheets and old magazines and sat down at his desk. He slid open the side drawer and was relieved to see that the manila envelope containing the *Child of the Gap* manuscript was where he'd left it.

With it in hand, he headed around his desk to the door. But a stray magazine slid under his foot and he sat down hard on the floor in the middle of the debris.

Great, he thought, getting to his feet and waiting for the pain in his tailbone to subside.

The *Gap* envelope was resting on a pile of junk mail. When he retrieved it, he noticed a smaller and considerably more wrinkled brown envelope underneath.

Inside was an official-looking document, unquestionably the same Trower J. Buckley birth certificate that Howard Bethune had barely glimpsed. It had fallen out of Nick Hobart's white couch.

Harry's curiosity was stronger than Bethune's. As he studied the certificate's contents he forgot all about his precious manuscript. He grabbed the phone and punched out a number. It took Terry a couple minutes to answer. "Figure out a movie yet?" she asked.

"Not yet," he said, and told her of his discovery.

She was as stunned as he.

"So, here's the deal," he said. "Check those proof sheets again, now that we know what we're looking for."

"We do?"

"Right. Forget about the struts and bolts and concentrate on windows."

Al Hewitt looked at the remarkable document that Trauble had just brought him. "There's no possibility this is a fake?" he asked.

"I think it's what got Nick Hobart killed," Harry said. "And there's a photo that backs it up. It's what T.J. was after."

"And you couldn't possibly have misunderstood the discussion the executives had about negating Buck's voting stock?"

"No chance."

Hewitt sighed. He was never going to get to sleep again. "You have the photo?"

"I can get it," Harry said.

"Better do that now," Hewitt said.

"What's the plan?"

Plan? Why in heaven's name is it up to me to devise a plan? Hewitt wondered. Even after discovering an adaptability he would never have thought possible in his cloistered former life, he still felt like a newborn in this truly amoral world. His wife's treachery had been his baptism. He wasn't sure he was ready for confession.

Still, what choice did he have?

"The plan," he told Trauble, "is to hold an emergency meeting of the stockholders. Then we lay all the cards on the table."

Trauble's look told Hewitt he'd expected something a bit more ingenious. Too bad. He was fresh out of ingenuity.

"What are you going to tell Mr. Buckley?"

"I'll think of something," Hewitt said. "Just get that photo."

55.

"What the devil is the copywriter doing here?" Milton Armstead asked Hewitt, as they stood at the doorway to the dining room of Buckley's penthouse suite. The large space with its heavy wooden table and high-backed chairs was being used in lieu of the conference room on the first floor where there was still blood on the tiles.

The question did nothing to raise Harry Trauble's comfort level. He was feeling queasy enough, sitting at the table with a short stack of folders on his lap. He turned his head from Armstead and stared at the frog statue at the center of the tabletop. He hoped the microphone was hidden well enough under its lily pad. In response to Armstead's question, he wondered if closing his eyes might possibly render him invisible.

"Harry has made a rather remarkable discovery, Milton," Hewitt said. "I want him to explain it to you and the others."

"I thought you said this was a meeting to discuss the violence that went on here last night."

"This references that general topic," Hewitt said.

Harry heard John Bingham and Ida Connor approaching from the elevator. She was trying to placate Bingham who was complaining about having to use the hidden entry at the rear of the building to avoid the reporters and TV cameramen that were gathered out front.

As they took their places at the table, the copywriter wasn't sure if he should stay sitting or stand or say hello.

He was waiting for Al Hewitt to give him a sign.

Kevin Dobbs joined the group. His index finger, damaged at the party the previous night, was wrapped in gauze. Seating himself, he asked, "Did anyone see what it looks like down there where the maniac was shot?"

Armstead shook his head. Ida ignored the question.

"It's like a slaughter house," Dobbs said.

"How bad is all this murder stuff on our image, Milton?" Bingham asked.

Armstead shrugged. "We'll ride it out. A little infamy could even be good for circulation."

"It all depends on who this madman was and what he was trying to achieve," Dobbs said. "If his motive was puritanical or maybe he was trying to protest what he perceived as our sexist dehumanization of the female—"

"Don't start with all that sexual politics crapola," Armstead said. "The guy was a loon with a hard-on for *Ogle*. He's dead. Case solved. The magazine is on the front page of newspapers across the country and any publicity is good publicity."

"On that note, we might as well get started," Hewitt said. "I've invited Harry Trauble to join us."

Harry stood awkwardly, keeping his hand on the folders, continuing to guard their contents.

"At a stockholders meeting?" Dobbs said. "That's pretty damned unorthodox."

"Isn't Buck coming?" Ida asked.

"He said to start without him," Hewitt said. "He's next door, getting dressed."

"I gather he scored last night with Moody's daughter," Armstead said. When the others reacted with disinterest or disdain to this morsel of gossip, he turned his attention to Harry. "What's in the folders?"

Harry waited for Hewitt's nod, then slid the folders across

the table to each member of the assembly.

Armstead was the first to flip open the cover and glimpse the top item beneath—a Xerox of a State of California birth certificate for one "Trower James Buckley, Junior, born this date, May 2, 1946, of Trower James Buckley (father) and Ida Simms Connor (mother)."

"What the hell is this?" Armstead asked, holding up the Xerox.

Harry was about to explain, but Hewitt shook his head.

"Ida?" Armstead asked.

Ida Connor looked at her Xerox copy and said nothing.

"Is this for real?" Bingham asked. "Jesus, Ida, you and Buck . . . have a child?"

She remained silent, staring now at Harry with no particular expression. He realized her eyes were red. From crying? If so, she'd run out of tears.

"I knew you two had a fling back in the day," Armstead said, looking for once like a man in pain rather than one who caused it. "But a kid you neglected to mention? And all this time Buck was aware of—?"

"Buck was aware of what?" Trower Buckley asked as he strode into the makeshift conference room. "That some bloke tried to kill one of our gals and got his ass shot off? Yes, Buck is bloody well aware of that, thanks to the phone calls, the newspapers, the TV. And the idiots perched like carrion birds in front of the building." He looked freshly shorn and shaved, clear-eyed and neatly attired in yellow LaCoste shirt and tan silk trousers.

He seemed relaxed and happy, beaming at them from his seat at the head of the table and Harry winced inwardly as he slid the remaining folder to the publisher.

"What's this?" Buckley asked.

Every eye in the room was on him, but no mouth spoke.

"I guess I'll just have to see for my . . ."

He looked puzzled for a few seconds, then he grinned. "This is a gag, right?"

He could see from their expressions that it was no gag.

His jaw dropped and the ruddiness of his face drained to a waxy grey. Harry could hear the man's breathing pick up its pace as he turned to face Ida Connor. "I have a son?"

"Ask Mr. Trauble," she replied coldly. "He seems to have all the answers."

The publisher shifted his attention to the only person in the room he didn't immediately recognize. "You're Trauble? What the devil is this all about?"

Harry felt his throat constricting. He swallowed and croaked, "A-according to that document . . ." clearing his throat, ". . . Ida gave birth to a baby boy nineteen years ago. And you officially went on record to acknowledge paternity."

"I did what?" Buckley turned to Ida. "This baby nineteen years ago, he was mine?"

"Not just yours, ours," she said flatly.

"How could I have acknowledged paternity? I didn't even know about it."

Ida Connor hesitated, then shook her head dismissively as if the question and her reply were inconsequential. "I . . . forged your signature."

"And you kept all this from me? What the fuck, woman? Did you think I wouldn't be interested?" She stared at him and said nothing more.

"Talk to me, God*DAMMit.*"

Ida Connor sighed. "Since you insist," she said. "All during the four years you were off fighting Hitler and Hirohito from the Navy Officer's Club in Newport, I waited for you. Because I was in love with you. When you returned home, I welcomed you into my bed. And then, you were suddenly too busy to see me."

"My grandfather put me to work in the bloody firm," he said, his voice an octave higher than usual. "You know that. I wasn't cut out to be a lawyer. I had to work three times as hard as the other clerks and even that didn't keep him off my back."

"But you had time for other women. Janet Boberry."

"The Boberrys were clients of the firm. My grandfather—"

"Please," Ida said. "You gave her an engagement ring."

"I didn't marry her. I give lots of girls engagement rings."

"Never me, Buck. Never me," Ida said. "What you gave me was a lot of nonsense about our friendship being more important than 'some temporary affair.' By the time I realized I was pregnant, you'd pushed me out of your life and you were engaged to the Boberry bitch. So fuck you."

"But if you'd just told me—"

"Bullshit. Why would you have cared about me or the boy? When have you ever cared about anybody but yourself?"

The vehemence in her voice made Buckley sink back on his chair. He was breathing even harder now, like a marathon runner pushing himself. "If that's how you felt why'd you help me start up the magazine."

"Help you? You self-centered jackass. They were making money faster in Chicago than the Great White Rabbit could think of ways to spend it. I knew the market was big enough for at least one more success story and *Ogle* looked like the ticket. I wanted to be a part of it."

Buckley was silent for a few seconds before asking in a much softer tone, "Where is he? Where is my son?"

"Why don't you take that one, Mr. Trauble?" Ida said.

Buckley turned to Harry, as confused and vulnerable as a child. Harry wasn't sure how to begin.

Al Hewitt stepped in. "Harry had a theory that the police confirmed earlier this morning," he said. "It's a pretty rough story, Buck, a terrible thing. One of God's tests. Can you handle it?"

Buckley straightened in the chair and raised his chin from his chest. Staring into Harry's eyes, he nodded. "Tell me," he said.

"The newborn identified on the certificate as Trower James Buckley, Jr.," Harry said, "had been working as a night watchman here, calling himself T.J. Muledeer. Trower James Muledeer. I guess the fake name was a play on yours. 'Buck.' 'Muledeer.' Anyway, he's the same guy who murdered at least four people and was killed here last night."

"Oh, sweet Jesus," Buckley said and closed his eyes.

"So much for your good publicity, Milton," Bingham said, a comment so inappropriate that Armstead responded with a mere look of disgust and even Dobbs, the ad man's closest comrade in the room, shook his head in dismay.

"He was the tall boy who worked here nights?" Buckley asked, gaining control of himself again. The question was addressed to Ida. When she chose not to reply, Hewitt said, "Yes."

"I must've walked by him a hundred times," Buckley said. "My son."

Ida blinked. "He was never your son," she said. "You merely supplied the semen. I was the only parent he knew."

"He told me his grandparents raised him," Hewitt said.

She wheeled on him, face flushed. "My father had money. I was in no position to care for an overactive child."

"I could have helped," Buckley said.

"Wake up, Buck. This was back when you were a certified flake, setting fire to the law firm's library. Anyway, what's done is done. My son—our son, if you want it that way, is dead."

Buckley's eyes were moist. "And I never even . . . Did he know I was his father?"

"He knew. He didn't much care."

"You turned him against me."

"He was an angry young man," she said. "He felt you had done me wrong. He was right about that. But he knew that I still loved you."

Milton Armstead groaned.

They were quite a crew, Harry decided. Buckley had turned a shade paler. Armstead seemed crushed. Bingham had backed away from the table, distancing himself from the discussion while being morbidly fascinated by it. Dobbs' twisted face suggested he wanted to be anywhere else.

Only he, Harry, and Al Hewitt knew where the tableau was headed. He chanced a quick glance at the *Ogle* statue, then faced Ida. "When did you find out T.J. was capable of murder?"

She faltered, but just for a second. "This morning," she said, "when I returned home from Milton's. There was a message from Detective Cardona. I called him and he told me what had taken place at the office."

"You had no idea what T.J. had been up to? All the other killings?" Harry asked.

"Of course not," she said. "Do you think I would have done nothing? What makes any of this your business, anyway?"

"Your son almost killed my girlfriend," Harry said. "He even took some shots at me out at a place called Nirvana. I'd say that kinda makes it my business."

"Why was he doing all these monstrous things?" Buckley said. "Was it to get back at me in some way?"

"That sounds like as good a reason as any," Ida said.

"But it's not the real reason," Harry said. "The real reason goes back to the death of Nick Hobart."

"Poor old Nick," Buckley said. "That damned incompetent sculptor."

"It wasn't Joseph Tobella's fault the statue fell," Harry said. "T.J. climbed out onto the marquee and pushed it onto Hobart."

"What?" Buckley said. "Why?"

"Because Hobart had secured a copy of the infamous birth certificate," Harry said. "I don't know how he came by it, or what he planned to do with it. Maybe one of you has some idea? Ida?"

Ida Connor smiled at him and said nothing.

"I don't understand any of this," Buckley said.

"Bear with me, sir, and I think things will clear up a little," Harry said. "Hobart's death kept T.J.'s relationship to you a secret for a while. Then the magazine threatened to sue Tobella, so he and his partner, Orlando Royale, climbed up on the marquee one morning to take pictures of the faulty construction.

"They took lots of shots, including one that threatened to expose T.J.'s identity. He killed Tobella and Orlando, trying to get the negative of that photo. Later, when Florence Proneswagger told him she'd seen the negative, he added her to his hit list.

"A copy of the photo is in your folder, underneath the birth certificate."

With a great weariness, Buckley reached out for his folder. By then, the others all had theirs open and were gawking at an 8 × 10" glossy black-and-white photo taken through the open blinds of Ida's private office just past the giant statue of the frog.

She was sitting on the couch. T.J. was lying down on it, his head in her lap. She was brushing back his hair and smiling down at him with a motherly affection matched only by Michelangelo's *Pieta*.

"I don't get it, Ida," Armstead said, still not seeing the big picture. "You must have some idea why the kid was so hell-bent on keeping his parenthood a secret."

She'd reverted to her silent mode.

"He was a mother's boy," Harry said. "He was only doing what mom told him to."

"What the hell do you mean by that?" Armstead bellowed.

"Ida wanted to take control of the company," Harry said. "To do that, she had to keep the relationship between Buck and T.J. a secret."

"I'm still not with you," Armstead said.

"This is some more bad news for you, Mr. Buckley," Harry said. "Your partners have been planning to have you declared incompetent so that they could take over the company."

"Unmitigated horseshit," Bingham bellowed.

"Oh, for Christ's sake, John," Armstead said. "Shut the fuck up."

"This is true, Milton?" Buckley asked.

"We were toying with the idea, Buck," Armstead said. "You've been so frigging obstinate about taking the company public."

"But none of you knew Ida had her own agenda," Hewitt said.

Armstead looked at her. "You were setting us up? Waiting to take over as soon as your lawyers arranged for Buck's shares to be passed along to his heir?"

Ida Connor gave him a bored look.

"And the thing between you and me?" Armstead asked.

"You and me?" Ida said scornfully. "That was simple sexual gratification. I assumed you, of all people, would understand that."

"Why bother to make me look incompetent, Ida?" Buckley asked. "Why not just have the boy—my son—kill me?"

"I didn't want you to die," she said. "I love you."

There was silence in the room. Afraid that Ida had not said enough to incriminate herself, Harry broke it. "I think you just wanted Mr. Buckley to be alive to see you take everything away from him. I wouldn't call that love exactly."

Ida Connor looked only mildly piqued. "I rue the day I hired you, Trauble," she said. "You really are an annoying young man." And she removed a small black revolver from her purse.

56.

Harry was about to shout "gun" into the hidden mike when Ida pulled the trigger. She seemed to be aiming at his midsection, but he felt a stinging sensation along the right side of his forehead. He fell backward, his head connecting against the seat of an unused heavy wooden chair.

Lying on the thick carpet he thought he heard more shots.

Then there was the sound of people rushing from the room. More shots.

And a scream. Fading away.

He wondered why he was still awake. Weren't you supposed to pass out when you were shot? Wasn't that one of the benefits? Instead, he was lying on the carpet in Trower Buckley's dining room, awake and in pain.

Had he been unconscious? His thoughts were a jumble.

Eventually he sensed someone beside him. He opened his eyes to Al Hewitt, kneeling on the carpet with a moist washcloth.

"I'm shot," Harry said.

"Not literally," Hewitt said. "In any case, medical assistance has arrived. They're in with Buck. Let's just see how things look under all the blood."

"Blood?"

"Head wounds," Hewitt said. "They bleed like crazy."

The washcloth was warm and rather comforting as Hewitt dabbed at his forehead. "Mmmm. A little nick. Maybe a stitch or two. How are you feeling?"

Harry sat up carefully. "Woozy," he said.

"Double vision?"

"No."

"Let's try standing up."

Hewitt helped him to his feet. He felt dizzy.

"How long was I lying there?"

"Maybe thirty minutes," Hewitt said. "With everything that was going on, we kind of forgot about you."

"I could have bled to death," Harry said.

"Oh, I checked to see if you had been shot. You're lucky. She was aiming for your vitals, but the bullet hit the centerpiece frog instead."

"And ricocheted along my head?"

"That was a piece of the frog's cocktail glass."

"A ricochet would have been so much cooler," Harry said.

"We'll call it that, if you prefer," Hewitt said.

"You said the emergency guys are with Mr. Buckley. Is he okay?"

"Ida shot him in the shoulder. Trying for his heart, I suppose, but she was on the run. It's a little more of a wound than yours. He's in his bedroom. He self-medicated with martinis while waiting for the medics, so he's feeling little pain. But I'm not sure I'd say he was okay. After today, it may be a while before any of us is okay."

"And everybody else?"

"Unscathed. In the editors' bullpen one flight down. The detectives want you there, too, if you can make it."

"What about Ida?" Harry asked.

"The police were a little slow to move. Detective Cardona chased her down the stairs to the first floor. There was some shooting back and forth, before he brought her down. She's dead."

"Oh. Cardona hurt?"

"I doubt that's possible," Hewitt said.

"I should call Terry," Harry said. "She's probably worried."

"Call your parents, too," Hewitt said. "They will have heard the news. This has become a very big story. And you're a part of it."

"Wounded by a frog's cocktail glass," Harry said. "Not quite like getting shot by a sniper in Vietnam."

Hewitt frowned. "I just realized: Ida died at almost the same spot where T.J. fell last night."

"I don't imagine Mr. Buckley will be putting up a plaque," Harry said.

57.

"Luu-cee, I'm home."

"Why do guys always say that when they come through the door?" Terry asked as she ran to throw her arms around him.

"Because they like to fantasize living with a beautiful, unpredictable redhead," he said.

That earned him a predictably passionate kiss that guaranteed dinner would be a bit late.

"I really missed you," she said after a while, the both of them side by side on the bed.

He closed his eyes.

"Well?" she said.

"What's for dinner?" he said.

"Get up, you unromantic lout and go set the table," she said.

"You realize we almost have matching bandages," he said.

"Aw, you are romantic after all," she said.

During dinner—sirloin burgers on fresh-baked buns—he told her of the events of the day.

"There was nothing on the news about T.J. being Buckley's son," she said. "All I've been hearing is that Ida was a mentally disturbed woman who passed along her craziness to her kid. She'd been fixated on Buckley since her college days and managed to worm her way into the *Ogle* organization. They were both ticking bombs that eventually went off."

"The 'ticking bomb' idea was Milton's," Harry said. "The

members of the board, what's left of them, decided to sweep all the stuff about paternity and the takeover plot under the carpet."

"Won't the police report tell all?" she asked. "Especially if they have the whole thing on tape?"

Harry shrugged. "I dunno. Milton had a chat with Cardona about all the false arrests and the sloppiness in letting a suspected accomplice to murder waltz into that meeting with a gun in her purse. My guess is a deal has been cut."

"And you're all right with that?" she asked.

"I don't see any reason to spread the word that the kid was Buckley's."

"Buckley's not this great guy, you know," she said. "He did use Ida and dump her."

"I'd say she more than evened that score."

"And don't believe for a minute that Milton and those other stiffs are doing the hush-up for Buckley's sake. They're only thinking about their precious circulation figures."

Harry nodded, but the talk of Buckley reminded him of the pain in the publisher's face when he learned that Ida had robbed him of fatherhood and turned his son into a monster.

Terry was staring at him, her brow wrinkled in concern. "Harry?"

What would it be like to have a child with this woman? he wondered. He saw the child as a boy, but a little girl would be just as wonderful. Still, bringing a child into this world . . . He flashed on T.J.'s body on the floor of the office, saw newsreel footage of the war in Vietnam, Larry Beagle gazing at the pop art painting of the Iwo Jima flag raising, Trower Buckley weeping over the loss of a son he never knew, Ida Connor pointing the gun directly at him and firing.

"Aw, hell," he said suddenly and he broke down, weeping uncontrollably.

Terry was around the table in a flash, leading him to the sofa where she sat close beside him, holding him tight until the tears stopped.

"I'm . . . I'm sorry," he said, not attempting to move. "I don't know where that came from."

"From the heart, I think," she said.

58.

The media insisted on labeling the killings "The Centerfold Murders," though the Eyefuls were in no way involved. Interest in the crimes peaked with an article penned by Kevin Dobbs that ran in the August, 1965 *Ogle*. It was the board-approved, abridged version of the real story but it still managed to make that issue the only one ever to sell more copies at the nation's newsstands than the monthly Armstead continued to refer to as "the rabbit rag."

On August 15, rioting erupted in the Watts section of the city and chased "The Centerfold Murders" and everything else from the minds of Angelinos, even those within the cloistered confines of the *Ogle* Building.

By the end of the year, the media had moved on to other more timely matters. The Vietnam War. The death of Albert Schweitzer. The meeting in space of earth-orbiting *Genesis 6* and *Genesis 7*. The rise of the Black Panthers. *Ogle* settled back into the still-comfortable number-two slot among men's magazines, but was keeping a weather eye on the new British upstart called *Penthouse*.

Harry did a little settling in, too.

He and Terry had talked about packing up and driving across the country to Manhattan where they could find jobs a little more grounded in reality. But Armstead offered him the position of Promotion Manager and the large bump in salary as well as the satisfaction of being able to make Maurice Grumbacher jump through hoops had been irresistible.

Instead of a coast-to-coat relocation, he and Terry moved up two floors into a larger corner apartment in their building near the ocean.

Their wedding in June of 1966 was a relatively small affair held on the sun-dappled, lovingly landscaped grounds of the Bel Air Hotel. Al Hewitt got his ministerial garb out of mothballs to officiate (with the help of a former judge whose presence was required by California law). Herkie gave the bride away. Harry's father and mother were in attendance, as were Terry's aunt and uncle and a family of swans who visited from a nearby man-made lagoon.

Milton Armstead surprised them with a gift—a weeklong honeymoon at a hotel on Lake Como. It was part of a barter deal the hotel chain had with *Ogle,* but that did not make their stay any less romantic.

For a while life was good and uneventful.

Then Harry began to grow restless.

He wasn't sure if it was Hewitt's effectiveness in keeping *Ogle* on an even keel or the influx of young business-minded types who, thanks to a rather bloodless new head of personnel, were replacing the magazine's eccentrics and oddballs at an alarming rate.

Or maybe it was the change that had come over Armstead since that dark day in which Ida Connor met her fate. In a metamorphosis that would have impressed even Franz Kafka, he had changed from a self-serving, lecherous, arrogant bastard into a more contemplative, if no less cynical, attentive business-man. His professional demands on Harry were logical and he was generous with praise when it was due.

"I might as well be working for Time-Life," Harry complained to Terry over dinner one night.

"Could be worse," she said. "*Reader's Digest.* Living in Pleasantville, praying for Barry Goldwater's comeback."

"You like sitting at that desk on three?"

"I can take it or leave it," she said. "If you're not happy, let's just blow that pop stand."

"You sure?" he asked, brightening. "We've got enough saved to take us through three or four months. Maybe a little longer if we don't eat."

"You have any idea what you want to do?" she asked.

"Well, that's the thing," he said excitedly. "I read in *Ad Age* about this guy in San Francisco who's just got the financing he needs to start a new magazine. I called him today. He said he's looking for an experienced promotion manager."

"What about his experience?" Terry asked. "He have any idea what he's getting into?"

Harry winced. "Actually, he's a brash young punk who dropped out of UC Berkley. But he's smart enough to meet with me as soon as I can get to San Francisco."

"Is it another girly book like *Ogle*?" Terry asked.

"Not at all. He's a rock and roll guy. The magazine is going to be about the new music scene."

"You don't know anything about the new music scene," she said.

"Before coming to *Ogle*, I didn't know anything about sex," Harry said, pulling her onto his lap. "We live and learn."

ABOUT THE AUTHOR

Dick Lochte is a *Los Angeles Times* bestselling author whose novels have been nominated for nearly every mystery book award and have been translated into more than a dozen languages. His *Sleeping Dog* won The Nero Wolfe Award and was selected as one of the 100 Favorite Mysteries of the 20th Century by the Independent Mystery Booksellers Association. His most recent novels include *The Last Defense* and *Lawless*, legal thrillers co-written with attorney Christopher Darden.